Hermann Buhl

Climbing without Compromise

Hermann Buhl

Climbing without Compromise

REINHOLD MESSNER AND HORST HÖFLER

THE MOUNTAINEERS BOOKS

BÂTON WICKS

Published by The Mountaineers
1001 SW Klickitat Way, Suite 201, Seattle, WA 98134

Published simultaneously in Great Britain by Bâton Wicks Publications, London. All trade inquiries to: Cordee, 3a DeMontfort Street, Leicester, England, LE1 7HD

Manufactured in the United States of America

Translated by Tim Carruthers
Edited by Donna DeShazo
Design and layout by Ani Rucki
Cover design by Amy Winchester and Ani Rucki
Cover: *Hermann Buhl on the summit of Broad Peak on 9 June 1957; his dream of the first ascent of an 8000-meter peak without the help of high-altitude porters and oxygen equipment has become reality.* © Kurt Diemberger. Inset: *Hermann Buhl* © Kurt Diemberger

Photo Credits: Thomas Aumann: p. 104, I2.4 right. Archive Eugenie Buhl: p. 12, 14, 16 bottom, 17, 18, 19, 22, 24, 26, 27, 35, 37, 39, 40, 46, I1.1, I1.4, I1.10, 44, 50, 51, 53, 56, 58, 59, 67, 82, 86, 95, 97, 103, 141, I2.1 bottom, I2.3 both, I2.4 top & bottom left, I2.8 top right, 158 both, 175, 191. Archive Eugenie Buhl/ S. Bray: p. 42, 118, 120. Archive Eugenie Buhl/H. Ertl: p. 149, 150, 152. Archive Eugenie Buhl/M. Schmuck: p. 162, 164, 166. Deutsches Institut für Auslandsforschung: p. 11, I1.16, 69, 128, 133, 134, 136, 145, 146, 151. Kurt Diemberger: Jacket shot, p. I2.8 top left, I2.8 bottom, I2.9, I2.10, I2.11, top, I2.12, I2.13, 176, 177, 179, 181, 182, 184, 185, 186. Horst Höfler: p. 43, I1.3 both, I1.5 both, I1.11, I1.12 bottom, 61, 77, 92, 109, I2.2 both, 159, 31 bottom. Eugen H. Hüsler: p. I1.5. Karakorum Expedition of the Austrian Alpine Club 1957: p. I2.6, top, I2.11 bottom, I2.14 top, 172. Walter Klier: p. I1.2 both, 48. Rudi Lindner: p. 114. Archive Karl Mägdefrau/H. Höfler: p. 65. Reinhold Messner: p. I1.6/7, I1.14/15, 131, I2.1 top, I2.6/7, I2.14/15, I2.16 top & middle. R. Obster: p. 73. Archive Siegfried Rabiser: p. 15 both, 16 top. Hans Steinbichler: p. 124. Archive Luis Vigl: p. 13, 20, 29, 30, 31 top, 106, 111, 153. Jürgen Winkler: p. I1.8, I2.5. Gerlinde M. Witt: p. 66, 168. Franz Zengerle: p. I1.13.

Library of Congress Cataloging-in-Publication Data
Messner, Reinhold, 1944-
    [Hermann Buhl. English]
    Hermann Buhl : climbing without compromise / by Reinhold Messner and Horst Höfler. — 1st English language ed.
        p.   cm.
    Includes excerpts from Hermann Buhl's diaries.
    Includes bibliographical references (p.   ).
    ISBN 0-89886-678-2 (North America)
    1. Buhl, Hermann, 1924-1957. 2. Mountaineers—Austria—Biography. I. Höfler, Horst, 1948- II. Buhl, Hermann, 1924-1957. III. Title.
    GV199.92.B8413M48 2000
    796.52'2'092—dc21   00-008990
                                                             CIP

British Library of Congress Cataloging-in-Publication Data
A catalogue record for this book is available at the British Library.
ISBN 1-898573-48-4 (U.K.)

♲ Printed on recycled paper

Acknowledgments

Our thanks are due in the first instance to Hermann Buhl's family—to his wife Generl, his daughters Kriemhild Lornsen-Buhl and Silvia Bögl. Generl Buhl kindly made available the diaries of her husband and many of the photographs, and our conversations with her and her daughters completed our "picture"of Hermann Buhl like the last little stones in a mosaic.

Our heartfelt thanks also go to Luis Vigl, Hermann Buhl's climbing partner and friend. Luis also gave us some important photographic material and provided the answers to many of our questions. Without his prompt help and advice we would have been unable to fill in the gaps in the original manuscript.

We would also like to extend our thanks to Kurt Diemberger, who not only provided us with his original photographs of Broad Peak and Chogolisa but also edited the captions.

A big thank you to the mountain guide Michel Darbellay from La Fouly, without whose help we would have not been able to write several important sections of the text.

Grateful thanks are also due to Walter Klier from Innsbruck for his many helpful tips and to the friendly ladies of the Library of the German Alpine Club for their invaluable help in tracking down much of the source material.

Thanks too to the Deutsches Institut für Auslandsforschung (German Institute for Foreign Research) and in particular to Manfred Sturm for permission to use photographs from his archives.

Finally, our thanks go to the photographers and above all to Kurt Diemberger for his contributions to the photographical portrait of Hermann Buhl and to Eugen H. Hüsler for permission to use his color shot free of charge.

Contents

PART 1
THE BEGINNING: THE MOUNTAINS AS A HOMELAND

PART 2
THE ASCENT: NANGA PARBAT AS THE GOAL

"The most dangerous time for the climber is the first year after starting to climb. He does not yet know the dangers well enough, cannot estimate things properly and is far too easy-going."

Hermann Buhl

PART 3
THE STAR AND THE DEATH: FROM THE CHALLENGE OF BROAD PEAK TO THE END

APPENDICES

Introduction

Who Was
Hermann Buhl?

A Man Driven

by Reinhold Messner

When I was a young lad, no other character from the world of mountaineering fascinated me quite as much as Hermann Buhl. I knew of his ideas and his name even before I read about him. In those days all the climbers were talking about him. There was no question—he was without argument *the* mountaineer of the fifties. Although some of his accomplishments were not undisputed, he was considered to be uncompromising, ambitious, and unrestrained in the desire to achieve his objectives. When Buhl was declared missing I cried, too.

The hero is dead; the myth lives on. The lasting proof of Buhl's ability, his enthusiasm and his commitment can be found in his routes: great deeds that he accomplished with an instinctive sureness and a feeling for his milieu, from the Mauk West Face to Nanga Parbat. In spite of the envy, opposition and arguments that sometimes marked his relationships with other climbers, all of which weighed heavily upon him, luck continued to remain on his side until that cornice collapsed on Chogolisa and he disappeared forever.

Those climbers who attempt the most difficult of Hermann Buhl's routes themselves, and those who conquer eight-thousand-meter peaks, are not the only ones who should be able to comprehend and evaluate Buhl's achievements—provided of course they place Buhl in the context of his times. All who read his words and those written about him should also grasp who this man Hermann Buhl really was.

For this reason, we publish here, for the first time, the "Hermann Buhl original version." We draw upon Buhl's original climbing diaries, journals, and articles written for mountaineering publications of his time, in order to present a more complete, or at least more balanced, picture of this man than has been available to this point. The first "Buhl book," *Nanga Parbat Pilgrimage—The Lonely Challenge,* was published in 1954 by the Nymphenburger press and was a bestseller. The book is an exciting read, and recreates the story of a small, weak lad, who, driven by his passion for climbing, becomes the best climber in the world. We do not wish to dispute that this was the case. But the text was created with the aid of a collaborator, Kurt Maix, who, as an experienced editor, gathered the early short stories and subsequent reports of Hermann Buhl into a single book manuscript. It is our contention that Maix has embellished certain parts of his "Buhl" and also omitted other parts, like any ghost writer

Hermann Buhl during the 1953 Nanga Parbat Expedition

"The mountains are silent teachers, and they teach us noble qualities: humility in the face of nature, modesty, courage, privation, and strength of will."

Hermann Buhl

Buhl was always seeking the challenge of man versus mountain—he is seen here climbing solo on the Direct South Arête of the Third Watzmannkind in the Berchtesgaden Alps.

wanting to give his story an unambiguous emphasis. (For more information on this, *see Appendix One: The "Original" Hermann Buhl*.

Buhl was not only smarter but also more fit—and thus more modern in his approach to climbing—than the romanticist Maix would have us believe. Indeed, Buhl was above all futuristic in thought and deed. It is true that Buhl questioned neither himself nor his climbing in the way that the noted German mountaineer Reinhard Karl would do twenty-five years later, but he did anticipate some of Karl's conclusions and doubts. Buhl was decades ahead of his time. The Buhl Crack on the Cima Canali demonstrates his style as a free climber; his ascent of Broad Peak gives us a glimpse of the super-alpinism of the future. Had Hermann Buhl been born forty years later he would surely have been one of the leading sport climbers, and a classic mountaineer without equal.

My admiration for Hermann Buhl grew during the course of my life. There is hardly a book I have written in which I do not come back to him. I sense an affinity with him as with few other climbers, not as a kindred spirit, but rather because of his willingness to commit himself completely. One of the things that drove Buhl was this need to make demands on himself.

Hermann Buhl was born almost exactly twenty years before I was. On 27 June 1957 he disappeared on Chogolisa.

On 27 June 1970 my brother Günther and I stood on the summit of Nanga Parbat. In 1978, 25 years after Buhl made the unforgettable first ascent, solo, in 1953, I stood for a second time atop Nanga Parbat. In 1982, 25 years after Schmuck, Wintersteller, Diemberger and Buhl had climbed Broad Peak, I retraced their steps in order to commemorate this pioneering act in my own way.

Alpinism has also continued to develop since Buhl's death, although the risks involved in this edge game have not lessened. Indeed they must remain for all those who seek the challenge of man versus mountain, as Hermann Buhl did in his time, or the great Austrian rock climber Paul Preuss before him.

How many of the best climbers have died during the past decades on the world's mountains? Reinhard Karl was lost in May 1982 on Cho Oyu; he was considered one of the best all-round mountaineers in Germany. Peter Boardman and Joe Tasker died shortly afterward on Mount Everest; they were one of the most successful teams in modern high altitude climbing. Alex MacIntyre was fatally injured by stonefall on the South Face of Annapurna in autumn 1982. Nobody had been more consistent than he in applying the modern style of super-alpinism to the most difficult eight-thousand-meter walls. Again on Mount Everest, in December 1982 Yasuo Kato disappeared.

He had already climbed Everest three times: in spring, in autumn and in winter. This most volatile of Japanese climbers did not return from his last summit attempt. In the spring of 1983 Nejc Zaplotnik, the exceptional Yugoslavian climber, was fatally injured by an ice avalanche at the foot of the South Face of Manaslu. He had gained admirers worldwide with his first ascent of the South Face of Makalu, the West Ridge of Hidden Peak and the West Ridge *integrale* on Mount Everest. Hironobu Kamuro died on Mount Everest in the autumn of 1983, a man who had climbed Dhaulagiri on his own. Naomi Uemura disappeared on Mount McKinley in February 1984. Uemura had climbed hundreds of high mountains solo and had made his way to the North Pole alone with a dog sled. He disappeared without trace during a winter ascent of North America's highest mountain. Then Jerzy Kukuczka, Wanda Rutkiewicz, Alison Hargreaves . . . it is not their number which dismays us, but the individual misfortunes.

All these women and men—just like Hermann Buhl forty years before—belonged to the dozen or so mountaineers who combined more success and experience in their few persons than did the many others of their generation. They belonged to the "Top Ten" of mountaineering greats. It is precisely for that reason that their deaths have had such a shocking—or is it a warning?—effect.

Has this great classical mountaineering tradition wound up to such a pitch that the risk can no longer be estimated? Has the margin between making it to the top or perishing become so narrow for those who are searching for these new dimensions, that only luck decides who should survive and who should die, in line with the motto "only every second or third survives"? If this were the case our actions could no longer be justified.

None of us climbs in order to be "The Best." There is no "Best Mountaineer in the World," no "Fastest," no "Most Modest." These attitudes are an invention. Perhaps some young climber may once have bestowed this sort of title upon himself, knowing that there are no gold medals or world championships to be won by the great mountaineers. Mountaineering cannot be measured in points and seconds, only differentiated to a limited extent in meters and degrees of difficulty; it can be expressed through the discipline of risk. Hermann Buhl understood this only too well—and he acted upon it. Success in mountaineering is a matter of constancy and of survival in increasingly more difficult borderline situations—and it is precisely that which killed Buhl in the end.

The greater the risk, the more difficult it is to do the right thing. And the right thing is what allows us to survive. To come back alive means everything. Anyone who stays at home because of the

It was not only in his homeland's limestone hills that Hermann Buhl constantly moved in difficult borderline areas of risk.

"Without a doubt Herman Buhl was the most significant German climber of the post-war era. His gaunt brown face and his large dark eyes were almost always smiling, even if his life was not always easy. Buhl was of average height, fine-limbed and always in top form."

Reinhold Messner

"The bundle of energy that was Buhl was not destined for a long life."

dangers or always sticks to the beaten track is not out there at the edge of things in the way that Hermann Buhl was.

At this point I once again ask the question: Have the opportunities which present themselves—the sum total of travel, mountain slopes, experience, equipment and knowledge—become so great that we run blindly into a trap? That we as human beings are too human, too flawed, clumsy and weak to be allowed to carry on playing our "game"? Have we interpreted Buhl's death on Chogolisa incorrectly? Mountaineering stems from an idea and from the great mountains. It has developed its own dynamic over a period of a hundred years, a dynamic that drove Buhl ever onwards—steeper and steeper, higher and higher, uncompromisingly upward! Mountaineering is only justifiable when we stop at the point where the discipline of risk stops.

Anyone who exposes himself to dangers from which he himself cannot escape is not a responsible climber. We should at least try to be responsible—and put more effort into this than we do into conquering all the summits in the world.

Hermann Buhl has disappeared, yet in spite of this he lives on in our memories because of his great routes, his stories, his friends—and even more because of his legendary will to push himself to the last. This driven man, who climbed higher and higher as if in a whirlwind of desire and the desire to prove something, at some point had to fall. That he died doing this was tragic.

What would have happened if Hermann Buhl had lived to be 75 years old? He would surely have continued to shape the face of climbing, much more than we can perhaps imagine. If, however, he had not stepped into that hole which had weakened the cornice on the ridge of Chogolisa, he would have fallen somewhere else, or frozen to death—"stayed on the mountain," as it was called in those days. The bundle of energy that was Buhl was not destined for a long life, and his early death made him a hero. Perhaps his death—painful as it was for his family and friends—freed him from the shackles of madness to which we mountaineers all succumb if we are prepared to go to the limits time and time again.

Climbing Was the Essence of Buhl's Life

by Horst Höfler

Mountaineering is a relentless pursuit. One climbs further and further yet never reaches the destination. Perhaps that is what gives it its own particular charm. One is constantly searching for something never to be found."—Hermann Buhl

ON A PERSONAL NOTE

When I stood on Mont Blanc for the first time, at the age of twenty, it had taken me only an hour to get from the Vallot Hut to the summit. I was pleased about this—it had, after all, taken me "only" a quarter of an hour longer than Hermann Buhl. In 1949 it had taken him three-quarters of an hour to do the same stretch.

I soon realized that our achievements were "worlds" apart, yet still I compared myself to him. Hermann Buhl had been my idol in the years of my youth—my hero since the day when I had been given his book *Nanga Parbat Pilgrimage* as a present at the age of thirteen.

I devoured this book and knew all the captions and many text passages by heart. At school I gave a talk about Buhl that captured the imaginations of many of my fellow pupils as well as my German teacher. I nagged my parents until they finally agreed to let me make a copy of the photo of Buhl that faced the book's title page. This photo then adorned my bedroom wall where it continued to keep its place even later on amidst posters of the Beatles, the Rolling Stones, Jimi Hendrix and Janis Joplin.

I was not good enough to be an extreme climber. But I was interested in the climbers who patrolled the borders of the possible, and I was pleased when I was able to climb routes that my heroes had also climbed in the early years of their climbing careers.

But above all I was interested in the real people behind the public images of these "rock stars." Thus my many conversations with Buhl's family—with his wife and daughters—became a very personal experience for me. These conversations also led me to form a completely different picture of Buhl in my mind. Now Hermann Buhl is no longer the "monument on a pedestal" to me but—with all the will in the world—a tragic hero. In this book we now hope to recreate this image of a strong-willed, creative and fragile man—to present the whole man with all his strengths and weaknesses.

Hermann Buhl's mother (right) came from the Grödnertal (Val Gardena) of South Tyrol.

Hermann's maternal grandmother (left), Hermann's mother in the center and on the right his sister Elfi.

CHILDHOOD, YOUTH, WAR

Hermann Wilhelm Buhl is born on 21 September 1924 in Innsbruck. His mother, Marianne—her maiden name is Rabiser—comes from the Grödnertal in South Tyrol.

Hermann's father, Wilhelm, is a master engineer in Innsbruck. Hermann has a sister, Martha (Elfi), born in 1923, and a half brother, Siegfried Rabiser, who is still alive today in Inzell.

When Hermann Buhl is four years old his mother dies, and he is placed in an orphanage. These orphanage years, which stretch on into the time of his youth, have a lasting effect on the boy. "This time must have been terrible for the boy as he was weakly and sensitive. The mental anguish and horrors which he had to endure during this part of his life must have been more painful than all the great physical pain which he resolutely took upon himself during his great mountain climbs as an adult," wrote Ulrich Aufmuth in his book *Lebenshunger (Lust for Life)*.

His father marries a second time but the new wife, his stepmother, shows Hermann no affection. Thus he much prefers to spend time in Innsbruck with his aunt and uncle, Marie and Rudolf Buhl, who own an electrical shop. Thanks to them—his nearest blood relatives—he at least gains some idea of what the security of a family can mean.

After leaving school Hermann is apprenticed as a forwarding agent. He also learns Italian and likes singing. Yet he is far more interested in the geography of the Alps and the people who have climbed their summits, ridges and walls. He reads the reports of those climbers whom he would like to emulate.

Buhl begins to climb, first easy routes then increasingly more difficult ones. He first achieves these as second on the rope but soon, with increasing confidence and ability, he becomes an ambitious leader. He trains in the "Höttinger Steinbruch"—a *klettergarten* in Innsbruck—"with radical persistence." (Aufmuth)

Hermann Buhl makes friends in the youth team group of the Innsbruck section of the German (it was 1939) Alpine Club. During the first years of the Second World War, when he is still too young to be drafted into military service, Buhl completes more and more difficult climbs until he reaches the magical VI level of difficulty. In 1943 he trains in the medical service in St. Johann, in Tyrol. During this time he achieves his first significant new route, the West Face of the Maukspitze in the Wilder Kaiser.

Buhl is sent to the front. During his leaves he undertakes wild climbing tours, often sailing very close to the wind. Is the soldier risking too much? Perhaps war and fear are a stimulus for his search

Hermann at about age six, with his aunt Marie Buhl.

Hermann Buhl in his homeland, Karwendel, at about age fourteen.

for danger away from the front. Very probably the hell of climbing Monte Cristallo, which Buhl survived, was more dangerous than what he faced as a soldier.

Karl Lukan, the popular Austrian climbing author, meets the soldier Hermann Buhl in 1944 in Terme di Valdieri, in Northern Italy. Lukan recalls, "I was told that there was a first-aider down in the dressing station who was also mad about the mountains. The climber was from the Tyrol. We chatted for a while then decided we could carry on our conversation while climbing around on the local granite blocks. This we did." His dream was one day to achieve something really great in the mountains, the Tyrolean told the writer from Vienna. Adds Lukan, "During the war each of us had his dream although neither of us knew how long we would remain alive. The Tyrolean's dream was to be fulfilled. In 1953 he achieved his solo ascent of Nanga Parbat."

GREAT ROUTES, MARRIAGE, FIGHT FOR SURVIVAL

Hermann Buhl is taken prisoner by the Americans, then, in the summer of 1945, he returns to his hometown of Innsbruck. Finding himself with no work experience and no job to go to, he gets by with casual work, first as a storehouse worker and later in a sports shop mounting ski bindings. With the money he saves, Buhl is able to finance his training as a mountain guide, which he successfully completes at the end of the forties. In 1947 Buhl does a whole series of new routes, mainly with Luis Vigl. The following year is shaped by a number of hard first winter ascents and by his first Western Alps trip; in 1949, together with Martin Schliessler, he accomplishes many great climbs in the Mont Blanc group.

In 1950 Buhl's climbing partner is Kuno Rainer, who is nine years his senior. Together they achieve the first winter ascent of the Marmolata South West Face, the Western Zinne North Face, the Walker Spur on the Grandes Jorasses and the first complete traverse of the Chamonix Aiguilles.

Also during 1950 Hermann Buhl gets to know Eugenie Högerle, from Ramsau in Berchtesgaden. She is a skilled climber who had been on very difficult routes with Hans Lobenhoffer, who, in 1939, together with Heinrich Harrer, Peter Aufschnaiter, and Lutz Chicken, had been on an exploratory expedition to the Diamir Face of Nanga Parbat. "Our Hermann skied fifty kilometers cross-country over the Hirschbichl to stand outside my little window," Generl (Eugenie) Buhl recalls. The couple marries in March 1951 and in the same year their first daughter, Kriemhild, is born.

Hermann Buhl in 1943: he was trained as a first aider in St. Johann in the Tyrol.

"His self-esteem was healthy and purposeful, and really stemmed from his natural survival instinct. He knew just how long his strength would last."

Sepp Jöchler

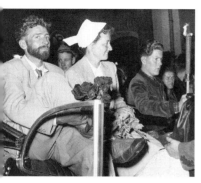

The parish of Berchtesgaden-Ramsau, from which Buhl's wife, Generl, came, prepared a grand reception for the summiteer on his return from the 1953 Nanga Parbat Expedition.

"The invitation to Nanga Parbat was a turning point in Buhl's life. With the successful attempt at the summit—which was due to him alone—Buhl became world-famous overnight. Because of his almost child-like honesty and his idealism he was immediately at the mercy of those who envied him."

Reinhold Messner

Hermann struggles to provide for his family by leading guided tours and, for the time being, is forced to put his own ambitions on hold. In 1952, however, he does achieve "great things": the Tofana Pillar, a solo ascent of the North East Face of the Piz Badile, and the North Face of the Eiger.

On a professional level, Buhl continues to be plagued by the matter of survival. His traveling by bicycle from Landeck to climb the Piz Badile, and return, is a feat referred to again and again. Many people admired Buhl for this, but it was done out of financial necessity rather than to set some kind of record: he simply couldn't afford any other means of transportation. Upon his return from the Eiger in 1952, Buhl and his young family are forced to vacate their flat in Innsbruck. They are able to catch their breath again only when the famous Munich sports shop, Schuster, employs Hermann—who is known much farther afield than Innsbruck—to sell mountain sports equipment and act as an adviser on mountaineering matters. That is in December 1952.

WORLDWIDE SUCCESS—NANGA PARBAT

Something far more important happens towards the end of 1952. Karl M. Herrligkoffer invites Hermann Buhl to join a German-Austrian expedition to Nanga Parbat that has been planned for 1953, in memory of Willy Merkl, the great German climber who died on Nanga Parbat in 1934. What happens on this expedition is the stuff of legend: from Camp 5, situated at about 6950 meters, the Tyrolean becomes the first man to reach the summit of this highly prized eight-thousander—"The Fateful Mountain of the Germans"—and overnight he becomes world famous!

Yet a true exposition of Buhl's achievement is at first hampered by certain clauses in the expedition contract giving the expedition leader the right to prepare the official expedition report. And Hermann rebels against this report. His notes in the margin of copies of Herrligkoffer's articles "Nanga Parbat 1953" and "Victory over Nanga Parbat" (in *Für-Euch-Bücherei,* a youth magazine) are an expression of this inability to come to an agreement. Herrligkoffer uses Buhl's achievement for his own gain and forces the summit conqueror out of the limelight.

In addition, profits made by Buhl and other expedition participants from lectures, essays and even books have to be given to the *Gesellschaft zur Förderung deutscher Forschung im Ausland* (Society for the Promotion of Research Abroad; later known as the Deutsches Institut für Auslandsforschung) in order to finance subsequent Herrligkoffer expeditions. For the majority of the team this does not present a problem: with the exception of Buhl, no participant has the chance of becoming a star climber. That Buhl tries to go solo with the marketing of his outstanding success is understandable, yet it brands him as an outsider. But this much must be said: on the one hand the Tyrolean had quite probably never even read the small print of the contract ("Hermann would have gone there with the devil," says his wife). On the other hand the success is his and his almost alone. If on 3 July 1953 Buhl had not "dared and won," the Herrligkoffer crew would have gone home empty-handed. Buhl does not want a fight, yet suddenly he is accused of envy, resentment and slander—even by some of the participants in the expedition. Newspaper and magazine editors of the day rush to exploit these arguments.

The sad climax of this mud-slinging is that Buhl's successful attempt at the summit is questioned by those who understand nothing of climbing—and yet it is undisputed. Richard Finsterwalder, who drew up the 1:50,000 Alpine Club (London) map of Nanga Parbat, writes to Paul Bauer, himself a Nanga Parbat veteran, on 21 October 1953: "A short time ago you were kind enough to send me the summit picture of Nanga Parbat from the Review No. 34/1953. Having checked with the help of the Nanga Parbat map, and also in particular with our new 1:50,000 Nanga Parbat relief map, it has been proven beyond any shadow of doubt that this picture really was taken on the summit."

Buhl finds it difficult to cope with all this argument, hostility and adversity. Above all he is affected by the human disappointments. In addition he is suffering from the after-effects of the frostbite sustained during his night spent bivouacking, standing up, above 8000 meters. He has lost both the big toe and part of the second on his right foot. He surely fears that he will never again be able to climb as well as he did during this expedition, and indeed his first attempts on rock afterward would seem not to be very promising. "He just stuffed his shoe and kept on trying," Generl Buhl recounts. On the other hand he is rewarded with financial success. For the 28-year-old and his family, the door to a secure future is opened.

Nanga Parbat Pilgrimage, first published in 1954, becomes a mountaineering bestseller. In addition, Buhl is in demand to give his captivating lectures: his listeners hang on his every word. He gives lectures all over Europe, even to the time-honored British Alpine Club in England. There are lectures in Switzerland, France, Yugoslavia, and in the then GDR [German Democratic Republic]. He gives

Hermann Buhl's first car. The Wolfsburg Volkswagen factory loaned the mountaineering star a "Beetle" for a year, a great help on his lecturing tours. One of his greatest "outings" was a lecture in Vienna on one evening and another the following evening in Nuremberg.

talks in Milan, Genoa and Rome. "There, in their enthusiasm, they carried him on their shoulders," reports the press. Buhl moves the souls of the Italians because he looks like one of them and because he gives his lectures in their mother tongue.

And at long last Buhl possesses a car. As befits the mountaineering star he has now surely become, he is given the use of a Volkswagen for a year by the VW factory in Wolfsburg. After this loan period is over, the Buhls accept the firm's offer to let them buy the "Beetle." Nowadays this might be considered a sort of cross between leasing and sponsorship.

BROAD PEAK AND CHOGOLISA

In 1954 the Buhls' second daughter, Silvia, is born, then in 1956 a third daughter, Ingrid, comes along.

Also in 1954 Buhl transfers to a different sports merchant, Sport-Scheck. His climbing in 1955 and 1956 is shaped by work, other mountain activities, and planning. He successfully does the great Western Alps routes, the most difficult alpine routes of the day, and he plans an expedition to the South Face of Aconcagua.

In 1956 Generl and Hermann go to Mont Blanc to take part in some movie-filming work. Gaston Rébuffat, the famous French guide who has also climbed the Eigerwand, is the director for climbing scenes in the film "The Son of Mont Blanc." The male lead is Adrian Hoven, whom Buhl has known since his youth. Buhl doubles for Hoven on Mont Blanc during the climbing scenes, and Generl does the same for the female lead. On days when there is no filming, Hermann and Generl climb the Brenva Face of Mont Blanc by the Moore route, and Hermann achieves the first—and a very fast—solo ascent of the Rébuffat Crack on the South Face of the Aiguille du Midi. Somewhat jealous, the first-ascent team was not exactly overjoyed by Buhl's achievement.

Meanwhile, Buhl has now climbed all the big-name routes in the Alps. Only his collection of first ascents is rather modest. But plans are in hand. His climbing companions Dietrich Hasse and Luis Vigl both know that Hermann is one of the first climbers to have attempted a "Direttissima" on the North Face of the Grosse Zinne. There is also a route description (translated into German) of the Bonatti Pillar on the Petit Dru among his pile of planning literature. It is clear that Buhl, who already knows Walter Bonatti's Grand-Capucin East Face and Guido Magnone's Dru West Face, wants to tick off the ultimate in granite climbs, the South West Buttress of the Petit Dru.

Buhl (center) intended to go on a Karakorum expedition with his best friends Luis (on Buhl's left) and Hugo Vigl (far left)—seen here at the Hahnenkamm downhill race in Kitzbühel.

But above all Buhl wants to return to the high mountains of the world. His dream is that the second time around, things would be run completely differently than in 1953. He would like to set off with just a few friends. He talks over his plan with his old climbing partner Luis Vigl and Luis's brother, Hugo. But the Vigls are both well established in their middle-class careers, Luis as a construction engineer and Hugo as a doctor, and they neither have the necessary free time nor are they fit enough for such a hard expedition. Buhl therefore introduces his bold idea to Marcus Schmuck. Marcus, from Maria Alm in Pinzgau, has partnered Buhl on the most difficult climbs in the Western and Eastern Alps. The plan is to attempt the first ascent of the eight-thousander Broad Peak in the Karakorum—without high altitude porters! The expedition party will also include Fritz Wintersteller and Kurt Diemberger, both from Salzburg.

It is tragic that on this expedition, too, right from the early stages, there are problems for which Hermann Buhl is not to blame. Once again an attempt is made to sideline Buhl. Nevertheless, on 9 June 1957, the four climbers are the first to stand on the summit of Broad Peak. Buhl, tired and drained, hampered by his previously frostbitten foot which is sensitive to the cold, makes it to the top only by virtue of his undiminished strength of will.

The original target, Broad Peak, is checked off, and Wintersteller and Schmuck have made the first successful ascent of the highest summit of the Savoia Group (later known as Skil Brum). Back at Base Camp, Kurt Diemberger and Hermann Buhl turn their attention to the seven-thousander Chogolisa, which they attack in Alpine style, carrying their small tent up with them day by day. At about 300 meters below the summit they are forced to turn back by a sudden snowstorm. In bad visibility Buhl tries to follow in the tracks of Diemberger, who is climbing down ahead of him, when he loses the trail and steps out onto a cornice jutting out through the snow. It breaks and Buhl falls into emptiness.

HERMANN BUHL'S SIGNIFICANCE AS A MOUNTAINEER

Hermann Buhl has fallen to his death! The fact that he will never be found makes him immortal. Buhl becomes a hero because he has disappeared forever on Chogolisa.

Buhl lived, above all, for and through his climbing. In his strength of will and in his self image, he was a professional climber—and all this during a period in alpinism when none even dreamed about making a living either directly or indirectly through top alpine

When there was no other option, Hermann Buhl was extremely resourceful with "technical tricks." First and foremost, however, he was a bold free climber—seen here on the vertical limestone of the Dolomites.

achievements. Only his successor, Walter Bonatti, became what one would now call a "professional."

Buhl was more of a rock climber than an ice climber, although he had at his disposal an all-embracing mountaineering ability. Above all he was a free climber. This is proved not only by his first ascents; many passages in his reports tell us about this, and it is substantiated by the comments of his climbing partners. Buhl's first ascents are, for the most part, free-climbing routes. As Buhl wrote in a letter to Walther Flaig after his first winter ascent of the South West Face of the Marmolata:

"There is a short traverse which the French [Jean Couzy and Marcel Schatz: publisher's note] rate as a VI. So we assume it must be damn difficult. It's soon behind me and I've done much harder traverses than that. Then there's a rope length of 35 meters: overhanging, extremely difficult, which the French classify as IV and V, as well as A2. ['A' stands for artificial; '2' for great difficulty when placing pitons or a great physical effort involved in order to overcome that section of the climb; two etriers necessary.] I think they did nothing but nail the whole thing—that's what it looked like from all the piton scars I could see—whereas I, I was leading at this time, was free climbing almost the whole way."

If Hermann Buhl enjoyed doing solo climbs during the early years of his climbing career, then this fervor reached an even greater peak after Nanga Parbat. He had become a loner, and was considered by many of his climbing colleagues to be a difficult man. It would seem that the wrangling with Herrligkoffer and his followers had made Buhl even more sensitive, even more egotistic (and on the mountains even more uncompromising), than he had been since his childhood. From 1954 on, Buhl climbed more often without a partner as he trusted nobody, since he felt that even Kuno Rainer had "betrayed" him with lack of support, simply for the sake of assuring himself a slot on a Broad Peak expedition with Herrligkoffer.

Buhl's first ascents in the Alps were not as significant as the new routes put up by Walter Bonatti. Hermann was too closely tied up with competitive thinking, or was before the Nanga Parbat Expedition, to make his mark across the Alps. He would have had the power and the drive to do new routes but he did not have the necessary creativity. His ambition drove him instead to try to exceed the achievements of his predecessors in style and time required, rather than to piece together his own great routes. The Italian, Bonatti, with his feel for magnificent routes and with his extreme toughness, was different. He would become the next climbing genius after Buhl. It was only at the time of his Karakorum Expedition in 1957 that Buhl possessed the vision and creativity necessary for demanding first ascents and innovations in mountaineering. Without a doubt he was at that time *the* mountaineer in the whole world. The way in which he attempted Broad Peak, and even more so Chogolisa, shows Buhl as a pioneer looking to the future. His fame, of course, is due also to the fact that he was the first man to achieve two eight-thousanders without Sherpas.

The race to collect the eight-thousanders had begun. . . .

HERMANN BUHL—ON THE DARK SIDE OF LIFE?

There is no question that Hermann Buhl was obsessed with climbing. He had—at least until the time of his marriage—hardly any other interests and he wanted nothing other than to improve his extreme climbing. Thus he made high demands not only of his partners but above all of himself. From his unrestrained youthful enthusiasm, he developed, in more mature years, an educated self-will and a great feel for the dangers on the mountain. The social scientist and climber Ulrich Aufmuth published, in 1996, a book entitled *Lebenshunger (Lust for Life)* which mainly focused on restless, "wild people" and their life stories. He paints a gloomy picture of Buhl's life: "Buhl was inwardly lonely. He lived only for his success. The fame he achieved did not satisfy his hunger at all. His inner self was despairing. As an adult he was no longer able to accept the love that could have redeemed and satisfied him, and which others were perfectly prepared to give him. His mountaineering death at the age of thirty-four [correction—this should have read thirty-two: publisher's note] brought his need to an end."

Aufmuth's analyses are important and should be taken seriously. And yet there was also a sunny side to Buhl's life. Luis Vigl recounts that Buhl was utterly optimistic and even extroverted. Yet he had—and this is underlined by his climbing diaries—a very subtle, not obvious, sense of humor. Among friends, when he felt good, he could be funny and would sing and play the guitar. According to Generl he never lost his positive attitude toward life even in difficult everyday situations. The image of a father as painted by his eldest daughter, Kriemhild Buhl [see following section], is also that of a man with a positive outlook on life.

Kriemhild added the following hand-written postscript to her text: "An acquaintance, who had gotten to know my father at a press ball in Munich, told me he had been a really good dancer and really charming companion. He had many admirers and was apparently

The two faces of Hermann Buhl—the melancholy . . .

well liked by women, although he was no lady-killer himself. Women were not all that important to him . . . too complicated and full of expectations . . . "

That Buhl had his rough edges is obvious, as is the fact that he made mistakes in his dealings with people in general and with his adversaries in particular. But it is this that makes the "hero" seem human and lovable to us.

One may care to consider expert graphological opinion, which may—quite rightly—be divided. On the occasion of the tenth anniversary of Hermann Buhl's death, a scientist from the French graphological society assessed the handwriting of the "Formula 1" climber with the aim of attesting to his honor. In this analysis, under the heading "Will and Character," it says: "Persistent and untamed will, fairly domineering, prefers to measure himself against the natural obstacles of the mountain world, rather than to bow to human pressure. The authority that people have tried to force upon him from time to time has prompted feelings of anger and rebellion. Knowing what he wants and where he is heading, he is capable of getting over this, totally convinced that he can prove that he is right. He does, however, force himself to submit to the hard and irreversible rules of his own discipline, which is severe but independent. He acts upon his own authority and makes no concessions, only conforming when absolutely necessary." And in summary the analysis says: "The behavior of the loner, Buhl, represents that of a fiery nature driven by an iron will. His entire strength, his comprehension, and his belief are in the service of an ideal, for which he is prepared to sacrifice everything."

To sacrifice everything—should that mean that even his very existence is thrown into the balance? I think not! Hermann Buhl lived intensely; he loved his family and "his" mountains. He loved life, and the kind of life he led meant that now and then he had to cross that delicate boundary high above the abyss between fear, hope, and luck.

Perhaps his quota of luck had run out on that fateful day of 27 June 1957, when the cornice broke. And perhaps the guardian angel, which his daughter Kriemhild suspected he had, had stopped paying attention just for a moment.

Hermann Buhl's wife Eugenie (she much prefers to be called Generl—the name to which she is accustomed) lives in Berchtesgaden-Ramsau, where she has been able to build up a livelihood for herself after the death of her husband by running a small guest house. And when the weather is good she almost always goes out into the mountains to go hiking or skiing.

The Buhls' youngest daughter, Ingrid, died in 1976. The eldest, Kriemhild (Krimi) Lornsen-Buhl, lives near Würzburg and works as a librarian; she is a successful author of both children's and detective books. Their middle daughter, Silvia Bögl, is married and living in Salzburg. She works in social services and is an artist with a preference for glass.

Neither of the surviving daughters is a mountaineer in the strictest sense, but from time to time they do go to the mountains for relaxation. At the age of about 14 or 15, Silvia went on climbs such as the Old South Face and the Barth Chimney on the Hochthron in the Berchtesgadener Alps. She also went on climbing trips with Luis Vigl in the Pala-Dolomites. And, along with Vigl—Hermann's old climbing partner and friend, who now lives near Kitzbühel in the Tyrol—Silvia and Kriemhild very cautiously retraced their father's steps to the Kopftörl Ridge of the Ellmauer Halt and the Hinteren-Goinger-Halt North Ridge in the Wilder Kaiser.

. . . and the confidently resolute.

What Kind of Father Was Buhl?

by Kriemhild Lornsen-Buhl

Hermann Buhl with his daughters Silvia (top) and Ingrid.

"Basically he was, in spite of many an aggravation, a bright man who enjoyed life. He made his mountaineering dream into the essence of his life."

Hans Seidel

He was not a whole-hearted family man, but rather a pronounced individualist with a need for family—a family who would remain in the background like a reservoir of peace. As a child he had not really known the family as a supportive arena for emotional exchange; in the same way, as a father he was soon out of his depth if we children clung on to him seeking devotion or a cozy little nest. He left the emotional side of things to his wife. Our mother is a very emotional person: it is surely not just coincidence that led him to choose her to be his partner. She had the qualities necessary to complement his: warmth of heart, thoughtfulness, a sense of family, and intensity of feeling, and she certainly used this dowry to fill a vacuum in him, to satisfy a longing.

He was not the kind of father who was madly in love with his children, or who became a slave to them. He always kept the upper hand and was a figure of authority rather than a pal. He was a father who wanted to be proud of his children. He had plans for the three of us: we should make something of ourselves. Although he knew us only as young children—our ages were five and a half, three, and one when he died—his wish was that of his three daughters, one would become a photographer, another a journalist, and the third having something to do with foreign languages. He wanted to push us further by demanding achievement from us rather than pampering us.

Mollycoddling, the gentle style of upbringing, was a thorn in his eye. Obviously he had had to do without it as a child. He would have loved to have had a son as well—a son out of his own mold, a son whom he could have shaped and supported according to his own ideas, and whom he would dearly have loved to see following in his own footsteps. Under his father's influence, any son of Buhl's would surely have found it difficult to make his own independent way.

Three daughters made him somewhat helpless. That was unfamiliar territory. Daughters probably embodied for him the emotional side of life—something irrational, perhaps also incalculable, because daughters would, of course, one day leave their father's ship and sail under a foreign flag. In spite of this he loved his "Dreimäderlhaus"—

his three-girl household, as he would call us to others—very much, and spent hours playing songs to us on the guitar if we were fretful or couldn't get to sleep.

When my mother went into hospital to have my sister Silvia in 1954, he stayed at home alone with me, Kriemhild, then aged two and a half, and looked after me in his own very special way. He sat me on the potty for hours so that we didn't have any little accidents, and played the guitar for me the whole time. I really liked that; Papa was playing just for me and I sensed the bond between us. We tamed each other then in the same way as the "Little Prince" and the fox. We really got to know each other.

There were not many such moments of familiarity, as he was a busy, usually distant father, totally absorbed in his own life plan. We children were a natural part of his life, but not the be-all and end-all. In order to get close to him, one had to be able also to leave him in peace. I admired him. To me he seemed strong and independent. I wanted to become like him and was proud when people discovered similarities between us.

As a little girl I noticed that he was pleased if I pulled myself together and persevered rather than whimpering. He took me and Mama on a couple of weekend tours to the Karwendel in order to make me gradually "mountain-worthy." Long climbs up to the huts at his pace were, of course, not my thing. There were too many distractions for me that tried his patience: paddling in mountain streams, picking flowers, collecting stones, and so on.

When he could stand it no longer he would put me on his shoulders and set off at speed. I really liked that. He, too, really liked my attempts at climbing on the bits of rock outside the huts. He was pleased about this and encouraged me, even though my mother was sweating blood and tears in the fear that her little girl might fall. His hope was to awake in me the desire, and at some stage also the ambition, to go climbing. For him the danger was of no concern. Perhaps he trusted his guardian angel. As a little daughter I soon learned how to win Papa's heart: by being willing to work hard and to suppress childish needs.

When he died I was not quite six years old. Mama was sad and cried a lot, and many people came to visit her. It was a strange and hectic atmosphere, which I did not understand. Papa did not come back again, but he had not been there much before anyway. I didn't really miss him. He was more like a dream of a father.

But his wish was fulfilled. He had shaped me. I studied foreign languages, have become an author and enjoy making my own first

"In spite of this he loved his "three girl household" . . . very much."

From the left, Silvia, Ingrid, and Kriemhild Buhl.

"Hermann Buhl was no loner or oddball, yet it takes understanding to accept his unusual way of life. At social events at the club or with mountaineering companions he was friendly, enjoyed telling stories, and livened up the atmosphere with his improvised drum-kit of spoons and pan lids."

Hans Seidel

ascents on sheets of virgin paper, just as he enjoyed his first ascents on rock and ice. Now and again I climb up to the mountains to catch my breath. Then I sense his presence, his energy and his good will, and I am grateful for this father.

How I Experienced Buhl

by Luis Vigl

It was a Friday in August of 1945.

Those returning home from the war were discharged in the large courtyard of the "Grüner Baum" public house in Innsbruck. With bare torsos and arms raised above their heads, they passed by the controllers one after another (they were looking for the blood-group tattoos of members of the SS). Suddenly someone in the queue facing us shouted out my name: "Luis!" It was Hermann, waving happily to me. He had returned from the Cassino front and I from the battle of encirclement in Belgrade. We had not seen each other for almost three years.

His first sentence was: "Hey, the weather forecast is good, we're going to the Kaiser. The 'Fiechtl-Weinberger' and the Mittelgipfel West Face would be good routes to start us off again."

I immediately started thinking about how to get hold of a motorbike to take us up to the Griesner Alm. It wasn't difficult for me to "organize" a bike. Because I was an old dispatch rider, the Americans and the French had used me to requisition motorbikes. In my mind I had already grabbed one of these bikes. . . .

We took the back roads, far away from the American checkpoints, and were soon heading up into the Wilder Kaiser. It was not long before we were standing once more at the foot of "our rock walls," the Totenkirchl, Fleischbank and Predigtstuhl. All the experiences of my youth passed before my eyes.

On the Scharnitzspitze I had climbed with Hermann for the first time. I had immediately felt at ease with his calm and friendly manner and we became climbing partners.

It was at the time when we had nothing. What we had we shared like brothers. Before we started to climb the walls we looked around for dropped pitons, carabiners, and rope slings. Thus our basic equipment was gradually extended. Frau Egger from Innsbruck stitched and glued the Manchon *kletterschuhe* together for us. We met again and again in the Kaiser and in the Karwendel.

At Whitsun 1939, on our first Kaiser Tour with the Youth team of Innsbruck and Hall, we went by train to Kufstein. Hermann stood out because his shoes were too big. He looked like a stork with his thin legs in these enormous mountain boots. We pranksters could think of nothing better than to take his shoes off him and throw them

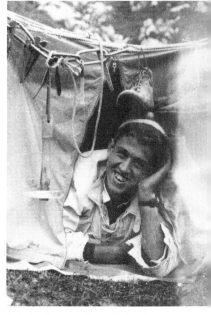

Luis Vigl at the time of his first routes with Hermann Buhl

out of the window of the moving train, one by one. We told the guard that the shoes had fallen out of the window and could hardly believe it when we got them back again, a few hours later, at the station in Kufstein. Luckily for Hermann he was able to take part in the Whitsun tour after all.

In 1941, again on a Youth Team Whitsun trip, our climbing friend Fred Schatz fell on the Predigtstuhl Ridge and was seriously injured. We young men carried him on an improvised stretcher over the Stripsenjoch and down through the entire Kaisertal to Kufstein in eight hours. After that we had not the slightest inclination to mess about on the homeward journey. We were all too exhausted.

We both experienced, and survived, our time at war in the high-mountain regiments. We sometimes met up on various training exercises of the high-mountain and medical corps. And wherever we were, we tried to find out the latest news about "our walls." Thus I also heard that Hermann had turned to extreme climbing. In the closest circles his ability was already highly esteemed.

The "Fiechtl-Weinberger" and the Mittelgipfel West Face became a real pleasure, and from our climbing partnership a real friendship developed. It went without saying that we were to plan all our weekend trips together. First of all we repeated all the new routes in the Kaiser and the Karwendel, all in the VI grade of difficulty.

Hias Rebitsch was on the "Laliderer Direct." His partner fell and thus Hias would not contemplate completing the route for a few weeks. Hermann and I noticed that the Bavarian climbers had their hearts set on this wall. Fairness in mountaineering circles was a "Holy Law"—we would never have dared to complete the Laliderer Direct without Hias' consent.

Hias gave me the green light. The route was planned for a Sunday just at the same time as a climbing friend of ours wanted to celebrate his stag night on Halleranger. We rearranged things so that we could go to the Falken Hut on Friday night and set off for the "Direct" at four o'clock in the morning. It took us ten hours to reach the summit; then we were able to join in the celebrations at the stag night the following evening. I had promised my mother that I would go to early Mass in Hall on Sunday. Thus Hermann and I set off again at four in the morning so that we would make it to church on time. My mother had no idea what we had achieved or where we had been. The breakfast table was set. Hermann was now part of our family, just like a brother.

Our mountain tours were extended to cover the whole of the Alps.

Stag night on the Hallerangeralm in Karwendel—on the day of the first complete ascent of the North Face Direct on the Laliderer Spitze by Hermann Buhl and Luis Vigl. Buhl (far right) and Vigl (left of Buhl) are pretending to be the bride and groom.

Mixed routes and pure ice climbs complemented our rock climbing. The various winter ascents gave us a foretaste of the Western Alps.

Hermann had to earn his money as a skiing instructor for the Americans in Saalfelden. During this time he got to know a girl in Ramsau in Berchtesgaden—his Generl. She came from a good middle-class family and was the daughter of a master engineer. Hermann and Generl fell in love, and when Hermann one day asked me about the price of my kitchen sideboard, I realized that it was serious. Now it was my turn to convince Generl's parents about his competence and reliability. The wedding was celebrated in Ramsau at the "Bierwirt." The Innsbruck and Hall Youth Team took on the responsibility for the music, which was very successful. Sepp Jöchler, known for his excellent accordion playing, was a guarantee for a festive atmosphere.

Hermann's ability and his great toughness helped him secure his triumph on Nanga Parbat. He finally came into money, thanks to his interesting lectures. He was invited to speak all over Europe. The times when we had to share each *schilling* were over. I needed a larger home for my growing family. After being paid for his first speeches Hermann shouted to me: "Luis, at long last we've earned some money!" and he pressed the amount needed for the deposit into my hand quite informally. My own professional success meant I was soon able to repay him.

When my son Luis was born, Hermann was determined to be his godfather.

My brother and I had settled for "middle-class" professions. Mountaineering became Hermann's profession. He managed to make this jump thanks to his intelligence and creativity. I think back to our joint holiday on the Adriatic with our wives. Hermann built himself a desk of sand and wrote for days on his portable typewriter. Thus the "original manuscript" for his book *Nanga Parbat Pilgrimage* came about.

Is it a mistake to be the best?

A climbing display had been organized on the local crags in Chamonix. People from France, Italy, Germany, and Austria took part. Hermann, in his enthusiasm and pleasure in climbing, beat all "nations" and stepped into the limelight without any diplomatic experience. The force-fields that this created became too great a handicap for any further peaceful development.

Hermann had suddenly moved into first place. Only old hands like

Buhl, left, with Luis Vigl, who is seen here driving Buhl from Munich to Berchtesgaden-Ramsau in 1953 after Buhl's return from Nanga Parbat. Vigl is linked to Buhl by a life-long friendship; they climbed the East Face of Monte Rosa together in 1955.

Gravestone in memory of Hermann Buhl in the cemetery in Berchtesgaden-Ramsau, Generl's hometown.

Terray, Lachenal, Contamine, and Cassin recognized these achievements as sovereign. Meanwhile, the young and ambitious started their battle. On their home areas they desperately defended their territory. Hermann had to defend himself on all sides. All at once people started talking about him as a "personality cult," a choice of words that was alien to us mountaineers.

As the old German saying goes, "Many dogs kill the hare." Hermann's fall at the age of 32 is indeed the result of this development.

Buhl in the Sella group, Dolomites; not one of the photographs from his early climbing years. There are no color photographs that show Hermann Buhl in his early youth.

It was on the Grubreisen Towers, an offshoot of the (Innsbruck) North Karwendel chain, that Hermann Buhl took his first climbing steps. Hermann's first entry in his first climbing diary (1 May 1940) concerns the South Tower-South Ridge, which can be seen on the left of the picture.

Buhl returned time and time again to the Kalkkögel. The line of the Auckenthaler Route on the West Face of the Riepenwand is roughly in the middle of the right-hand part of the photo. On 5 July 1942 Hermann Buhl and Waldemar Gruber accomplished the third ascent.

The Schüsselkarspitze in the Wetterstein mountains (with the "Erinnerungshüttl" or Memorial Hut in the foreground) was the setting for various stages in Hermann Buhl's development as a top-flight climber. The route list includes: in 1940, the Spindler Route; in 1942, the second winter ascent; the "Herzog-Fiechtl"; the "South-East" (Peters/ Haringer); the "Direct" (Kuno Rainer/ Paul Aschenbrenner); the East Face (Schober/ Kleisl) and—in October—the first solo ascent of the classic Herzog-Fiechtl Route.

In August 1943 Hermann Buhl climbed the Dülfer Route on the West Face of the Totenkirchl in the Wilder Kaiser, doing all the traverses without tension from the rope. Buhl's ascent was thus one of the first free ascents—if not the first—of this VI+ Kaiser classic.

"Buhl was light, wiry, and
very fit. He had the ideal
climber's build. He moved
languidly, like a cat, but
fast and steady. Over the
years he also developed an
instinct for danger in the
mountains. It was on loose
rock that Buhl's real
mastery was apparent."

Reinhold Messner

Hermann Buhl in the 1950s,
seen here free climbing
on the Herzog-Fiechtl
Route on the South Face
of the Schüsselkarspitze
(Wetterstein).

The first ascent of the West Face of the Maukspitze (the prominent smooth wall in the right-hand third of the photo) in the Wilder Kaiser was Hermann Buhl's first significant new route (climbed in 1943 with Wastl Weiss and Hans Reischl).

Together with his lifelong friend Luis Vigl, Hermann Buhl made the first complete ascent of the Direct North Face of the Laliderer in the Karwendel, in 1947.

The Brenva Face of Mont
Blanc and the Peuterey Ridge.
Between 1948 and 1951, and
in 1955 and 1956, Buhl succeeded in climbing some of
the most difficult routes in
this region, among them the
second ascent of the North
face of the Aiguille Blanche
and the first complete
traverse of the Chamonix
Aiguilles.

The first winter ascent of the South West Face of the Marmolata (on the left-hand side of the photo) finally fell to Hermann Buhl and Kuno Rainer, after two previous attempts, in March 1950.

"Hermann climbed like a cat."

Luis Vigl

Left:
During their first trip to the Western Alps in 1948, Hermann Buhl and Luis Vigl made the fifth ascent of the North Face of the Aiguille de Triolet in the Mont Blanc group.

In 1950, the Walker Spur on the Grandes Jorasses (left of center) still held the reputation of being the biggest mountaineering challenge in the Alps. Hermann Buhl and Kuno Rainer made the seventh ascent that year.

"It all went too slowly for him out there in France. He was a restless spirit. He was a man obsessed."

Kuno Rainer

Right:
An ascent of the Cassin Route on the North Face of the Cima Ouest (right of center) in the autumn of 1950 was a fitting end to a successful year for the Buhl/Kuno Rainer partnership.

The North East Face of the Piz Badile (in the Southern Bergell). Buhl made the first solo ascent in just four and a half hours.

Also in 1952, Buhl and Jöchler climbed the "Tofana Pillar." Theirs was the fourth ascent.

In 1952 Hermann Buhl and Sepp Jöchler climbed the North Face of the
Eiger (eighth ascent).

Nanga Parbat. This aerial photograph shows Buhl's line of ascent via the Silberplateau (the Silver Plateau) (left of center), the False Summit, the Bazhin Gap and the Summit.

"Buhl would still have gone to Nanga Parbat even if he had known in advance what Herrligkoffer and his cronies would later make of his [Buhl's] success. Nanga Parbat was his mountain of Destiny, the peak and the proof of his achievements. It was up there that Buhl's rise to fame ended. His fall began when he returned to Base Camp; the fall that all those who envied him—and a few who attempted to capitalize on his success— had seen coming."

Reinhold Messner

The ladder through the ice fall on the Rakhiot Glacier (1953) which provided the fastest access to Camp 2 on Nanga Parbat.

Part 1

The Beginning
The Mountains as a Homeland

Herman Buhl's climbing life begins in September 1934 with a hike up the Glungezer in the local Tuxer hills. His father accompanies him on this trip to celebrate the lad's tenth birthday. On the summit, Hermann is fascinated by the peaks and towers of the Inn Valley chain of the Karwendel that the people of Innsbruck call the "North Chain" because it rises north of the town.

A few years later these mountains become Hermann's adventure playground. Sunday after Sunday he runs around and jumps about among the peaks. He finds the scrambling and climbing rather easy. Here on the silvery gray Karwendel ridges, towers and needles, Buhl equips himself for his later career as a climber. During these early years, exploring alone on the paths and grassy slopes, in the snow, and on crumbling and solid rock, he acquires—in a similar way to Paul Preuss's youthful climbing experiences—a feeling for sure-footedness in the mountains.

Down in the town Hermann stands in front of the display windows of the sports shops. Yes, if only he had a rope! But he does not have the money for that, so he has to take his stepmother's washing line. The young lad uses this to undertake his first simple climbing tours with friends: the South Ridge of the Brandjoch and the Normal Route on the legendary rock tower "Frau Hitt."

In 1939 Buhl discovers the Grubreisen Towers for himself. Alone, wearing ski boots, the fourteen-year-old tests himself on the Melzer Tower—any ascent of which is usually graded at least as a lower IV. Hermann begins to climb, and manages to get a fair distance up, but then he can't go any farther. Some climbers have been watching the lad from below and offer to help him with a rope, but Buhl refuses this help and fights his way back down, from handhold to foothold, until he is once more on solid ground.

The other climbers are impressed by this independent retreat, and invite him to climb with them on the North Tower (III+). And then the boy realizes who his guides are: Peter Aschenbrenner, Wastl Mariner, and Sepp Douschan, household names among climbers in the area.

During the descent the experienced climbers show Buhl the Southern Ridge of the Grubreisen South Tower. He learns that it is a difficult climb and is told that he is not yet ready for it, but just a

The beginning: Hermann Buhl (left) and Ernstl Vitavski, a youthful partnership on the Grubreisen Towers of the Karwendel North Chain. Vitavski fell to his death in 1940 when attempting to solo the Auckenthaler Crack on the South Ridge of the Grubreisen South Tower.

week later Buhl and his school friend, Ernstl Vitavski, are standing at the start of the route. Above them on the ridge a couple is already climbing. One of them calls down to ask whether the lads could bring their rope, which is lying at the start of the climb, up the Normal Route to the top of the South Tower.

The rope. What a temptation! Hermann and Ernstl tie themselves into the rope and climb up to the others via the South Ridge (V- and IV), catching up with them at the foot of the summit wall.

That is the gist of what it says in Buhl's bestselling book, *Nanga Parbat Pilgrimage,* which was, of course, edited by Kurt Maix. We choose the word "gist" quite consciously here! This is because in the book it also says that Ernstl Vitavski fell to his death while attempting to solo climb the Auckenthaler Crack (VI-/A1) a few weeks after their South Ridge climb together and—according to *Nanga Parbat Pilgrimage*—this must have taken place in 1939. This, however, cannot be true given the time span, because according to Buhl's climbing diaries, he and Vitavski climbed the Vorderes Brandjoch, Frau Hitt and the Sattelspitze on 26 May 1940!

It seems editor Maix has not read Buhl's climbing diaries. Perhaps Hermann did not want to part with these diaries, which he kept so lovingly and which without a doubt represented a personal "treasure trove" for him. Be that as it may, we do not know how Buhl coped with or came to terms with the death of his early climbing partner.

In 1939 Buhl joins the Youth Team of the Innsbruck Section of the (former) "German Alpine Club." On 1 May 1940 he begins to write his first climbing diary. On the title page, in pencil, Buhl has drawn a picture of the Matterhorn; written underneath it in German script are these words: "The mountains, they are my homeland."

First Diary:
1 May 1940 to 20 June 1941

(Extracts)

The first climbing diary of the fifteen- and sixteen-year-old Hermann Buhl covers his early years as a mountaineer, as he writes of his experiences first on easier, then more and more difficult routes, on which he survives often dangerous situations.

The first attempt by Hermann Buhl and Karl Glätzle to climb the South Ridge of the Grubreisen South Tower was a hair-raisingly adventurous event. Buhl was almost struck by a falling slab of rock.

The extracts from Buhl's texts are presented here "unvarnished," that is, without attempting to edit or clarify except where it seemed particularly needed for the reader's understanding. Apart from adjusting some of the punctuation, we have purposely left them in essentially their original form.

1 May 1940
GRUBREISEN TOWERS, KARWENDEL
South Tower, South Ridge

Now the time has come when the skier enjoys the splendid glacier downhills but the climber, too, can follow his urge for the cliffs that soar heavenwards. I, too, am one of those who can no longer wait to go climbing and so I decided to undertake a climb this coming Friday with Karl Glätzle.

On 1 May I left my flat at 4:00 a.m. and headed towards the Seegrube, which I reached at 7 o'clock. There I waited for my mountain companion, who came up with the train at 7:30. We traveled straight on to the Hafelekar cirque. Here it was bitterly cold. The descent into the cirque demanded great care due to the deep snow.

Soon we were over at the start of the route. After a little snack we changed our shoes. Our intention was to do the South Ridge of the Grubreisen South Tower. Glätzle soon set about the vertical wall of the first pitch. He was soon up at the loose slab. I thought to myself, hopefully it will hold. As Karl was pulling himself up on it, the slab broke loose and both of them flew down towards me. But the piton that was a few meters below Karl held the fall. I was ripped from the stance and dragged up against the wall and thus escaped the death-bringing missile. The slab hit the ground exactly where I had firßn belaying. Luckily, everything had gone all right. We turned back and waited for our Youth Team leader Hannes Schmidhuber, who was coming down from the cirque. Then, with him, we climbed a chimney that led to the South Ridge and along this by varied and very nice climbing to the summit.

Hannes was in a real hurry and immediately descended a snow-filled gully straight back to our rucksacks. Karl and I were still roped up and slid down the steep gully in this way. It got faster and faster and we could not brake enough with our rubbers [rubber-soled climbing shoes]. Then it was down over rocks to the cirque. That was a tough test for the leather on our backsides! We changed our shoes, raced across onto the Hafelekar cirque, and from there returned down to Innsbruck.

"He didn't have much to eat."
Luis Vigl

2 May 1940
GRUBREISEN TOWERS, KARWENDEL
South Tower, South Ridge, Auckenthaler Crack

On the second day of the holiday I wanted to go up to the Grubreisen Towers again, the "School of Karwendel Climbing." My companions were again Hannes Schmidhuber and Karl Glätzle. This time we left somewhat later and only got to the entry pitch of the South Ridge at ten o'clock. [Mathias or "Hias"] Rebitsch was already there with some of his friends from the army. We waited around at the start until it got a little warmer. In the meantime, Rebitsch climbed and descended the South Tower South Ridge on his own.

Towards midday we started climbing. The entry pitch was hard going for us. Since the slab is now down below it is no longer as easy to reach the ring peg. After a few rope maneuvers we had managed it. Up to the Auckenthaler Crack everything went smoothly. Here, we searched out a good place to belay, then Hannes set off up the pitch. . . . The crack was badly nailed. There were only four pitons in place, so we had to place most of them ourselves. Hannes said it reminded him of being on the South East Face of the Schüsselkar. At the overhang he had to come back down once, and then he overcame it.

Now it was my turn. The waiting had made me cold. But with the hard climbing that soon went. At the overhang I needed a pull from above and then that part was behind me. Glätzle now came up and had to hammer out our pitons. After a short bit of climbing we reached the summit. . . .

17 May 1940
BRANDJOCH, KARWENDEL
Ascent: South Ridge, Descent: East Ridge

This Sunday I was on my own again and so I decided to do the South Ridge of the Brandjoch. There was still a lot of snow lying everywhere and the seracs were glistening in the sunlight.

On Sunday morning I had already left the flat by 4:00 a.m. and made for the Achselkopf. The hut located there was managed by a guardian. I called in. When I announced my plan to the people there they advised me against it and said that I would not make it with all the new snow. But I refused to be dissuaded and soon left the hut.

After strength-sapping trail-breaking in deep snow I reached the Brandjoch. Here the South Ridge started. Everything around me was

"And then you try to get a feel for the rock again. The first pitch is mostly still rather hesitant, but then the rock again becomes that same old companion. And you stroke it again, like a delicate thing."

Hermann Buhl

On the Brandjoch in the Northern Karwendel, the 15-year-old Hermann Buhl braved tricky winter conditions.

white. The rocks were covered with ice and snow. Thick fog enveloped me and flakes came down from the heavens. I was soon standing on the first big cornice and kept myself well back from its edge. It was a place for the greatest caution, since the new snow lay on top of hard snow and ice. Also, the light was so diffuse that you could not see the edge of the cornice from just a few meters' distance. The cornices had a height of eight to ten meters. They were hung with thick icicles covered in hoar frost.

I had soon put the first gallery of cornices behind me. Then came rock and after it the second big cornice. After a further stretch of rock the third and last big cornice gallery followed; this one was especially steep and hard. After this came a difficult bit of rock, the chimney. I could not get into it from the side, had to climb down and could only gain entry to the chimney from below, through a tight crevice filled with ice. I was worried all the time that the ice would fall into the depths and take me with it. Shards of ice broke off with every blow from the ice axe. I bridged up the chimney. The little cornice that roofed it over had a hole in it that I slipped through. Now came a sharp snow ridge with double cornices, a traverse across a steep snowfield, and then followed the summit slope. Soon afterwards I was standing on the summit.... Because of the cold and the wind I soon descended via the East Ridge. Here was smooth, ice-covered rock with little snow. So an ice axe belay was not really possible. Suddenly I slipped—the axe could not find enough purchase in the thin covering of snow—and I was off. I thought I would come to a stop at a rocky outcrop but I slid over it. On my stomach, then up on my legs, then somersaulting over, I whistled down a steep snow gully on the North Flank of the Brandjoch. Farther down lay more snow. Here I came to a stop by ramming the pick of the axe into the snow with all my strength.

Ten meters below me was a vertical precipice dropping 50 meters down to the cirque. The snow that had slid down with me thundered down into the cirque. I had slithered down almost the entire North Flank of the Brandjoch. Rather more carefully, I then traversed across to "Frau Hitt." As far as the Höttinger Alm I had to stamp down quite a lot of snow and often I broke through the snow, which came up to my chest. Totally soaked through, I arrived at the Alm at about four o'clock in the afternoon. I warmed myself up and then walked back down into the town. I had never seen the Brandjoch like that before and never imagined it to be like that. Now another adventurous Sunday had passed and I am fully satisfied with my mountaineering route.

Hermann Buhl, aged about 16, outside the Memorial Hut on the Scharnitzjoch in the Wetterstein. He was already a member of the Youth Team of the Innsbruck Section of the Alpine Club.

4 August 1940
SCHARNITZSPITZE, WETTERSTEIN
South West Face

At seven o'clock Sepp Fuchs, Herbert Eberharter, Herta Maier and I left our cozy little home in the Leutasch and walked up to the start of the route. At 10 o'clock we started climbing: Herbert with Herta; Sepp and I. I led the Welzenbach Overhang and the following pitches. The whole face is now split by a chimney. Lovely, varied and airy climbing up this and we reached an area of bulging slabs, which offered the last pitch. We made alternate leads. Here, Franz Hermann [who had been soloing the route and had overtaken the two parties] fell 250 meters to his death. We were very shocked by this and climbed rather more cautiously. Soon we climbed out onto the summit and shook hands. We met the others on the Wangscharte and told them about the accident.

18 August 1940
SCHÜSSELKARZSPITZE, WETTERSTEIN
South Face, Spindler Route

Kuno Rainer and Herbert Eberharter took us along on a really big route: the Schüsselkar South Face. On Saturday we walked up to the Memorial Hut, so as to be near the wall the next day. On Sunday the weather was fine, so we were already climbing by 8 o'clock. Kuno led me and Herta up it and the second party was led by Eberharter. We were soon at the traverse. It went smoothly. Now came pitch after pitch of very nice climbing up to the top. We were soon down below again, via the West Ridge. We picked up our things from the Memorial Hut and walked back down to the Leutasch.

In 1940 Buhl managed several other easier routes in the Ferwall and in the Karwendel, attended a climbing course in the Kaisergebirge with the Youth Team and took part in a mountain rescue exercise on the Olperer in the Zillertal Alps. In the autumn he climbed a route on the Steingrubenkogel and one on the Kleine Ochsenwand in the Kalkkögel. This climbing area is part of the Stubai Alps and it was on these—often loose—walls that a mere two years later Buhl was to mature into an extreme leader.

For Hermann Buhl, these 1940-1941 climbing years alternated between carefree—and thus often hair-raisingly dangerous—days on the

The new generation of Innsbruck climbers poses in front of the Memorial Hut. With Herta Maier (right), Buhl (second from right) climbed many extreme rock routes in the Wetterstein, the Wilder Kaiser, and the Kalkkögel.

rock and light-hearted hours spent in the company of the *Jugend-mannschaftsblas'n* (the musicians of the Youth Team). His climbing diary reveals that although Buhl was never really the initiator of bois-terous pranks he would observe such antics with great pleasure.

The ascent of the South Face Cracks on the Martinswand (V+/A1) was to become a defining experience for Buhl, one that finally showed him the way to pull off difficult ventures of his own, inde-pendent of his mentors.

At the start of his extreme mountaineering career, Buhl gained admission to the fa-mous "Karwendler" climbing club, founded in 1904. Buhl's membership card was signed by none other than the great Erwin Schneider.

16 February 1941
ALPENKLUBSCHARTE, KALKKÖGEL

Glätzle, Franz, [and Glätzle,] Karl and I intended doing a winter ascent of the *Gipfelstürmerweg* on the West Face of the Kleine Ochsenwand. The rock conditions could not have been better for this enterprise. The *föhn* [warm] wind had blown all the new snow off the walls. Due to the warmth these were now free of ice and quite dry.

In order to get a good start the next day we went up on Saturday [on skis] to the Adolf-Pichler-Hut. On Sunday we left the hut at 9 o'clock. Soon we were breaking trail up to the start of the climb. The weather was very *föhnig*. The new snow had been blown into a hard crust and we were worried about the danger of windslab. Karl was almost at the entry pitch, Franz was a little way below him climbing up with herringbone steps, and I was right out away to the right. Suddenly Karl shouted, "Avalanche, avalanche." I could already hear it roaring and then it came down, like a raging torrent five meters high.... To my left there was a rock spur and I reckoned the ava-lanche went thundering down behind it. It had already swept Karl away; I could no longer see him. The avalanche had increased in size tremendously. I watched as the slope split into plates, leapt into the air and shot out to the left. Down below, the avalanche cone was over one hundred meters wide....

In vain, I looked around for my companions. I was just about to descend when Karl, who was standing on the rock spur, shouted to me where Franz was. Soon afterwards a figure churned his way out of the debris cone. It was Franz. He had only lost his skins [ski coverings for climbing], otherwise everything had gone all right.

Karl then told me that he saw the slope go up there, shouted and then shot behind the rock spur, where he braced himself against the avalanche, which still took him down with it. Luckily, he was able to stick a ski pole in a hole and so hang on to it. The whole avalanche went down over him.

Because he was right inside it Franz could not get out. . . . Soon everything went black in front of his eyes. The loose powder snow forced its way through his clothing and into his air passages and he ran out of breath. Suddenly everything grew lighter around him and straightaway he set to, to dig himself out and clean the snow out of his mouth and throat. He had been swept down about 300 meters.

So the day had been thoroughly messed up, even though the weather had turned out fine. We could not do anything else, since it was now too late for that. [Franz] Glätzle showed off his skiing skills by doing adventurous turns.

2 June 1941
PREDIGTSTUHL, WILDER KAISER
North Summit–North Ridge, Middle Summit,
Descent by the Botzong Chimney

Fred Schatz and I got permission from Hannes to do the Christaturm Arête. But when we were at the start of the Predigtstuhl Arête we decided to do that with Wastl. Weber was also with us. We were up at the top of the first chimney quickly. Then it went rather slower, since one of the ropes was only 20 meters long. Curtains of rock followed, then came the vertical arête. At the foot was the Matejak Traverse, followed by chimneys and cracks. After that came easier ground and finally the summit headwall, which still held a few nice sections.

Then we were standing on the North Summit. Wastl was already a bit ahead. We climbed the Middle Summit and wanted to get onto the Main Summit. Fred, who had not allowed me to lead any of the route, went first here as well. Now came the most difficult section. We were able to get a good belay. Fred did not see the piton and went past it, but soon had to come back again and spent a long time hanging onto a hold. He probably ran out of juice, for suddenly I saw a shadow flashing down the wall. I was just about able to let Weber know and together we held the 15-meter fall.

Fred was groaning a lot. Weber went down to him and I notified Wastl. He said we should lower Fred down the Botzong Chimney. We started doing this straight away. Fred had injured his knee and had also bruised his feet, so at first he could not even stand up. I abseiled down first, looked for a good belay and let Fred abseil down—using a classic abseil and belayed by Weber—after me. Then Weber abseiled down. Thereafter, the rope was pulled down and the whole maneuver started again from the beginning.

The only things to abseil from were blocks. On one section only

It was down the Botzong Chimney on the Predigtstuhl (the dark fissure on the left of the picture) that, in 1941, Buhl and his climbing partner, Weber, had to lower the injured Fred Schatz, who had fallen 15 meters when attempting to cross from the Middle Summit to the Main Summit.

there were three pitons in. There was a waterfall coming down the chimney and furthermore there was ice and snow in the back. We were soon soaked to the skin and everyone was shivering with cold. The rope was like a steel cable, we could hardly pull it through and the friction around the body was so great that we could hardly make any headway. There were four or five abseils and we required three hours for them. Back down at the bottom, Wastl, Pauli and Hans took over, who had been watching us. Fred was then carried over to the Stripsenjoch. I had to walk across there with one shoe, since the other one lay right down at the bottom.

Completely soaked and frozen through I arrived at the hut and was looking forward to dry clothes and some decent grub. However, the hut was completely full and the rucksack was still at the bottom of the first pitch of the route, so I just lay myself down. Early the next day I went to fetch the rucksack. In the afternoon we transported Fred to Kufstein and took the train back to Innsbruck.

29 June 1941
MARTINSWAND, KARWENDEL

The Sunday finally arrived when my long-yearned-for wish was to be fulfilled. We were off to the Martinswand. I felt fit and the weather also seemed to be good enough for it. At half past eight we drove over to Kranebitten. From there we walked up to the start of the route.

At half past eleven we started up the first pitch. Since I was the lightest, I led. And we were soon at the top of the chimney on the lower part since I knew it well from earlier in the year. At the beginning of the groove we deliberated for a long time whether we should push on through or turn back, but decided to carry on up. It was now that our equipment—double ropes and 15 carabiners—were pressed into service. The first pitch gave us a foretaste of the wall. Each successive rope length now got harder and harder. Grass rendered the climbing more difficult. However, there were six to ten pitons in place on every pitch, all of them placed by the practiced hand of Hias Auckenthaler and all of them reliable. The groove is loose in parts and very exposed in its upper reaches.

After five pitches, of which the last two are the hardest, we stood beneath the overhang. It is festooned with nine pitons and I ran out of carabiners. Now, the wall lies back. We did everything without a tight rope. After two pitches, which called for great care due to the poor belays, the looseness and the grass, we stood at the first trees.

The ascent of the South Face Crack on the Martinswand near Zirl in the Inn Valley was a milestone in Hermann Buhl's early years as a rock climber.

Now it was up through the woods to the Jägersteigl and across this and down to Zirl.

Totally dehydrated, we arrived at the road at seven o'clock. Since there were no more trains we marched on foot back to Innsbruck.

6 July 1941
SCHARNITZSPITZE, WETTERSTEIN
South West Face

Auckenthaler memorial day. Around 20 young men met up on Saturday in the Leutasch, where we spent the night. The next day we were up early and off to the Wangalm. A wreath was woven, a ceremonial fire built and lit and two of the lads did one piked vault after another over the fire. Albert gave the cows no peace at all, of course. Our new rescue appliance was tested. It failed the test and was soon in bits.

In the afternoon everyone went off to do their routes. Karl and I did the "Kadner," which we polished off in an hour. Then it was the memorial celebration. The wreath was hung and candles were lit. Karl and Hans said a few words in remembrance. Then it was back down into the Leutasch again. Hans let the wheel from the rescue appliance roll down the slope. It picked up more and more speed, the cows could just jump out of the way in time. The wheel made 10-meter leaps into the air and came to rest in a gorge, damaged, of course. From the Leutasch it was back to Innsbruck by bike, where we arrived at 11 o'clock at night.

"The climber who sees only the rock experiences Nature just as little as the hiker who sees only the flowers."

Hermann Buhl

BEGINNINGS . . .

Hermann Buhl was not only the first man to climb Nanga Parbat, the first "Westerner" with two successes on 8000-meter peaks; he was, above all, one of the best rock climbers of modern times. The decade between 1939 and 1948 is every bit as important in Buhl's "career" as the nine years afterward, the years that were to make him famous, first in Innsbruck, then in the German-speaking world, and finally in the worldwide mountaineering scene. Buhl was first and foremost a rock climber and, moreover, he climbed his routes free, insofar as this was possible given the footwear and the training methods of the day. That Buhl was in direct competition with his contemporaries was all too understandable. There were Erich Streng and Manfred Bachmann in North Tyrol; Erich Abram and Otto Eisenstecken in South Tyrol; Martin Schliessler and Hermann Köllensperger in Germany. Later, Buhl was to measure his skills

Hermann Buhl lovingly kept a climbing diary. Here, the entry for 11 October 1942 of the second volume. On this day Hermann climbed on the bizarre needles of the Erlspitz group in the Karwendel Mountains.

"Now the time has come when the skier enjoys the splendid glacier downhills, but the climber, too, can follow his urge for the cliffs that soar heavenwards. I, too, am one of those who can no longer wait to go climbing."

Hermann Buhl

against those of the most successful climbers around: Lionel Terray, Gaston Rébuffat, Guido Magnone, Walter Bonatti . . .

To be sure, it cannot have been easy for his predecessors—Hias Rebitsch, Anderl Heckmair, Rudolf Peters, Riccardo Cassin—to watch this "new star" in ascendance. Yet most of the young climbers of the future took their direction from Buhl: Toni Egger, Kurt Diemberger, Joe Brown. Or Lothar Brandler and Dietrich Hasse, who dedicated their first ascent on the Rotwand in the Dolomites to Buhl. It was the kind of gesture Hermann Buhl could no longer simply dismiss.

It was only with his successes farther afield than the mountains of the North Tyrol—from the Marmolata in the Dolomites to the Aiguille de Triolet in the Mont Blanc region—that Buhl achieved widespread recognition as one of the finest climbers of the post-war period. Suddenly it was "Buhl did this; Buhl did that." On limestone and on granite, on ice and snow, he could move like few others. He was also lucky, and developed his will, his instinct and ideas to achieve greatness. His rise was unstoppable, even by those who simply could not believe that this poor man, returned from the war, was capable of such an impressive run of success.

The climbs that the twenty-five-year-old Buhl preferred were the "big name" routes: the Soldà (Marmolata), the Walker Spur, and the Cassin Route (Cima Ouest). He wanted to demonstrate that he was faster than his predecessors and yet he paid them due respect: Auckenthaler, Allain, Lachenal. Hermann Buhl was an extreme climber in the classical sense: deeply rooted in the free climbing tradition yet with his sights set firmly on future deeds.

THE RISE OF THE STAR

Buhl rapidly became a legend: "Badile solo"; "Eigerwand in a storm"; "Bivouac on the Tofana Pillar." Yet the fact that with these sensational headlines the curiosity of the public at large grew while the accuracy of the reports suffered went unnoticed by Buhl himself. He wanted to go farther, higher. Despite all the difficulties and dangers he wanted to go to the boundaries of what was possible. Buhl wanted to go to the Himalaya.

"He was very lean and looked really hungry—not only for food . . . there was fire in his eyes . . . "

Mathias Rebitsch

Hermann Buhl on the summit of the Badile after the first solo ascent of the North East Face (1952).

Second Diary:
1 January 1942 to 21 November 1943

(Extracts)

Buhl's second climbing diary reveals more about his development as an extreme mountaineer than any other document. It contains, after several descriptions of ski-mountaineering tours, the entry for the second winter ascent of the Spindler Route on the South Face of the Schüsselkarspitze, the record of an ascent of the South Cor-

In 1942 Hermann Buhl and Waldemar Gruber made the eighth ascent of the North West Corner of the Riepenwand (center) in the Kalkkögel.

ner of the Schüsselkarspitze incorporating the Auckenthaler Crack, and the following remarks about the Herzog-Fiechtl Route on the Schüsselkarspitze South, a climb he had long wanted to do and finally achieved on 10 May 1942: A long-yearned-for wish was fulfilled! I was in top form; everything went without a hitch. My partner was Herbert Eberharter, who was on leave here from the battle front. Manfred Bachmann and Waldemar Gruber were also on the cliff. Time: 4+ hours."

Six days later Buhl climbed the "Auckenthaler" on the Martinswand in two and a half hours, and on 24 May he succeeded on the South East Face of the Fleischbank in the Wilder Kaiser. A few days later Hermann "ran" up the South East Ridge of the Christaturm in an hour, with Waldemar Gruber, and subsequently the two men climbed the Dülfer Route on the East Face of the Fleischbank in just three and a half hours.

On 5 July Hermann Buhl and Waldemar Gruber became the third party to climb the West Face of the Riepenwand in the Kalkkögel—Buhl's first grade VI route! They started the climb at three o'clock in the afternoon and by 10 o'clock, as darkness was falling, they had done it. Also in July, Hermann—again with Waldemar Gruber—climbed the North West Corner on the Riepenwand. This was the eighth ascent and the route "counts as one of the most difficult climbs in the Kalkkögel. . . . Waldi fell off the last corner pitch six times and could get up it only by using prussik loops. Hats off to Hias Auckenthaler," writes Buhl.

August 1942 also saw a series of grade six routes in the Kalkkögel, as well as the South East Face of the Schüsselkarspitze. After six lines of his diary entry ("Rock on head—hole; otherwise everything went well" . . .) Hermann quotes poetry:

> Rest on the summit
> Fairy hands fill the valleys with clouds
> Raising them higher and higher.
> The mountains slowly sink.
> Over the peaks and the tops
> A second, glistening, far-off range builds.
> —L. Lang

The progression continues in linear fashion: Schüsselkarspitze South Face Direct, Schüsselkarspitze East Face, Öfelekopf South Face. A total of seven extreme routes within four weeks are recorded. In September 1942 Hermann Buhl and Waldemar Gruber climb their first big Karwendel route.

6 September 1942
LALIDERER NORTH FACE, KARWENDEL
Auckenthaler Route
7th ascent

> "In the heart of the Karwendel there is a rock face whose form and whose frightful smoothness and steepness are unlike any of the many other walls I know."
>
> Hermann Buhl

With Waldi Gruber; height of face: 1000 m, time: 10 hours, with 2+ hour detour after going off-route, exceptionally diff., best mountain route in Northern Limestone Alps; incredibly long. Weather: bad, red sky early morning, wind, mist, cold.

Saturday 8:00 a.m. by bike from Innsbruck up to Karwendelhaus, then on foot to Falkenhütte. Arrived 6:00 p.m. No hut guardian.

Sunday up at 5 in the morning, started the route at 8 o'clock; on the summit at 6 o'clock in the evening; descent by Spindler Gully in mist; back at hut at half past seven in the evening. Only party in the Falkenhütte area. Back to Karwendelhaus in pouring rain and pitch darkness; spent night there. Monday morning ¼ meter new snow and snow storm. Back to Innsbruck by bike during morning.

The seventh ascent of the Auckenthaler Route on the North Face of the Lalidererspitze was a great experience for Hermann Buhl and Waldemar Gruber.

From now on, the entries in the diary provide a record of further notable stages in the 18- and 19-year-old Hermann Buhl's climbing career: from the second ascent of the Auckenthaler Route on the North Face of the Praxmarerkarspitze in the Gleiersch-Halltal range of the Karwendel, right up to Buhl's first important new route, the West Face of the Maukspitze in the Wilder Kaiser.

The entries are powerful evidence and written in an engaging manner. Here, for example, we find the emotional outburst of Kuno Rainer after he had seconded the crux pitch of the North Face of the Praxmarerkarspitze: "Bua, bua," he shouted to Buhl [translator's note: "Phew!"], a comment which expressed both worry and respect in equal measures. Or note the few terse lines about the first solo ascent of the Herzog-Fiechtl Route on the South Face of the Schüsselkarspitze, which encapsulate in a single sentence the huge free climbing talent that Buhl possessed. And Buhl's original account of his 50-metre fall on the East Face of the Fleischbank makes for an exciting read!

The free ascent of the Dülfer Route on the West Face of the Totenkirchl, on the other hand, must be rated almost as a minor mountaineering sensation: "All traverses climbed free; without tension from rope," Buhl wrote in his climbing diary. This means that the Tyrolean must have done the "Nasenquergang" (VI+) free in 1943, and that in 1979, Sepp Gschwendtner, Andreas Kubin and Herwig Sedlmeyer were only the second team to repeat this feat! (Sedlmeyer reckons that it is entirely possible that Buhl did the route free.)

Then there is Hermann Buhl's account of the first ascent of the West Face of the Maukspitze. Nowhere else is climbing at the absolute limit of what was then possible more excitingly represented: a hair-raising description!

13 September 1942
NORTH FACE OF THE EASTERN PRAXMARERKARSPITZE, KARWENDEL
Auckenthaler-Schmidhuber Route
2nd ascent

With Kuno Rainer. Bachmann and Knoll as second rope. Height of face: 600-700 m, time: 6-7 hours; exceptionally difficult, madly loose; typical Karwendel route; must count as one of my hardest routes and one of the most dangerous faces I have been on. Lower section climbs a pillar of overhanging, red/yellow rock. The wall made a huge impression on me.

Saturday . . . to the Hallerangerhaus; waited out the storm there and then pressed on to Lafatscher Hochleger; pitch-dark night, lost the path; we did not have a lamp with us. After a lot of up-and-down and to-and-fro in the wild Karwendel woods we gave up and lay down on the soaking wet ground, but could not get to sleep because of the cold.

The morning finally arrived and we soon had the path again. We

In September 1942 Hermann Buhl and Kuno Rainer made the second ascent of the Auckenthaler-Schmidhuber Route on the loose North Face of the Praxmarerkarspitze (Karwendel, Gleiersch-Halltal range). The eighteen-year-old Buhl led the crux.

still had 2 hours to the Hochlegeralm and then another 1+ hours with no path up to the Praxmarerkar-Reissen. We reached the start of the route over loose rubble. By coincidence Bachmann and Knoll were coming up the hill and we met at the start of the first pitch. For ten years the wall had enjoyed peace and quiet, and now there were suddenly four candidates on it.

There were no arguments; we simply agreed that Kuno and I would go first. It was all very pleasant up as far as the pillar. Then that sinister wall really reared up: 250 m, all of it overhanging. While I set about the thing, the others had to take cover and bide their time. Salvo after salvo of loose rocks fell into the awful void. There were hardly any pitons at all. I was certainly happy when I stood on the ledge after the first two pitches. It was now a matter of crawling along a ledge to the right, a bit of face climbing and another pitch up below a corner. Suddenly there was a terrible crack, as if the wall was exploding. For a good quarter of an hour the rattling did not stop. The second party had probably found a little tower of rock barring their way.

Now for the crux: a 40-meter corner, overhanging, holds all sloping the wrong way, loose rock and not a peg in place anywhere. Carefully, I climbed higher; this was no place to run out of strength. And I made it. Below me the face overhung all the way down to the cirque. "Bua, bua," said Kuno as he got to the top of the pitch. The last man up broke off a narrow little finger edge in the middle of the corner but he was seconding and just slumped onto the rope. We reached the summit over easier rock.

Bachmann and Knoll walked over the Jägerkarscharte into the Hinterau Valley and we went via the Arzlerscharte back to Innsbruck. The shot Kuno had taken in the stomach really made itself felt. Through the pitch-black night and across the Arzlerscharte.... Kuno got a rock on the foot and could hardly even hobble. Arrived home at 1:00 a.m.

6 October 1942
SCHÜSSELKARSPITZE SOUTH FACE, WETTERSTEIN
Herzog-Fiechtl Route
1st solo ascent

Time: 3 hrs. Set off early for the Wetterstein, Erinnerungshüttl, with Werner Fischer and Sepp Fohrsinger. Started route at 2 o'clock; on summit at 5 o'clock. Back at hut at 7. Everything climbed without rope, except pendulum and slabby corner. "8 meter wall" climbed with no pegs and no carabiners. Madly hot. No worries at all. Ate like a bear at the hut. Left a visiting card on pendulum and an entry in the summit book. Everything went well.

14 June 1943
FLEISCHBANK EAST FACE, WILDER KAISER

A new route up the East Face of the Fleischbank, first climbed by Aschenbrenner and Lucke in 1930. Four ascents to date. Weather fine. We wanted to go straight up to the start of the West Face of the Middle Summit [of the Predigtstuhl], but at the "Tor" I caught sight of the Asch-Lucke; it was looking back at me, too. So we did that. We went up to the overhang unroped. The overhang itself was still wet and what a sight it was. 45 m high and leaning out about 5 m; every meter overhangs. So it is all peg-pulling. You could not have free climbed it but neither could we see many pitons and usually there are almost 50 of them in place. As luck would have it, I had plenty, and plenty of long ones. The constant rope drag and having to place pegs all the time made me dog-tired. Then, from my scanty little belay ledge, I had to give Waldemar a tight rope since he had to knock the pegs out again. I had rarely been as exhausted as I was up there.

After a pitch with a real pig of an overhang I came to a chimney; a few pitches up this landed us a hundred meters below the North Ridge. Now, a smooth, overhanging chimney blocked further

A bold and self-confident-looking Hermann Buhl on 6 October 1942 just before the first solo ascent of the "Herzog-Fiechtl" on the South Face of the Schüsselkarspitze (Wetterstein).

While attempting the Aschenbrenner-Lucke Route on the East Face of the Fleischbank (Wilder Kaiser), Hermann Buhl and Waldemar Gruber mistakenly took the wrong route and ended up in a blind alley, a smooth chimney (which was later to provide the line of the "Schmuckkamin"); here a little shelf of rock broke away under Buhl's feet, causing him to take a 50-meter fall.

progress. No pegs, no peg holes. I realized immediately that it was a blind alley. 20 m above the stance there was a little shelf in the chimney. The whole world seemed to be nailed shut and barred. I bridged up onto the pulpit but hardly was I standing on it than it broke off underneath me. I could not hold on any more, had the presence of mind to jump backward away from the wall and fell— down into the chimney. A 50-meter fall. I was fully conscious. Felt everything. Bounced four or five times in the chimney, hitting it head first. Suddenly there was a tug as I was dragged upright again, but the fall went on. I did not think of much at all, just that the flight seemed a long one.

Soon I came to a halt, standing upright on a tiny little ledge in the chimney, 30 m below Waldemar. In the first few moments I felt nothing and was even in quite a good mood. I felt myself all over. Blood on my head; that meant a hole. The fine new velvet breeches were torn, and that was the thing I was most sorry about, since I had always looked after them. Knees and hands ripped to pieces, waist badly chafed by the rope.

I was about to climb up to Waldi. No strength in my left hand. The metacarpal bone was broken. Waldi was just amazed that I was still alive. His belay peg had ripped out, he had been pulled off with it and just as he was dragged to the furthermost edge of the rubble ledge—he could picture both of us taking the big fall—I came to a stop in the chimney. In actual fact neither of us had been frightened, it all went so quickly. Quite calmly, Waldemar said we had to carry on up. But he could not get beyond my stance.

We now abseiled off. We were soon at the big overhang. With no protection we stood there, two of us on a tiny belay ledge. Or rather, I stood with one foot in the foothold and the other in mid-air and he sat on my knee. We both clipped in to the same peg and tried to pull the ropes down. Then I set off with no protection, abseiling into the wild blue yonder. The rock soon curved inwards and I was hanging free; first one, then two, three, four, five meters out from the cliff. I was spinning around in circles. The seam of my anorak split and I had the rope running over my neck. The weight of the two ropes, hanging free in mid-air, almost pulled me over backward.

I was soon level with the belay, there was no more rope left and I was still hanging in space. It was now or never. I started to pendu-lum, swinging farther and farther but still spinning. Just at the right moment I lashed out, got my feet on the belay ledge, swung my upper body after them and stood up. Waldi now followed me down;

he had it easier, I simply pulled him in to me. I would not have been able to hold out much longer in that position; my hands were hurting from hanging on and I had a nice rope burn on my neck.

Just to cap it all, a thunderstorm now came in. The rope was wet and could not be pulled through. It was as if we were stuck in a mousetrap. We could not go up and without a rope we could not go down either. We tried every trick in the book to get the rope back. He swung on it, while I pulled in as much as I could. . . . Slowly at first, as it fought against its own weight, then faster and faster, the rope came down. Then it flew down in a great arc. We were happy when we had it in our hands. Another 40-meter abseil and we were in the Steinerne Rinne, just as the storm really broke. But what did we care? We were happy just to have got down off that wall at all.

It was now that I really noticed the bruises on my feet and waist for the first time; everything hurt when I walked. Since I could make only slow progress I went ahead, while Waldi coiled the ropes and had something to eat. When our companions saw me coming back down alone and so unusually slowly, they knew there was something wrong and came up to meet me. When they saw my blood-encrusted face they feared the worst and asked if Waldi was dead. They soon calmed down when I told them everything and they saw that things were not quite so bad. First I got tons of food to eat and a bed to sleep in. The next morning my feet were so painful I could hardly get up. Our company doctor prescribed four weeks rest confined to barracks.

"Climbing is not a matter of hauling oneself up with brute strength, but of gliding elegantly upwards."
Hermann Buhl

8 August 1943
TOTENKIRCHL WEST FACE, WILDER KAISER
Dülfer Route

With Herbert Eberharter; 2nd rope: Ernst Waldhof, Fr. Glätzle.
Mist and rain on the way from the Stripsenjoch to the start of the route; mist then cleared, giving way to fine weather. Start hard to find from the Winklerschlucht [on the West Face]. Route well marked to first traverse: pitons like barn door nails. Climbed without rope; wonderful climbing, solid rock. All traverses climbed free; without tension from rope; airy and exposed; exit cracks fantastic; very long. Height of face: 600 m. Rates as one of the finest routes in the Kaiser. Mist on the summit, storm brewing; descent via Führerweg [Guides' Route]. Time for West Face: 5 hrs.

22 August 1943
MAUKSPITZE WEST FACE, WILDER KAISER
1st Ascent

The West Face of the Maukspitze in the Wilder Kaiser. Kitzbühl climber Wastl Weiss was "mad for it." Together with Hermann Buhl and Hans Reischl he made the first ascent.

On the Maukspitze in the Eastern Kaiser there is a totally smooth, vertical wall bounded on the left by the Spengler Chimney and on the right by the South Corner—this is the West Face. It had already been attempted many times by the best climbers from Innsbruck, Munich, and Kitzbühl but the featureless traverse on the upper half had repulsed every party.

The wall's keenest suitor was certainly the top Kitzbühl climber, Wastl Weiss. At 31 years of age he was the equal of many a younger man. This summer he had already attempted the wall several times. He had already done the traverse once, but took a 20-meter fall just before completing the crux when a piton snapped. All the pegs pulled, apart from the belay peg. . . . When he heard that a Munich team had designs on the wall—after he had placed all the pegs—he abseiled down the entire 500-meter face from the summit without knowing whether he would reach the cirque, and knocked all the pegs out. The Munich lads did indeed start up the route but they had to turn back on the lower part, at the strenuous, overhanging chimneys.

Wastl would have given his life for that wall. As a Kitzbühl man and guardian of the Ackerl Hut, which lies directly beneath the West Face, he considered it a matter of honor to make the first ascent. Wastl did not think that there were any other serious candidates and so he was just waiting until he found the right partner for the Wall. It was left in peace for almost the whole summer.

I knew about it, to be sure, but I was not interested in it, since it was clear to me just how much Wastl had invested in the Wall. Then, one day, Hans Reischl, with whom I had done the Mühlsturz Arête, persuaded me to try this last great problem in the Kaiser. The route returned my gaze—again—and so the following Saturday was earmarked for this wall. I was not, of course, going to get authorized leave to go climbing, so I just took off anyway.

We were at the Ackerl Hut early and used the afternoon to study the Wall. We sat on a boulder near the hut and considered the Wall. The route was pretty much pre-ordained. On the lower section, a series of chimneys or cracks, then an easier part with patches of grass and finally the big roof, which blocked access to the entire headwall. Here was the big question mark. Below, above, to the left and to the right of it was all smooth plates of rock; we were unable to make out even the smallest crack or other feature, even with our binoculars. And even if a traverse across to the right were possible, we would still have to climb up and right of the bulge. We could look at it as much as we wanted, even in the better light of evening, but we saw nothing. We would just have to give it a try, we said.

Meanwhile, Wastl had arrived. He had been watching us for a while. He knew immediately what was going on and was quite obviously annoyed about it. If we started on the route tomorrow he would shoot us down, he said. I did not want to fight with Wastl and I would have cancelled then, but my partner remained firm—he intended to do this route. After long discussion—I had to use all my rhetorical skills—I eventually succeeded in getting Wastl to the point where he agreed to come with us. And so we were three. A great weight was lifted from my shoulders; we were all happy with the solution. I would have actually preferred to do it as a rope of two, with Wastl.

Wastl sorted out all the gear, his own "special stuff." We got a big meal at the Ackerl Hut and then lay ourselves down to sleep. The next day we were awakened at 5 o'clock in the morning. Another big, sustaining meal was ready for us, and at 6 o'clock we left the cozy little hut.

We started climbing at 7 o'clock. My climbing rubbers were several sizes too big for me, so I had to stuff them with bits of cloth. The route starts 15 m right of the Spengler Chimney. There is an easy pitch up to a cave. From the outset, Wastl let me do the leading; I was to keep the lead up to the crux. He climbed last.

The first pitch goes all right, in spite of the fact that the cliff is overhanging and the rock very brittle in parts. But then come the chimneys, the like of which I had never done before. Three pitches of them. Exceptionally strenuous and strength-draining. One section I remember in particular. The chimney is really narrow at the back, but it widens outwards, with totally smooth walls, and as if that were not enough the whole thing overhangs nicely, too. I did not know how I was going to get up it. I jammed my feet in the chimney, and with my left hand reached a hold so small that I could just pull myself up by my fingertips. And all that with almost no runners, for the pegs just would not go in.

After several very difficult pitches—at one point I had to move leftward out of the chimney—I stood below the crack running down from the bulge in the middle part. It was 10 o'clock. We all felt hungry and had something to eat, since this was our last chance to

Mauk West Face, first ascent. Wastl Weiss on the crack leading up to the traverses.

sit down and eat in peace. How was the crux going to be? I could not imagine it getting any harder.

Soon I tackled the climbing again. The crack up to the first traverse went quite well. I now brought Wastl up. I traversed to the right under the roof, on quite badly placed pegs, until I finally gained a hold. I now hammered a peg in as high as possible behind a flake—carefully, only a few centimeters deep, so as not to shatter the rock. A long ring peg farther down on a totally smooth slab bore testimony to another attempt; it was one of [Hias] Rebitsch's. Now I tackled the traverse. Carefully, thinking about every move, I slowly went across. After 5 m there is a little foothold almost at the same level as the peg on the traverse. It was all about reaching it. I could reach it, but only with my hands. That was no use to me; I could not get onto it, since everything was smooth below it. Suddenly the peg on the traverse pulled out and I did a nice swing back to where Wastl caught me.

Soon I am up there again, hammer the peg on the traverse back in a little deeper and start the traverse again from the beginning, but somewhat higher than before. It is a completely vertical traverse, really smooth, with little rugosities for the fingernails. It puts every other traverse I have ever done in the shade. Finally I am across it; I pull up and stand with one foot on the foothold and the other in mid-air. Stroking the rock with my hands, I manage to keep my balance.

Above me is a smooth wall, four meters high, devoid of foot- and handholds. I place a wooden wedge in a little pocket and place a special peg, short and square-shaped, in the wedge. It sits well. Then I tension off the placement, stand on the peg, stretch up and hammer two pegs into a crack—only one, maybe two centimeters in—tension quickly again, reach up and get the first hold. I then climb up a few meters and I am at the stance beneath the bulge. "Stance" is good, it is more a matter of hanging off the peg. With the help of a bit of tension from me, Wastl and Hans soon joined me. I remind Wastl to leave the peg with the wooden wedge in place, otherwise it would be impossible for others to climb. It stayed there, as I was later able to verify for myself. [On 26/27 December 1948 Hermann Buhl, together with Peter Hofer, made the first winter ascent of the Mauk West Face.]

The sun was now burning down hot and making us sweat hard. But we paid it no attention at all, our thoughts were only on the climbing. I now roped down to a little stance where I waited until Wastl had brought Hans up. Standing around on the little belay was too strenuous, so I traversed a few meters left to where there was a little niche on the wall. I just had room to get my body inside it. With the heat and the tiredness, I soon nodded off. When I opened my eyes and took stock of my airy position I was rather more careful. But tiredness got the better of me. Three times I nodded off, until the whole thing got too dangerous and I returned to my old stance. Wastl soon followed. I now went on, ten meters up a crack, another abseil down to the right, a short rightward traverse and yet another abseil. I was now at the lowest point of the traverse and right above me was the crux.

A short time elapsed before we were all gathered here on the little stance. Not in the least expecting that the crux was coming next, I set off up the next pitch. I did not have many more pegs and had run out of the short ones in particular. After a short traverse right I reached a shallow groove which soon ended in a smooth face. The odd short crack was visible on it. I reckoned my climbing skills had run out at this point and so asked Wastl what I should do. "Yes, just carry on up there," was the answer. So I said to myself, if he had got up there then so could I.

Trusting to luck, I set off again. There were no holds, and I could only gain height by using pegs, which bottomed out after one or two centimeters. I had to trust my whole weight to them. If one of them had pulled out, the rest would have followed suit. In this fashion I got up the 10 meters to below an overhang. This was the icing on the cake. Underneath the overhang there was a little flake crack where I could place my shortest peg, hammered in upside down and only in about a centimeter deep. If only the peg holds, I thought to myself.

Carefully, I tensioned out off the peg, stretched up past it over the overhang and reached a small hold with one hand. The other hand came up to join it. With the rope now slack my rubbers kept skidding off the smooth, overhanging rock. Just do not let go now, and with all the strength and energy I had, I pulled through and stood on the belay.

Two ring pegs went in and Wastl could then come up. Some of the pegs came out as I took the rope in, others fell out when they were merely touched, among them the last, short peg. There were hardly any pitons left in for the third man, we had to really haul him up and he was absolutely finished when he arrived at the belay.

Wastl now told me that that was the crux. I was naturally pleased about that. Wastl now took over the lead from me, and I was happy for him to do so. We had taken 9 hours for the pitches after our rest.

Mauk West Face, first ascent. Hermann Buhl, leading, photographed by Wastl Weiss just below the crux. Buhl's original route is only very rarely repeated.

"He felt at his best when operating right at the edge of what was possible. He was the typical 'only just' kind of man. The fact that he never overstepped this boundary was one of his outstanding characteristics on rock."

Marcus Schmuck

The sun was already sinking and we had to hurry if we were to reach the top before it got dark. There were now two very hard pitches, but they were nowhere near as difficult as what had gone before, and then we were above the main difficulties. Climbing over easy rock, we reached the ridge leading to the summit—just as it got dark, at 9 o'clock in the evening.

We had been on the route for 14 hours. With that, the hardest wall in the Karwendel—and also the hardest route I had ever done—was in the bag. There was a great reception for us back at the Ackerl Hut and we could first fill our stomachs.

Third Diary:
21 June 1944 to 3 August 1950

(Extracts)

Hermann Buhl's third climbing diary begins with the entry "Holiday from the front—summer 1944." Buhl was a medical orderly in the High Mountain Regiment and in 1943 was transferred from the Training Unit in St. Johann/Tyrol to the Italian front. Between 21 June and 16 July 1944 he was on leave. During this time he climbed eleven routes, mainly with Herta Maier, his form improving all the time. Together with Herta Maier and Fritz Stadler, Buhl did the West Face of the Middle Summit of the Predigtstuhl, establishing a new variant on the Haslacher-Behringer Route:

1 July 1944
PREDIGTSTUHL MIDDLE SUMMIT,
WEST FACE, WILDER KAISER

With Herta Maier and Fritz Stadler.
  Must be about the hardest route on the Predigtstuhl. It was damned cold in the morning. Easy up to the West Gully, then every pitch getting harder and more exposed; did a diligent piece of work: climbed the crack direct instead of traversing right onto the face. Crazy hard; overhanging, small holds and all without any pitons; was at the limit of my strength; on the crack, where Rittler and Brendel fell off, even had to give Fritz a tight rope. Height of face: 300 meters; last four pitches exceptionally difficult.

Nine of Buhl's eleven holiday routes were in the Kalkkögel. Along with several amusing episodes, there is an account that illustrates the uncompromising way in which Hermann Buhl would go about his climbs—that of the North East Face of the Kleine Ochsenwand. Storm on the summit, lightning, thunder, and hailstones—nothing could prevent him from mastering the unprotected crux, a difficult traverse. From the following text we can construe, however, that Buhl did not record this undertaking in his diary immediately after the event, but included it only as an addendum two years later, in 1946, about one year after his return from captivity.

On the Predigtstuhl Middle Summit, West Face (left of center) in the Wilder Kaiser, Hermann Buhl, Fritz Stadler and Herta Maier climbed an exceptionally severe crack variation on the Haslacher-Behringer Route.

7 July 1944
GROSSE OCHSENWAND, DIRECT EAST ARÊTE, KALKKÖGEL
Rebitsch Route
3rd ascent

With Herta Maier. Herta had to carry the rucksack and two pairs of shoes; still have to listen to this two years later! Terrific route. Height: 600 m, exceptionally difficult; crux a 40 m corner, overhanging, no pegs; lower section very airy; did a new variation despite Herta's objections, straight up the arête and the ridge to the summit. Wonderful day. Sat for a long time on the top, singing.

8 July 1944
KLEINE OCHSENWAND, NORTH BUTTRESS, KALKKÖGEL
Schmidhuber Route, Hand Traverse

"He was a 'climbing-only climber.' For a long time he knew no other alternative pleasures."

Hans Seidel

With Herta Maier. A little dispute over tying-on at the start of the route. My order was to tie on "short" due to the lack of rope; she is pigheaded about it and ties on "long," with a shoulder sling system. Wonderful stemming up the chimney. Big bridging move across from the top of the pillar to the opposite wall; short, hard wall section followed by the hand-traverse; this is, in the truest sense of the words, "between heaven and earth." Feet dangling almost in mid-air, 30 meters with few pegs, across under roof.

I have to have another moan. Herta was really "shitting it" and did not trust herself to second it without a back-rope. And so things turned out like I said they would: the rope ran out and she could not get across; I had to climb back and unclip the ropes. Finished up the original route; exceptionally difficult.

9 July 1944
MITTLERE ZINNE (SCHLICKERZINNE) NORTH WEST ARÊTE
KLEINE OCHSENWAND, NORTH EAST FACE, KALKKÖGEL
9th ascent

With Herta Maier, Ernst Pertl, Walter Laichner. At the fork in the path up to the Alpenklubscharte we stopped for deliberations. I want to do the Kleine Ochsen North East, they fancy the Schlickerzinnen. Everyone says they don't really care but everyone has their own route in mind. For Herta, the Kleine Ochsen NE is not enough; it is not a "top end grade six." She has been spoiled. After half an hour we draw lots. We decide on the Schlickerzinnen. Slog up to the start. Crazy loose. Two hard pitches, crazy overhang (lasso manoeuvre). I climb it free, without pegs. Walter is seized with ambition, he also does it free. Did a terrific traverse, then stayed on the arête all the way, over several overhangs, to the summit. Whole pinnacles wobble. The dissatisfied Herta did the Schlicker North Tower with Walter, I went over to the Alpenklubscharte with Ernst. I descended without a rope and Herta again had a few words to say about that.

Afternoon, did the Kleine Ochsen NE. Height 250 m, almost vertical, exceptionally difficult. Time: 1 hour. All of it without pegs. There were only two pegs on the face. Caught out by a heavy thunderstorm halfway up. The wind blew like crazy over the AK Scharte and lashed the rain horizontally into the wall. It nearly threw us off the little stances. We climbed on in spite of it. The rope hung in a loop out into mid-air. The mist rolled in, thunder and lightning crashed all around us and just as I was hanging on the crux it started to hail like mad. In no time at all the holds were full of hailstones and ice. I was dripping wet, my fingers were stiff with cold and damp. I debated whether or not to place a peg but could not find a suitable pocket and so did the traverse free. The rope arched down 40 meters to my friend below. He followed it free but nearly fell off when he broke a hold. One more pitch and we were out of it, on the rubble terrace. The other two were already back down in the cirque, sitting down and protected by a big boulder, and were getting worried about us. But in an hour we had done the route. A crazy time, especially in this weather. The rain relented on the descent, but we arrived back at the hut, dripping wet. Soon, it cleared and in the evening the weather was beautiful.

The Kleine Ochsen NE Face is probably the best route in the Kögel. The rock, in contrast to the other routes, is as solid as iron and full of good holds.

"Start. Summit. The two most impressive moments."
Hermann Buhl

16 July 1944
RIEPEN WEST ARÊTE, KALKKÖGEL
Solo

My last holiday climb. I am wandering around below the Riepen, looking at the cliffs. I solo up to the hand traverse of the corner and back again, then decide on the West Arête. The start is to the right of the arête. There's one very hard and overhanging pitch up to the arête and then it's lovely, airy climbing up the edge. Ernst and Walter follow on behind but turn back as a result of the imminent storm. The rock is wet and I have to climb carefully. The upper face climbing sections are very exposed, since one climbs directly above the overhanging West Face.

It is hard to bid farewell to the Kögel, but it has to be. Tomorrow I travel back to Italy.

Back to Italy meant back to the front. The next climbing diary entry is under the title "Summer 1945!" And: "On 16 August 1945 returned from imprisonment in Tarent; soon afterwards I attempted my first climb."

With Herbert Eberharter, Buhl sets off up the North East Face of the Kleine Ochsenwand, but he notices "that my skill and my sureness had suffered badly." Shortly thereafter, on the Scharnitzspitze, Hermann is "in better shape again" and the very same month he climbs the "Herzog-Fiechtl" on the South Face of the Schüsselkarspitze.

In late autumn, Buhl, having regained his old ability, succeeds in making the second solo ascent of the Auckenthaler Route on the Martinswand:

1 November 1945
MARTINSWAND, KARWENDEL
2nd ascent, solo

"Whoever really wanted to 'have' Hermann Buhl had to go with him to the Karwendel."

Marcus Schmuck

After a longer break from climbing we wanted to do the Martinswand as a threesome, on 1 November—a real November day, cold and misty. W. Gruber and another Innsbrucker were my daring companions. I was thinking, I hope Hias Rebitsch does not come along, otherwise there will be another disgraceful performance.

I climbed the chimney unroped, intending to wait in the corner. But it all took too long, so I climbed on, pitch by pitch, from one stance to the next, always with the intention of waiting there. In this way I finally did the whole face, solo, in a time of 1 hour. When I got back down to the road the others were just about in the middle of the wall.

A little anecdote, related by the man whom Buhl admired, Mathias Rebitsch, is most appropriate here:

"Curiously enough, it is a brief and inherently unimportant encounter with Hermann Buhl that I recall most vividly; it left a

far stronger impression than our later, almost dramatic, ascent of the North Face of the Grands Charmoz together. It was still at the time when he was struggling to make a name for himself. We had met by chance on the road. It seemed to me that he held me almost in secret awe. He gave the appearance of being reserved, almost a little inhibited. Perhaps he suspected—mistrusting those around him because of some unfortunate experience from his early youth—that I would jealously regard him as a 'competitor' and wished to stand in the way of his burning desire for fame. He was very lean and looked really hungry—and not only for food . . . there was a fire in his eyes. . . .

"I invited him for lunch. In those days, right after the war, that was not so simple and it meant something. Everything was still on ration coupons and everyone had to keep a careful watch on what they did with the little they had.

"We talked about climbing, naturally. I spoke a few friendly words, commending him on his bold rock climbs. And as I spoke, his eyes suddenly took on a different, softer shine, a damp shimmer almost, or so it seemed to me. Suddenly, he gave the impression of being relaxed, happy, approachable, almost soft and boy-like. There, sitting before me, was no longer Buhl the hard-man rock climber with the nerves of steel, the man who climbed the steepest faces. It was the other Hermann; the sensitive, sentimental, emotional man. Suddenly, this side of him had emerged from within this youth who, with his unbridled urge to reach for the heights, often remained alone, feeling himself misjudged and unappreciated. He had not had a good childhood and thus he now hungered after good words, after understanding and recognition. This he craved. This was a man for whom—in the madness, the storm, and stress—the construction of a bourgeois existence at first meant nothing, and who thus held the deepest hatred for the warning forefinger that was raised at him perhaps once too often. He sought and found the compensation, his dream world, and his happiness in the mountains, and that is where he then remained. . . .

"I had never before experienced Hermann so relaxed as over this simple lunch-time meal, and never did so again. And he thanked me so nicely and in such a heartfelt way for the little invitation that I, too, had a warm feeling."

Mathias Rebitsch certainly did regard Hermann Buhl as a young competitor, but nevertheless sent a card to the Broad Peak Base Camp congratulating Buhl on his second eight-thousander.

Hermann Buhl's third climbing diary, although containing entries right up to the summer of the year 1950, is incomplete. It is very probable that he simply lacked the time to keep the diary up to date, for

During the course of their first trip to the Western Alps, Hermann Buhl and Luis Vigl, accompanied by Hias Rebitsch, climbed the 900-meter-high North Face of the Grands Charmoz on the Chamonix Aiguilles.

it was during this period that Buhl made a whole range of important first ascents. There was, for example, the first complete ascent of the Direct North Face of the Laliderer Spitze (with Luis Vigl); his two routes on the Lamsen-Hüttenturm (with Luis Vigl and Rudolf Schiendl); the Direct North Face of the Rotwandlspitze East Summit and the Direct West Face of the Speckkarspitze North West Corner (both with Luis Vigl), and the roof crack on the East Face of the Sagzahn (with Fritz Stadler) in the Rofan mountains, to name but a few new routes.

The only one of his first ascents from this period that he wrote up in his little cloth-bound *"Büchl"* was the "Direct West Arête of the Rofanturm" (25 July 1946, climbed with Wolfi Girardi). Thereafter, we have only a few brief entries in note form including, among other climbs, an account of a solo ascent of the Melzer Route (V) on the North Face of the Pflerscher-Tribulan.

In 1948 Buhl made his first trip to the Western Alps, accompanied by Luis Vigl, Erwin Schneider and Mathias Rebitsch. Conditions were poor. Despite this, there were successes on the North Face of the Grands Charmoz (Buhl/Vigl/Rebitsch) and the North face of the Aiguille de Triolet (Buhl/Vigl).

In 1949 Hermann Buhl ticked off several early repeats of big Dolomite routes. In the summer of the same year he again travelled to the Mont Blanc range, this time with the young and talented Mannheim climber Martin Schliessler. A sudden worsening in the weather thwarted their attempt to climb the Walker Spur. Buhl and Schliessler then tried their luck on the Peuterey Ridge, but after having climbed the famous South Ridge of the Aiguille Noire in record time, they were driven back down to the Noire Hut by a heavy storm.

Under the thin blankets, Schliessler caught a cold. In the morning of the following day he and Buhl descended to the campsite at Entrèves. They organized their equipment and climbed up to the Brenva Bivouac. Unable to sleep and bathed in sweat, Martin Schliessler lay on his bunk. He was seriously ill, yet still set off shortly after midnight with the unwavering Buhl to do the North Face of the Aiguille Blanche (second ascent), followed immediately by the summit of Mont Blanc via the Peuterey Ridge.

Again, bad weather threatened. Schliessler managed the difficult ice wall and dragged himself—it was snowing meanwhile—up to the Col de Peuterey.

They climbed up to the summit of Mont Blanc and escaped back down the Bosses Ridge to the Vallot Hut. No blankets, no down jackets—the night was spent lying in a bivi bag on the iron grating, and was just like a bivouac in itself. For the sick man, Martin Schliessler, it was hell: "Shivering with cold and with a raging headache, I could find no sleep."

The next morning dawned bright and fine. Buhl did not want to descend via the Normal Route but to go back up over the summit of Mont Blanc and return to the Torino Hut and Entrèves via the Col de la Brenva, Mont Maudit, Mont Blanc du Tacul and the Géant Glacier. "On that day I switched off all feelings and just walked, walked, and kept on walking. For twelve long hours I saw only my own tracks, then I crawled into the tent like a sick and dying animal." (Schliessler)

Two days later, Schliessler attempted to pull himself together one more time and climb the West Face of the Aiguille Noire with Hermann Buhl. But it was no longer possible. Up at the Gamba Hut the sick man collapsed, shivering violently and with a below-normal temperature. "It was only by taking artificial stimulants that I got myself back down to the campsite. A few days later I drove home with a group of Innsbruck climbers. Hermann stayed in Entrèves for several more days; he wanted to try another route or something."

So much from Martin Schliessler, the man who achieved the unimaginable. This story reveals like no other the way in which Hermann Buhl would demand the utmost of his partners, with no compromises made. For him there were no "bad days," and only occasional brief periods of tiredness. Before Nanga Parbat, the never-satiated Buhl would completely spend himself to the point of

"His whole body weight rested on the tiny front points of his crampons, the pick of his ice axe, and the tip of one ice piton, which he was holding in his left hand. He placed no pegs for running belays. . . . Hermann climbs totally without compromise."

Martin Schliessler

Hermann Buhl (second from right) in the early '50s in front of the Taschachhaus in the Ötztaler Alps. To the left of Buhl is Sepp Fürreiter, and next to him, Rudolf Schiendl (Buhl's partner on first ascents in the Rofan); on the far right is Rudl Steinlechner.

near-fatal exhaustion only once. That was during a terrible storm on the snow- and ice-plastered North Face of the Eiger.

From 1951 on, Buhl began to publish articles on his big routes in the mountaineering periodicals—mainly in *Bergsteiger*. Whether and to what extent these essays were edited, and possibly altered, by the then chief editor Josef Julius Schätz is no longer possible to determine. However, if we compare the few remaining original Buhl manuscripts with those pieces by him that appeared in the magazines—and later in the yearbook of the German Alpine Club—we may, with confidence, assume that we are reading "Buhl originals." Following is a selection of four of Buhl's articles from these mountaineering publications.

First Winter Ascent of the South West Face of the Marmolata

By Hermann Buhl

4 MARCH, 1950. The mountains lie under a cloak of new snow but a steel blue sky stretches out above them. A foursome, we flash up the Brenner Pass road in the car of a fellow club member. Our companions are Theo Plattner and Rudl Seiwald. From the wintry Brenner the road drops down into the green and sunny Etschtal. In Bozen we take a break. We call in at an acquaintance's to make careful inquiries about the conditions on the Marmolata, but he advises us against it. There is too much avalanche danger and we ought to leave it be. Naturally, we do not mention anything about our true plans.

A wonderful car journey through the Fleimstal to Predazzo leads us back into winter again. To the right and left of the road walls of snow several meters high obstruct our view. After a punctured tire we arrive at four o'clock in the afternoon at Canazei, the starting point for the walk to the Contrinhaus. We enquire after the guardian and are directed to the Hotel Maria. Herr Dezulian receives us with a most friendly welcome. He was once a mountaineer, too, and so he understands. When we announce our

request for a key to the Contrinhaus he is at first not very enthusiastic. The hut belongs to the Milan section of the C.A.I. and he says he does not have permission to hand over the key. After a few impractical suggestions we find a way round it: a mountain guide will accompany us and entrust us with the key up at the hut. After heartfelt well-wishes we leave that hospitable house. The skis sink deep into the virgin powder snow and the rucksacks press heavy. At seven o'clock in the evening we reach the hut.

During the night, I look out of the window. Above the Marmolata the mists hang heavy and a violent wind shakes the hut. But at eight o'clock in the morning it is fine again. Now, for the first time, we see the South Wall of the Marmolata. She looks impressive in her winter dress; we had not imagined her to be so terrible. Nevertheless, we want to attempt her just the once. The climbing rucksacks are packed, and then Kuno Rainer and I haul the heavy sacks the three hours to the start of the Face. A violent north-easterly drives the loose powder snow from the North Side over the ridge to us, where

With Kuno Rainer, Hermann Buhl climbed some great routes in 1950; at the beginning of the year, they did the first winter ascent of the South West Face of the Marmolata.

it trickles down the Face like silver snakes.

It is bitingly cold. The double ropes link us together, each of us has an extra 30-meter length of rope and the ironmongery draped about him, plus a 10 kg climbing sack. And so Kuno starts climbing. The rock is coated in ice, every hold covered with spindrift, and our fingers are soon without feeling. The way forward is a 40-meter-long, leftward-leaning chimney. It, too, is partially full of snow and farther up it becomes narrow and smooth in places. With the utmost care, I climb this impeding chimney. Moves that are given IV and V in the route description demand everything we have got. Of course, IV and V on this Face would mean maybe grade VI anywhere else. We arrive at a series of snow-covered slabs. With no protection at all I set off up them and climb 30 meters up to a stance. Hands rummage around in vain in the powder, searching for holds, feet perched on the icy slabs. I hardly dare to breathe. If the snow had not held, it would have been impossible to climb.

And then this, the worst part of the route so far, is also behind me. Kuno leads on through and soon disappears into a crack over to the left. Snow trickles down toward me uninterrupted. The crack continues for 30 meters to below a zone of overhanging, smooth plates of rock. Despite the tremendous steepness we are up to our chests in snow. When we look down into the abyss we see nothing but snow. The start of the route lies invisible beneath the overhanging sections of the wall. Black roofs and slabs of rock look down on us from above. It is five o'clock in the evening. In the previous six hours we have managed only 150 meters, hardly a quarter of the wall. We calculate that we will possibly get as far as the second terrace, maybe even the overhanging corner, but the subsequent traverses, which count among the hardest pitches—these three rope-lengths of holdless, snow-covered slabs—we will, in all probability, not have time to do. To say nothing of the summit gully. And so we decide to retreat. We leave the greater part of the ironware here. Since the rock overhangs so severely in the direct fall-line from where we are, we have to dispense with an abseil and down-climb the route. Darkness has fallen by the time we feel our way down the last pitches.

We intend to wait a few days until most of the new snow has melted from the wall and then make a new attempt. . . . While Kuno waits for me at the Contrinhaus I drive back with our friends to Innsbruck to stock up on provisions for a longer siege. On 9 March I go south again. The eye infection I picked up on the Marmolata makes its unpleasant presence felt. Every ray of light is like a stab with a needle. Wearing the darkest glasses I can find, I arrive at the Sellajoch, where an icy west wind greets me. On the south side of the Pass the snow is rotten right down to the ground; keeping to the side of the road it takes me a full two hours to get down to Canazei. Just before the sun goes down I set off for the hut. Kuno has been expecting me and soon busies himself making something for my stomach. We set the alarm clock for four o'clock and soon go off to sleep.

THE NEXT MORNING my eyes are considerably better, thanks to the household remedy prescribed by Frau Dezulian; namely, stiffened egg white applied to the eyes overnight. The inflammation has gone. At half past four we leave the hut. The sky is covered in a light veil of clouds, but these soon disperse. At eight o'clock we lay hands on the rock. The wall looks much different today. Although there is still enough snow cloaking the rocks at least the cold new snow has gone. Instead an icy west wind is blowing directly onto the Face. After two hours we are already back at the point from which we retreated. We divide up the ironware we had left behind, then I attack the first extreme pitch of the wall. Above a roof I reach an overhanging crack which leads in 20 meters to a little projecting ledge. The rock is wonderfully sound. A vertical crack follows. Kuno has a hard job on the crack, which goes up for 40 meters interrupted at intervals by overhanging bulges. We meet up again on the top of a pillar, where we study the route description: "Descend a few meters and traverse ten meters left to a hidden crack." With a little tension from the rope I push myself leftward across the holdless slabs. We encounter the first piton on this wall, but it does not look very trustworthy. Moving down and around a bulge, I get to the start of the thin crack, which soon loses itself among smooth, overhanging bulges. Ten meters above me I can see a peg. With my hands in the crack and feet bridging out wide, I slowly move up toward the peg. Meanwhile the warming rays of the sun have now reached us. Again and again, overhangs block the way. Several pegs help me gain a little height but soon the crack becomes just a crease, will not accept pegs, and is quite holdless. "No more rope," comes the call from below, and I can just about stand and make an emergency belay. When I'm hauling the rucksack up, the whole side of it rips open and only the tent sack inside prevents the entire contents from making a break for the freedom of the ground below. Strapped up like a parcel, it goes back on my shoulders. . . .

At two o'clock in the afternoon we are standing on the roomy snow ledges of the second terrace, amid holdless, overhanging

"Why climb? For the natural experience; for the danger that draws us ever on; for the feeling of total freedom; for the monstrous drop beneath you. It is like a drug . . . "

Hermann Buhl

sweeps of rock. To the west, heavy clouds have formed and are drifting threateningly towards the Etschtal. We take only a short rest, since the huge yellow corner at the left-hand end of the terrace awakens our curiosity. We traverse across snow to get to it. It is only in the Dolomites that one can find such impressive bits of climbing. The right-hand section of this corner is a huge slab of rock, as if cast in a single piece, while on the left tremendous roofs overhang the corner. Another 200 meters higher and 20 meters out from the terrace we can make out the exit from the gully. In between, the cliff lies back a little—that must be where the traverses are. We decide to carry on up. The corner pushes me violently outward. I feel like a spider; hands and feet almost level, bridging out wide, I feel my way up on friction alone. Holds are scarce. Back-and-footing against the slab, then bridging once more, I drag myself up 30 meters. At a little knob of rock I prepare to bring Kuno up but he urges a retreat. The wall of cloud has got nearer, he says, and, for sure, the weather is about to change for the worse. I drape a rope sling around the knob and lower myself back down, while Kuno uses the second rope to pull me into the rock. Meanwhile, over in the Rosengarten, it has already begun to snow. Over the Pala, a serious storm is brewing. A dense gray bank of cloud comes out of the west, heading straight for us. Hurricane cloud. As we are getting ready to continue our descent, the mist is racing over the Ombretta Pass. It is six o'clock in the evening.

WE TIE THE TWO 40-meter ropes together, belay ourselves with the extra 30-meter lengths and start off down. It is mostly a mid-air trip. Again, I glide down on a carabiner brake. I cannot see the ends of the rope, but I do know that the rope will not reach the next stance. I am at the traverse. Like a pendulum I swing to and fro until I reach the top of the pillar. While Kuno pulls down the ropes, I am already hammering in the next abseil piton. The straight-down abseils are finished now. On the very next abseil we have to descend the face by the same route we climbed it. And meanwhile the wind has risen; it has started snowing, and the ropes arc out from the wall in a sweeping curve. At eight o'clock in the evening we are standing back at the foot of the route with our skis. . . .

We have one more winter Sunday at our disposal. The weather is still holding. On 18 March at six o'clock in the morning, six of us "Karwendelers" meet up: Kuno Baumgartner, Dr. Fischer, Hugo Vigl, Karl Gombotz and we two. Again we head for the Brenner.

19 March, three o'clock in the morning. The sky is overcast but

Buhl and Rainer got up a wintry Soldào Route (it runs up the left hand section of the face) on their third attempt.

despite this we sort the equipment for the big route. This time we have reduced the gear to the bare minimum in order to facilitate more rapid progress. Only one rucksack comes along for the ride, with less ironware, one bivi bag, no spare clothing and provisions for only two days. This means we either have to get up it in two days or turn back yet again. At six o'clock, at the start of the first pitch, the sky is black and threatening. Civetta and Pala are both veiled in mist. The sun comes up blood red. All this weighs heavily on our souls as an icy west wind blows across, making the coldest day we have had seem colder still. We make faster progress than the last time and arrive at the second terrace about midday. Despite the unchanged weather none of us speaks of retreat. Above us, only yellow roofs and huge overhangs. . . .

GRADUALLY IT begins to snow, as the mist rises from the Ombretta Pass and envelops us in a monotone gray. After the next pitch we are at the start of the traverses. The slab to the right of us is tilted back slightly but still completely smooth. I climb up diagonally rightward, mostly trusting to the friction of my rubber soles, which perform brilliantly, and reach a small platform. The route continues for 20 meters below a bulging overhang; there are no pitons. The weather is deteriorating still further; we have to hurry if we are to still reach the summit gully. Meanwhile, the new snow has again covered the hand- and footholds. After a 15-meter abseil we again reach climbable terrain, a ramp which runs up left to right. I belay beneath a smooth, overhanging corner and bring Kuno up. This is the last big obstacle before the bivouac site and it really causes us some trouble. Then I am standing on a commodious ledge, but the real bivi spot, the niche, is two pitches farther right. At six o'clock in the evening we are at the summit gully. Little avalanches of new snow slough down the gully and pour over our heads; the weather situation, furthermore, is threatening. We still have to equip the pitch into the gully today, the most difficult on the whole wall, if we do not want to become prisoners of this Face. The rock is plastered in ice and snow lies everywhere. After the effort of doing half of the pitch, darkness forces me to turn back. We leave the ropes hanging, and

by the light of our torches look for a place to bivouac. The niche to our right, the usual bivouac, is unusable, full of snow and ice. On a hand's-width ledge a little way below we find the only possibility of spending the night in a halfway-sitting position. A few pitons are knocked in, sit-slings and ascenders clipped in and the bivi sack pulled over us. It is more like hanging than sitting; the bivi sack only reaches down as far as our knees and the spindrift trickles down out of the gully and pours into our climbing boots. We cannot cook in this position and so have to make do with a cold meal. We warm our hands a little on a candle. Our situation is grim. We reckon that if it keeps up like this there will be half a meter of new snow by morning. Will we be able to climb out then? Retreat has been cut off now.

The time passes unendingly slowly. The feet have long since lost all feeling, the legs have gone to sleep. At last, the monotonous pattering on the bivouac sack grows less. Around midnight we take a look out of the sack: it has cleared up. It is becoming noticeably colder but this is still better than the snow. We are now brimming with confidence again. At five o'clock in the morning we give the pre-arranged torch signal to our companions down at the hut. At six o'clock we crawl out of the icy sack and make a quick hot-chocolate drink. It is only now that we notice just how exposed our bivi site is. At seven o'clock we continue on up. It was good that we had prepared the next pitch the previous day. In today's freezing cold temperatures it would otherwise have been impossible to continue; added to which, ten centimeters of new snow have fallen during the night. Wearing mittens over my hands I work my way 20 meters up the rope. This warms my hands and I can start climbing again. It is more like fire-brigade training than climbing: nailing up the wall since the new snow forbids the use of any of the holds. Finally, I am in the gully. It does lie back a bit, to be sure, but it is all the smoother for it. After only 30 meters an overhanging, heavily iced bulge arrives. The rock here is extremely smooth, with the holds all sloping the wrong way, and even in summer it is a matter of pure friction. In today's conditions this section represents the most demanding part of the entire route. Often, just when I think I am standing quite safely, I suddenly find myself dangling from the last peg. Thus, I can never run out over a greater distance without protection; the risk would be too great. But placing pegs here is in itself an art form, harder, it seems, than the climbing as such. The weather has again taken a turn for the worse; it is icy cold, the ironware literally sticks to my fingers. After a further hard pitch the gully leans back somewhat and we can see up onto the ridge.

At three o'clock in the afternoon we stand on the summit of the Punta Penia. We can hardly believe that the wall now lies behind us. A strong, hearty handshake says more than many words. Over there, on the summit of the Punta di Rocca where the famous standard descent goes off down, our companions stand and wave to us. But the route across to them is not easy. The ridge, the North Flank—with smooth ice beneath the powder snow—and the traverse into the notch are dangerous enough. In the mist, we arrive at two rucksacks and our boots that two of our friends have brought up for us. And soon we are with them. In the little hut below the summit we find shelter and room for the well-deserved night's rest. The next day it is down, in bad snow, to the Fedaja Pass. Again we are the guests of Herr Dezulian in Canazei, who this time had not reckoned with our success. Full of joy and pride at having climbed the most difficult wall in the Dolomites for the first time in winter, we drive home.

"When he was up on the rock face it did not matter what was happening around him. For him the only thing that existed was that rock face."

Marcus Schmuck

The North Face of the Western Zinne

By Hermann Buhl

[Translator's note: It is common in English to refer to the mountains in the Dolomites by their Italian names. Buhl, however, is a German-speaking Tyrolean and for this reason I have retained his original nomenclature. The Western Zinne is better known to English-speaking climbers as the Cima Ouest di Lavaredo and the Drei Zinnen as the Tre Cime.]

WE ARRIVE AT the Umberto Hut late in the evening. The night is short; at 4 o'clock we step outside the hospitable little house. Crossing the Patternsattel we reach the north side of the Drei Zinnen and follow the little path that leads beneath the walls. We keep on craning our necks, hardly believing that human strength could measure up to the all-powerful Nature on show here. And yet we had done routes like this before. We stop under the North Face of the Western Zinne. Here human imagination is no longer sufficient; only iron will and unshakable courage can make a goal of such a route. Massive roofs hide the upper part of the wall from our view. Somewhere above them the climbing must go on. With great respect, I think of the men who had done the hard pioneering work until, finally, two audacious young Italians, Cassin and Ratti, completed the job their predecessors had begun. Only

after three days, and with the pair of them close to madness, did the wall finally release them from captivity. In the meantime it has been repeated several times, yet to this day it has still kept its reputation as a route "at the bounds of what is humanly possible."

We rope up in silence. It is still bitterly cold. We have to keep warming our cold-stiffened fingers in our trousers pockets. The rock is very brittle. I reach a chimney. From here I think I have to traverse out left. Narrow ledges lead out onto the smooth face. I try my luck everywhere but always climb back again with the same result: "It won't go that way." The route description is very poor. Overhead a mighty roof blocks the view upward. It can only go out right. I climb up to below the roof. A thin crack leads horizontally rightward to a pulpit on the overhanging wall. The stance is very airy. But after it the route continues in an almost

"No haste, no unnecessary moves, his was more a very exact kind of climbing style, even though it all went so fast that my eyes could hardly follow. He missed nothing, no possibility remained unused. Truly, Hermann Buhl was a master on rock."

Marcus Schmuck

reasonable fashion. We climb over a ledge and arrive at a rock tower. It must surely go out left here. We have to get out onto the exposed face somewhere. Yellow, impeding rock. Brittle, too. "This can't be right." I climb still higher—that much I manage—and we reach a ledge that leads out to the left onto the yellow, overhanging wall. We could have had things easier if we had started the route up on the right around the arête, but of course we want to do the North Face!

From the end of the ledge a crack shoots up vertically. A few rusty pitons look down at us reproachfully as if they are trying to say, "You are going to need us yet." Soon I am hanging from them. I have difficulty pulling the rope through the carabiners. Sitting in a rope sling, I bring Kuno up. The pitons are not exactly confidence-inspiring. The change-over at the belay proves to be rather awkward. Kuno has to swap stances with me. Yes, "stance" is rather exaggerated; it is more a case of hanging in a sit-sling clipped to two pitons, with the feet, likewise in slings, splayed out wide against the smooth, featureless wall. Right below our feet the cliff breaks away into huge roofs. The cirque is 300 meters below; we cannot see the start of the route. On the smallest of holds, I manage to gain a few meters. Looking at the way ahead, cold shivers run down my spine. It does not look very cheering.

The points of reference to catch the eye are a few pegs, heavily bent downward and with only their tips biting in the rock. More numerous still are the hammer-marked piton scars into which the little iron spikes have been forced against their will.

I remain hanging there, in the same extremely exposed spot, for perhaps two hours. I can't get back, since Kuno is occupying the stance. I manage to place a piton, hardly a centimeter deep, in a cranny above me. I hang a rope sling on it. Carefully, I put some weight on the peg. But what if it comes out—could Kuno hold me? I look across at him, observe the drop below, drop a rock off and watch as it hits the cirque 20 to 30 meters out from the base of the wall. Kuno's belay looks very questionable to me. Bent double, I hang on one peg. A few times I try to straighten up and grab for the sling, hoping to hold myself in on it, but each time I return to my original position since it seems much safer. But I am not making any progress like this! No other possibility remains. Now I simply do not care, and give it a go. Very carefully I put my weight on the sling, step into the foot loop, straighten up and knock in another piton, not too different from its predecessor. "Tension. Carefully," I call down to Kuno. Or rather, I almost whisper it, so as not to scare the piton. My feet balance on the smooth rock face. Each move is executed with the

In the autumn of 1950 Hermann Buhl and Kuno Rainer climbed the Cassin Route on the North Face of the Western Zinne (far right). At that time the route was still reckoned to be among the most difficult climbs in the Dolomites. At one point, Buhl was just a hair's breadth away from taking a serious leader fall.

"Build your houses on the rim of Mount Vesuvius. The greatest satisfaction! One stands literally above the Earth, like an eagle above his empire."

Hermann Buhl

utmost precision, for a sudden jerk would undoubtedly rip the piton out. At last, I reach an old piton and snap in a carabiner. "Tight on Perlon"; a short breather and I set off up again, not wanting to spend too long hanging on that peg. With tension from the rope I reach up and bang in another peg, but have a hard job clipping in the carabiner and, as I am doing so, the last piton, with its carabiner, goes sliding down the rope. And so the grueling game repeats itself until I finally reach a narrow ledge where, first of all, I take a breather and massage my fingers.

NOW IT IS KUNO'S turn. He is happy to be able finally to leave his uncomfortable stance. It is very hard work for him, since every time he unclips a carabiner he swings out from the rock. With help from the rope he gets up it quite well, however. We stand on the narrow ledge and untangle the rope salad. The ledge runs across leftward out onto the yellow wall, but soon peters out and reappears in the shape of a roof. The first few meters are still reasonable, but soon the sharply overhanging rock above pushes my upper body far out from the face. Instead of a ledge I now have only little wrinkles for footholds. After 10 meters the roof projects so far out that I can barely reach the holds above it any more. I am actually hanging almost horizontally on the rock.

And I have to go down a meter. Not as simple as it sounds. I cannot reach the holds under the roof, my arms are too short. And so I hit upon a strange idea. With my feet braced quite high against the wall I slip my head beneath the roof, still hanging on to the holds above. Then I press for a moment with my head against the roof and find I can hold the weight of my body for just a few seconds. I am now lying in an almost horizontal position beneath the roof. I let go with my hands, make a grab below the roof and my fingers curl themselves around good, solid holds. This is acrobatics on the rock. I climb down just a few more meters and soon reach easier ground.

IF WE THOUGHT that the difficulties were now behind us, we were very badly mistaken. We are now slightly to the right of the exit of the great couloir, whose black streak cuts through the whole of the upper part of the face. Ice splinters whirr down past us. It is a wonderful picture; thousands upon thousands of glittering shards against the background of a blue sky. Extremely severe face climbing, hand-traverses, and exposed traverse pitches follow one another, as the weariness in my fingers starts to make itself felt. Often, very often indeed, just when I think I will manage to climb a section without any great trouble, I have to back-climb to the last stance. Vertically below us in the cirque some Italians are sitting, watching our antics with intense interest.

We are now on the big ledge in the middle of the wall. One last overhang bulges out above, then the wall finally angles back. I climb 20 meters out leftward to where there is a weakness in the zone of overhangs. The rock still leans sharply outward but what is there that does not overhang on this wall? Our eyes have become accustomed to the situation; it is nothing special any more. I climb a little wall to reach a narrow ledge and follow it to the left. Five meters farther on a chimney splits the face. Every step I take pushes me farther outward. I am literally hanging only by my fingertips. Suddenly I become aware that they are gradually deserting their duty, as a terrible tiredness overcomes me. One glance down makes clear to me the terrible nature of my situation. I am hanging well clear of the ledge, while below my feet the undercut wall breaks off clear to the cirque far below. I can't go back; I haven't got enough strength to do that. Kuno is standing on the ledge 20 meters away to my side, with the rope hanging in a big loop down to him. He has not even got a peg in for a belay. "Kuno, I'm coming off!" I shout, as my fingers open out and lose their grip on the rock as if they were made of butter. With my last ounce of energy I just manage to hurl my upper body across into the chimney, where I can wedge myself precariously and take a few seconds rest. The overhanging rock is pushing my body too far outward, but each time I am right at the point of slipping off I am just able to find a bit of friction with one part of my body or other to keep me on. This desperate fight lasts a few minutes; the sweat of fear trickles down my forehead until finally I am inside the chimney and can place a rock peg. I look across to Kuno, who has been following my antics with remarkable composure. The rope runs between us over a flake. "Underestimated it," I tell Kuno.

The wall has, it seems, robbed me of much of my energies. And in any case, different standards apply here. Under normal circumstances it would not have been a problem. I manage to take a little comfort in the fact that Kuno, at least, does not find it such easy going up here. The route up the Wall is now clearly visible, right up to the summit. The big couloir and the right-hand containing wall are clad in huge cascades of ice, which cover the whole rock face. It is here that the projectiles originate that buzz down occasionally. The difficulties now diminish noticeably, and we have no objections to that. Occasional patches of water ice stand in the way but this no longer bothers us.

AT SIX O'CLOCK in the evening, eleven hours after starting up the route, we shake hands on the

"On some occasions I had the feeling that it was only the coming together of as many unfavorable circumstances as possible—bad weather, loose rock, mist and the resulting difficulty in finding one's way—that made him really happy."
Marcus Schmuck

summit. We start the descent straight away, since the light has already begun to fade. Kuno knows the way. Soon the night has us in its clutches, but we carry on down. Everything seems uncannily steep. We come to a col, slide down a chimney and soon find ourselves in a scree-chute. I want to follow my instincts and go straight down the gully, but Kuno reckons it breaks off into a big drop and we must keep to the left across the rocks. These are, however, very steep. We climb down from ledge to ledge. We can see nothing. We make our way down by touch alone. The rocks get steeper. Finally it all gets too risky and we sort ourselves out a bivouac. It is only 8 o'clock and our friends would be waiting for us, but it is no use; the dangers of descending through the night are too great. We can hear noise and the sound of motors drifting up from the Umberto Hut. We also hear someone shouting our names. Down in the cirque someone is wandering about with a torch, shining it over the ground; one of our companions. We make it understood that we will have to bivouac. The night is long and the morning cold. At first light we peel off our bivouac sack. And . . . what must our faces have looked like as we saw, only 20 meters farther to our right, a debris-chute leading down easily to the cirque! Half an hour later we were back at the Umberto Hut.

On the Walker Spur of the Grandes Jorasses

By Hermann Buhl

THE OPPRESSIVE heat of a midsummer's day weighs heavily on the Chamonix Valley. The sun has reached its zenith as we stride up the Mer de Glace towards the Leschaux Hut. A pleasant, gentle wind blows down from the glaciers and cools our sweating bodies. The icy giants of the Mont Blanc group gleam blinding white. But right at the back, at the edge of the Leschaux Glacier, a black and gloomy wall pierces the azure blue of the sky.

Two days ago we had admired this face in all its grandeur from the summit of the Petit Dru. Faint-heartedness had crept up on us as we gazed at the view, since we were indeed of a mind to face up to it. It is a rampart of rock and ice perhaps unique in the Alps, this North Face of the Grandes Jorasses. Fortune had favoured us more this time than on my Mont Blanc sojourns of the previous two years. Kuno Rainer was my companion again, and we had succeeded at our first attempt on the North Face of the Petit Dru, by way of the fourth ascent of the exceptionally difficult Allain Crack. After the traverse across to the Grand Dru and an adventurous descent, we had finally accommodated ourselves in a second bivouac out on the ice of the Mer de Glace (the first had been at the foot of the North Face).

In the late afternoon, we reach the Leschaux Hut, perched at the foot of our "little beauty." We are soon identified by several like-minded occupants as candidates for the Spur. Before we go to sleep we persuade ourselves once more that the weather is indeed satisfactory, and we study the route description again. Before the sun sinks behind the row of rock pinnacles of the Chamonix Aiguilles, its warming rays stroke the precipices of the Grandes Jorasses one last time, laying bare the secrets of the face.

The Spur drops abruptly from the main summit of the Jorasses —the 4208 m high Pointe Walker —a 1200 m buttress set at an average angle of 70 to 80 degrees, plunging to the savagely riven ice of the Mallet Glacier. While the North Face contains a harmonious balance of power between rock and ice, the Spur is so steep and smooth that rock predominates. It was only due to the disfavor of the weather over the last weeks that ice had formed in the cracks and crevices of the face,

Kuno Rainer at the start of the "30-Meter Corner" on the Walker Spur of the Grandes Jorasses (Mont Blanc group)

decorating the wall with its filigree patterns and making the whole thing appear all the more cold and distant.

It was at the same time as the battle for the first ascent of the North Face of the Matterhorn that the first recruits began to arrive at the North Face of the Grandes Jorasses. Up to 1934 the most successful partnership had been Rudolph Peters and Haringer, who had been forced to retreat from a point only 150 m below the summit of Pointe Croz when bad weather suddenly set in. Haringer fell to his death, while Peters fought his way down, alone, amidst the raging elements. The following year Peters, this time with Martin Meier, was finally successful, climbing the whole route to the summit. The spell had been broken but the ideal solution—the direct route to the main summit—still remained to be climbed. In those days this last great problem was not yet believed possible. Attempts made by French teams failed as low down as the first big corner, just above the start of the route.

When, in the summer of 1938, victory over the North Face of the Eiger caused widespread astonishment in the world of mountaineering, an Italian party—themselves Eiger candidates—prepared for an assault on the Jorasses Spur. It was none other than the outstanding Dolomite climber Riccardo Cassin

from Lecco, with his companions L. Esposito and U. Tizzoni. Theirs was an outrageously daring undertaking. The three men were in the Mont Blanc area for the first time, and it was perhaps for this reason that victory was theirs at the first attempt, since they judged the face by Dolomite criteria. Their battle with the difficult rock and ice lasted three days. On the last day they were caught out by a storm, finally reaching the summit of Pointe Walker in wind-driven snow. As a result of their lack of knowledge about the descent they were obliged to bivouac for a fourth time, on the summit, before the mountain released them from its grip. Thus, in a single year, the two last great problems of the Alps had been solved.

Although the Walker Spur on the Grandes Jorasses is considerably more difficult technically than the North Face of the Eiger, it is the latter that has the greater objective dangers. Further attempts were made, but a repeat ascent had to wait until the French pair of Frendo and Rébuffat came along in 1945. The pair avoided the first big corner—the hardest bit on the whole route—by climbing out to the left, a variation which still involved exceptionally difficult climbing. This team also required three days for the climb. Further ascents, all of them made by Chamonix guides, soon followed, yet none of the parties was able to reach the summit in one day. The sixth, and first non-local, ascent was made by an Italian team from Monza, near Milan [Walter Bonatti, Andrea Oggioni, Emilio Villa and Mario Bianchi].

THE DATE IS NOW 29 July 1950. At 2:00 a.m. we close the door of the Leschaux Hut behind us. Still drunk with sleep we stumble down across the screes to the moraine and, jumping over the rough-hewn boulders, are soon standing on the main stream of the glacier. A clear, starry sky arches out above the giants of the Mont Blanc range. In a deathly silence, broken only by the crunching of the soles of our climbing boots, we leap across a few torrents, turn off to the right and start up the Mallet Glacier. As we reach the end of the névé the crevasses grow more numerous, reminding us to be careful. A labyrinth of crevasses, criss-crossing each other, holds us up for a long time. The only means of crossing a seemingly bottomless rift—via a collapsed snow bridge—nearly proves to be our undoing. The glacier now steepens, but becomes more compact. To the east the sky slowly takes on a gray hue. We make our preparations for the hard climb ahead of us; this year we are very well equipped—above all, our wall gear is much lighter. We traverse below the house-high bergschrund at the foot of the great couloir that splits the mountain between the Peters Route and the Spur to reach the start of our route.

The climbing is initially quite easy. As far as possible we try to stick to the rocks. We soon reach the place where we had turned back last year. We zig-zag up over steep and very smooth slabs to the foot of the "30-Meter Corner," the first of the extremely severe pitches on the face.

I CLIMB INTO THE left-hand of the pair of ascending cracks—the Rébuffat Crack. Now things really do start getting extreme; this is noticeable on the first few meters of the corner. A grade VI pitch on the Jorasses is by no means easier than in the Kaiser or the Dolomites; if anything, it is even more strenuous. Soon the thin little crack peters out into smooth slabs. A short hand-traverse on an outward-sloping rounded edge brings me to the parallel crack, the "Allain Crack." The entry into the crack is severely overhanging and terribly strength-sapping. We turn an arête and now easier-angled ground lies ahead, but this is heavily coated in water-ice and snow.

We climb several pitches of mixed ground up and right to reach the edge of the Spur.

Here, the wall again rears up vertically above us. A slightly overhanging corner system, colossal in size and with smooth outer walls, rises up above us to

"And how economical were his movements, how precisely he used each hold! With what measure of certain instinct did he transfer his weight! To be sure, this was the high art of the climber!"

Marcus Schmuck

lose itself in a crown of overhangs and the blue of the sky. We are now in the grip of climbing fever and I can hardly wait until Kuno joins me. A treacherous, barely visible glaze of ice lies over the granite slabs. A narrow crack runs up the back of the corner, making upward progress possible. With my hands wedged in the crack and feet bridged wide, I work my way slowly upwards.

The rucksack and the ice axe strapped to it severely hamper my freedom of movement, and the granite, poorly supplied with hand- and footholds, does not allow elegant climbing as on limestone. At many places the only thing that helped was a quick layback—a move which I, whom Nature has equipped with modest biceps, always find particularly hard. My breath comes in gasps, while the rubber soles of my lightweight climbing boots skitter off the lichenous rock and my fingers grope for holds among every slight unevenness on the walls. The climbing sometimes borders on the impossible. And there are still two more pitches with several overhanging sections to battle with. The few pitons remind us of the early ascents. The route description is very exact, with a chimney running up until a roof blocks any further upward progress. I traverse right, where a steep slabby ramp cuts through the overhangs. After three pitches we stand once more below a

mighty roof. Two abseil pitons point the way down. Fifteen meters down, beneath an overhang, is a narrow ledge, but the rock pushes my body so far out I cannot reach it. By swinging like a pendulum I reach a little stance away to the right. Above a black, ice-covered overhang a more comfortable belay beckons and Kuno joins me, using the rope as a handrail. We glance upward but still can see no end to the difficulties. The weather seems to be holding.

CLIMBING SLIGHTLY to the left we manage to reach the second steepening of the Spur, the "Black Slabs," the crux of the route. Pitons strewn everywhere bear testimony to the fact that here each party had gone for a slightly different line, though the individual variations were pretty close to each other. By climbing an overhanging crack, I manage to reach a line of handholds leading out left beneath a roof to a small stance. A rusty peg with a rotting sling tempts me to use it. Thereafter, overhangs alternate with slabs until I am greeted with a thin crack, which ends 20 meters higher at another belt of overhangs. Over to the right I can see some pegs in place. But what lies between is just smooth, outward-sloping rock. Beneath a roof I discover a narrow crevice; a piton sings as it goes into the rock, and by means of a tension traverse I manage to get across the seemingly unclimbable bit. It is a traverse that would in no way dishonor a route in the Kaiser, and this with heavy boots, a climbing rucksack and ice axe! A crack, overhanging in stages, leads on upwards. First of all it is a matter of getting through the overhangs to reach it, and in order to save both time and strength I free climb through them. The afore-mentioned crack is extremely smooth and holdless. Just a few meters separate me from the next stance when the rope jams. I have to down-climb the whole of that hard-won section to below the roof, pull through enough rope, and attack the crack again. And again the rope gets stuck. Twice more I have to go back down again until finally, at the end of my strength and patience, I reach the belay stance, the first proper one for about 150 meters. While I take a breather to recover from my strenuous efforts, I cast a glance down to the open crevasses of the Mallet Glacier—seeming almost flat from up here—with their black and gaping mouths turned upwards. The exposure is terrific. Kuno, perched on the tiniest of belays, is no less happy to finally be climbing again. We climb an ice ramp to reach a roomy, snow-covered terrace, protruding out from the wall like a bay window—the second bivouac site used by the first-ascent party. It is past midday, but the "Black Slabs," the hardest part of the climb, now lie behind us.

The face breaks off vertically down into the Great Couloir, where from time to time volleys of stones go clattering down. We settle down for a short rest, but our uncertainty about the con-tinuation of the route and the difficulties that await us do not allow us to linger for long. An in-ner urge forces us on toward the summit, which we still hope to reach today. The rock rears up vertically now. After three pitches we are on the edge of the buttress again. At this point it forms a sharp arête and we are able to glance over at the north side of the Spur, falling away in tremen-dously steep ice-slopes, then, far below, becoming rock again and disappearing from view. At last, the rock becomes a little more juggy and the climbing absolutely beautiful.

SUDDENLY WE ARE shocked out of our reveries. A huge block has detached itself from the sum-mit wall of Pointe Whymper and is tearing down the 1000-meter-high face to the couloir below with a terrible din and a trail of sulphurous fumes. We instinc-tively take cover, even though we are well out of the danger zone. When we have the time we can cast a glance over the top of the Aiguille du Tacul to the Chamonix Aiguilles, with the sight of a thunderstorm brewing up over them, and farther on down to Monténvers, where the whistle of the rack railway signifies the

"The best is the hour on the summit with a pleasant companion; with your thoughts still on the cliff you have just climbed, your gaze roams farther, to yet another objective."

Hermann Buhl

Kuno Rainer on the morning of the second-day's climbing, on a traverse on the upper section of the North Pillar of Pointe Walker (Grandes Jorasses)

proximity of so-called "civilization." Pitch by pitch we wrest the height from the face. Level with us, across the big couloir, the second ice-field of the Peters Route rises high, a sharp arête of névé standing out from the face. It is only now that we are able to get a real impression of the dimensions of this wall.

Rolls of thunder fill the air as the mists descend from the summit, enveloping the wall. The very next moment we are at the center of a thunderstorm, which breaks over us. Lightning flash follows lightning flash, and the walls echo with a thousand thunder-claps.

The heavens open their sluice gates and drench us with showers of hailstones. In an instant we are standing knee-deep in a shifting morass. It seems as if the wall is sinking beneath our feet. Avalanches of hail and snow gush down every crevice in the mountain like foaming waterfalls. An uncanny din fills the air around us, and we can hardly hear ourselves speak. The storm gathers yet more speed and we can but hope that it will soon blow over. For a brief moment the raging of the elements abates, only to begin again with renewed and greater violence, one storm chasing the other. A savage northwest gale whips at the ropes. We search feverishly for a place to shelter. A little notch on the edge of the buttress is the only possible place to wait out the storm. We pull the bivouac sack over us and feel a little safer. It is three o'clock in the afternoon and 250 m of climbing separate us from the summit. My altimeter shows 3950 m. We wait and wait, but the raging of the storm does not lessen any.

Only now do we get the chance to supply our bodies with something edible. Tiredness is slowly beginning to make itself felt. My feet in particular are hurting from all the hard climbing. After some considerable time, Kuno takes a look at the watch and is horrified to learn that it is already half past seven in the evening. We need to sort ourselves out a bivouac. We put on every available article of clothing, although we do not have much. My down jacket is pressed into service and performs extraordinarily well. A few pitons give us the necessary security, and with the rope we fashion a back-rest of sorts, while our feet dangle free over the 1000 m abyss. Finally we pull the bivi sack over us, by no means an easy thing to do in this storm.

WE DOZE LONG INTO the night, listening apathetically to the organ music played by the storm. Finally sleep overcomes me, probably caused by sheer weariness. But the cold jerks me awake again and I am ruthlessly brought back to reality, astonished that it is already daylight. Through the little window in the bivouac sack I look out onto a scene like a laundry room. The rocks in our immediate vicinity are glazed with ice and hoar-frost. The storm is raging as it did yesterday, but the hail has given way to snowfall. We do not know what to make of the weather and decide to wait things out at first. Kuno tells me he has had a very bad night of it, for the cold had induced constant shivering fits.

About nine o'clock, with no change in the weather, we decide to press on with the climb, since we have no wish to become prisoners of the wall. It requires a great effort to crawl out of the sack and take up the fight anew with the difficult climbing and the weather, for our bodies are quite

"Just what is it that drives a man to pursue this audacious game? We live in an age where each of us is robbed of his freedom by legal requirements and society's rules. One has to find a way out of this straight-jacket of civilization and one escapes to the natural world, to the peace and remoteness of the mountains."

Hermann Buhl

stiff and our muscles cramped. We strap the steel rims to our boots and sort out the Perlon rope—by now encased in a thick coating of hoar-frost. Then we remove the pitons, now partially buried in the ice, and I set off back along the traverse into the steep ice gully, from which we had fled yesterday in the face of the torrential hail and rain. I hack my way up the 60-degree ice slope, zig-zag fashion, until I am directly above our bivouac ledge. Then we stamp up the triangular snow-field to the start of an overhanging section. I have to remove my gloves, for better or for worse, since the holds on the rock are too small. After an extremely severe traverse to the right I reach the start of a steep fissure. The rock here is smooth and outward-sloping, and brittle in the bargain; every hold has to be cleared of ice first—our steel rims do sterling service here—and several overhangs make the whole thing that much harder. After two pitches the fissure becomes an ice gully and Kuno takes over the lead. Step by step, he hacks his way up the brittle ice that covers the rock in a thin, treacherous layer, while I become the target for chunks of ice raining down from above. I am merely curious about how we will get out of this cul-de-sac, for up above black overhangs festooned with huge curtains of ice glower down at us, making further progress seem hopeless. Kuno disappears behind

a rocky corner. The rope, a dumb messenger, goes up and down in jerks, allowing me to guess at the difficulties he is having up there.

A curse escapes Kuno's lips, I hear something fall, hurtling down through the air, and grip the rope tighter but—thank God —it is only the ice axe that is swallowed up by the abyss. It gradually dawns on me what consequences the loss of the axe might still have for us.

We traverse now for two pitches across smooth sweeps of slabs perched beneath mighty overhangs, until the structure of the rock again allows upward progress. Whenever the mists lift a little we can see the summit ridge of the Jorasses quite close by. After one more not particularly hard overhang, steep ice-covered fissures lead up to the edge of the buttress. The climbing now grows markedly easier and we want to quicken our tempo, but the thin air does not allow this. The higher we climb, the more brittle the rock becomes, a sure sign that we are nearing the summit. There still seems to be no end to this wall when, suddenly, something light appears through the monotone gray and begins to take shape—the summit cornice of Pointe Walker. At half past four in the afternoon we shake hands on the highest point of the Grandes Jorasses.

THE SPUR IS behind us, yet the route is not yet over, not by a long chalk. We have no mind to descend, like all the others who had climbed the Spur, to Courmayeur. We want to link in the traverse of the summits of the Grandes Jorasses massif and then descend from the Col des Jorasses directly back to Chamonix, thus sparing ourselves the long detour by the Col du Géant. And so, although the traverse of the Jorasses is a full day's outing in itself, we set off on our way to the Col des Jorasses, hoping that we might find the bivouac shelter there before the day is over. The weather is slowly taking a turn for the better, but we are still in thick mist. From Pointe Walker we climb down southward along the glacier to the notch between Pointe Walker and Pointe Whymper, which we then climb by a very exposed and corniced ridge. Everything goes well as far as Pointe Croz, where the ridge narrows to a knife-edge. Kuno doubts that we will be able to keep to the ridge much longer, and so we descend onto the South Face, where the slabs that break away from the ridge keep forcing us farther and farther down. I do not like this descent one bit, since we are getting too far away from the ridge. So I duck around a corner to take a look at the gully beyond, in the hope that it will take us back up to the ridge, but it proves to be unclimbable and we have to retrace our steps back to the ridge. Only now do we really begin to feel the effects of the last two days' hardship, as we gasp our way back up, making good our route-finding mistake.

We climb a very exposed, sharp ridge leading to Pointe Margherita. The rock is unusually rough here and our fingers, painfully sore from all the climbing, leave bloody prints on the rock. Now and then, when the mist lifts a little, we can just make out the mighty North Face. The ridge now becomes very jagged. We have to make several abseils from Pointe Margherita, and even before we reach Pointe Elena we are caught out by darkness. Down the smooth slabs we slide, abseiling off into the night. The northwesterly gale has increased in strength again. The ropes, far out from the rock, are whipped by the wind. The last ascent to the summit of Pointe Young arrives, just a little above the 4000 m mark. This, the last peak of the Jorasses, breaks away steeply on all sides. In the darkness, we can do nothing more and so we decide to bivouac again, just 100 meters above the Col des Jorasses. We locate a roomy spot out of the wind, of which there are, luckily, more hereabout than on the Spur itself.

AT FIRST LIGHT WE are on our feet again. We cannot climb down to the Col, since a steep ice field blocks the way and our lack of instruments for dealing with this brittle element does not allow it. So we descend an endless rock rib cutting down the North Face. We use the last rocks and some boulders frozen solid into the ice to abseil from, and in this somewhat awkward, but safe, way we arrive on the upper reaches of the Mallet Glacier, directly below the gigantic bergschrund of the Col des Jorasses. We are happy to feel solid ground beneath our feet once more. The sun, too, feels more kindly disposed towards us.

As we descend the heavily crevassed Mallet Glacier, we keep casting a glance back up to those unearthly heights where mighty bastions of rock soar heavenwards, aloof yet at the same time seductive—the Walker Spur of the Grandes Jorasses.

First Complete Traverse of the Aiguilles de Chamonix

By Hermann Buhl

FOR THE CLIMBER on his first trip to Chamonix, whiling away the hours in the town and taking pleasure in the majesty of this world of mountains, the sight of Mont Blanc, the highest point in the Alps, with its brilliant white fields of névé and huge bastions of ice, will of course prove deeply impressive. Yet what will hold his gaze even more and cause him to crane his neck again and again, what will fill him with awe and wonder, is the chain of peaks in front of Mont Blanc—the Aiguilles de Chamonix. . . .

I got to know this range better on the occasion of my first stay in the Mont Blanc region. Then, the conditions were so wintery as to banish all thoughts of big routes on the 4000-meter peaks, but climbs on the Chamonix Aiguilles proved to be just the thing. And so it was that I climbed the various faces of the Grands Charmoz, including the Direct North Face (my first route in the French Alps), made the acquaintance of the Grépon Traverse and the Blaitière and, as a keen cragsman, developed a particular taste for these adventurous needles of rock. They combine the jaggedness of Dolomite towers on the one hand

with the generous route length and the seriousness of the Western Alps on the other. . . .

After a day of relaxation and rest, we again flee the turmoil of the streams of people who inhabit Chamonix, for we want to make the most of the last few days of our holiday. The weather, unfortunately, is rather unsatisfactory; gray banks of cloud hang over the slopes of the mountains and a light rain soon begins to fall from the heavens. In Monténvers we meet some French climbers on their way back from the Aiguille Verte; they advise us to accompany them down to the valley, but we press on. We know the walk sufficiently well. We turn off right where you meet the ice-falls of the Géant Glacier. A little path, hard to make out, zig-zags up steep slopes to the right that are covered by a wonderful carpet of flowers. The color of the flowers slowly gives way to the green of a lichen-covered sweep of rocky slabs. We are still separated from the cliffs of the East Face of the Grands Charmoz, the easterly outpost of the Chamonix Aiguilles, by a small hanging glacier and have to cross a wide, gaping crevasse to reach their foot. Terraces and

"Hermann is driven by a feverish impatience, always urging us to set off. The uncertain, the new, the chaotic view of the route we have to take—all this makes him fidgety, like a young racehorse under starter's orders."

Kuno Rainer

In 1950, the successful partnership of Buhl and Rainer succeeded on the first complete traverse of the Chamonix Aiguilles. The photo shows a section of this chain of sharp granite spires (left to right): the Aiguille de Blaitière, with the Aiguille des Ciseaux next to it, then the Aiguille du Fou, Pointe de Lépiney, Dent du Crocodile, Aiguille du Plan and the Glacier du Plan.

"The featureless granite wall rears up vertically. A tight, perpendicular crack splits it right up the middle and Hermann, beaming with pleasure, shouts down to me, 'I've got it—the Mummery Crack!'"

Kuno Rainer

sweeps of slabs alternate constantly with each other as we make our way up. It is an approach in typical Mont Blanc style. We arrive at a smooth, vertical groove, the crux of this so-called "hut-walk." Kuno is most impressed by this "path." The groove would be a grade IV climb in itself. Meanwhile, it has stopped raining, but the weather remains consistently poor. Kuno is equally surprised when he suddenly catches sight of the hut, the Tour Rouge Hut, perched on a little projection on the steep rocks. "Hut" is probably rather exaggerated, since it is nothing more than a shed made of wooden planks and stuffed with a bit of straw. . . .

The next day, four a.m. reveille. We look out of the hut. The clouds hang heavy, mist obscures our view of the cliffs, and the rocks are still slick with rain. Still we decide to set off. We traverse to the right across broad ledges until a long series of cracks and corners leads on upward. Yet another rightward traverse and we reach the North East Ridge of the Charmoz, a little way below the two rock pillars of the Cornes de Chamois. We turn them on the Mer de Glace side and start up the flanks of the Aiguille de la Republique. The climbing grows more difficult and we are sometimes compelled to use the rope. The rock here in parts is most deceptive; seemingly easy sections often give the greatest difficulties, and vice-versa. We climb up the steep wall for about

200 or 300 meters till we see the notch behind the Aiguille de la Republique above us and to the right.

LEAVING THE rucksacks at the notch, we drape the rope around our shoulders and storm up the 150-meter-high needle of the Aiguille de la Republique, climbing together. We avoid the overhanging face opposite the notch to the right, and reach the East Ridge of this sharp needle, up which we climb—several pitches of airy climbing, and by no means easy. Just 40 meters separate us from the summit. On a broad shoulder beneath the monolithic summit block we hold a council of war. The steep upper section of the needle has not yet been free climbed. The French used a kind of harpoon affair here, with which they projected the rope over the summit and onto the north side. This they then used for aid to reach the summit. What we find strange, however, is how they managed to reach the rope on the overhanging, barely accessible North Face. It is a method of conquering a peak that seems alien to us, yet the French have often employed it and consider it perfectly fair; indeed, the uniquely smooth and featureless formation of many a summit in the Mont Blanc region would appear to require such methods.

First of all we attempt to throw the rope over the top by lassoing it Wild West style, but this proves to be hopeless. Then, after searching around for a bit, we discover a roll of string with a small lead weight on the end. Again, all attempts with it fail and we have to resort to trying to free climb the thing. The right-hand wall—a completely smooth slab set at an angle of 70 to 80 degrees—no longer gave any friction for our rubber-soled boots, so I try reaching out onto the left arête, which plunges down onto the North Face. It overhangs tremendously but at least it has a few well-spaced little edges on it. I manage to throw the rope over a protruding knob on the arête, fix it in place as a hand-rail and slither across the smooth, impossible slab to gain the arête. After pulling the rope through and re-tying, my retreat is cut off. And I have made an error of judgment with the little edges, too; they turn out to be too far apart for me to stand up on one and reach the next, as I had hoped, so I have to free climb the smooth and overhanging intervening bit. I get about ten meters up it, the rock forcing me out backward and calling for delicate balancing tricks, but eventually my artistry fails me— and this with only 15 m separating me from the top of the Aiguille de la Republique! I want to place a peg but only then do I notice that I haven't got any with me. Kuno was relying on me and so all the ironmongery is lying safely in our rucksacks back at the notch. So there is nothing else for it—Kuno has to knock out his belay peg and pass it and the hammer across to me on the rope. In vain, I try to find a placement for the too-thick piton in one of the thin cracks. I see how hopeless it all is and am about to climb back down without protection, but every time I try to reach down to the edge I am standing on, the rock threatens to push me off balance. My feet are slowly beginning to shake, and the "sewing-machine legs" known to all climbers threaten to hurl me off the footholds. I need all my energy just to stay calm. Finally, I think I have found a suitable crack for the peg; it goes in, none too deeply, and I heave a sigh of relief, while down below Kuno presumably does the same. To be on the safe side I test the piton before trusting myself to it. A few hefty tugs, and it flies out, hitting me full in the face. I can feel the warm blood running down my cheek and neck; a little injury to my nose and there is blood everywhere. I notice that my strength is slowly fading and shout down to Kuno, "Watch me, I might be off here!" I take another look at the terrain below me and, with not a little concern, establish that in the event of a fall I will be hurled against the opposite wall before falling free 20 meters to land on a terrace. Again I try to place the piton, and with the strength born of desperation manage to get it in. Since we also have not got enough carabiners and I do not want to sacrifice one

"Hermann pauses, takes a good look at the chimney above, and looks back down the face. Then, with a few words of warning, 'watch me here, it's as smooth as a window pane,' he pushes, twists and contorts his way up the thing."

Kuno Rainer

here, I untie from the rope, thread it through the peg, tie back on again and have Kuno lower me down, hanging free, to the offending terrace. With Kuno's help I then manage to regain the Shoulder, a very happy man indeed.

Our efforts have robbed us of precious time—by now something like three hours have passed. We gladly do without this particular pinnacle and instead set off back down to the notch. A steep, almost vertical wall leads us round to the other side and upward. The ridge is endlessly long but the climbing nice and varied. The nearer we get to the summit of the Charmoz the narrower the ridge becomes, although it does decrease in steepness. We have to turn several of the pinnacles on the North Side, until finally we find ourselves in the col below the summit rocks, at exactly the same place we had emerged from our ascent of the Direct North Face all that time ago. Cold showers run down my back as I cast a glance down that fearsome wall with its steep black runnels of ice, and I can barely believe that we had found a way up it. However, we are now back on familiar ground and making faster progress.

ON THE DESCENT from the Aiguille des Grands Charmoz (3480 m), we are slowed down slightly by a tight squeeze chimney. On this peak you generally just have to follow the bits of waste paper and empty tin cans to stay on the right route. From the col between the Charmoz and the Grépon, an ice gully runs up to join the Mummery Crack. The start of the Crack, itself the most difficult part of the entire Grépon Traverse, is no easy matter. Hats off to Mummery, I think to myself as I worm my way up the fissure. Two years previously I had done the Grépon Traverse with Luis Vigl, but in the other direction, and we had had to resort to some hard free climbing on the abseil sections. This time, a rock window gives access to the west side of the mountain and a line of juggy cracks leading to the top of the first pinnacle on the ridge. We attach the rope to a huge, wobbly block, half of which protrudes out over the abyss. It is only the many old rope slings, bearing testimony to its reliability, which induce us to put our trust in the block, and it is with some suspicion that I slide down the arête. Forty meters down, we are reunited at a little col. We pull the ropes down and traverse onto the east side, onto the so-called "Bicycle Ledge." One could indeed ride a bicycle along this terrace, but the awesome sight of the 900 m drop to the Mer de Glace might perhaps prove rather distracting.

Unfortunately, we are now in the mist again, as we had been two years ago, and the midday storm is not lacking either. Through a tight squeeze we traverse back onto the west side, and here we are greeted by the gale. Diagonal cracks lead up to the main summit of the Grépon and its life-size statue of the Madonna. A last abseil, a short traverse, and we are back on the ridge again. We cross some short patches of snow and clamber over notches on the ridge, from which gloomy rifts drop straight to the Mer de Glace, until we find ourselves at the foot of the summit rocks of the Aiguille de Blaitièr.

This ridge I know well also. A knife-edge arête forms the hardest part of the climb. After a lot of back-and-forth and up-and-down we arrive at the traverse of the couloir that falls from the col between the summits of the Blaitière to the Nantillons Glacier. The ice is quite brittle. We strap on our steel rims and cut our way across, step by step. Unfortunately, the 40-meter rope is not long enough and we have to move together on the traverse, each trusting the other. Up to now we have been stuck in the mist, making the route-finding questionable at times. And now we are on new territory again, with only the sketches in the French Mont Blanc guidebook to give us any indication of the correct route to take. Yet like a wish fulfilled the clouds suddenly part for an instant, giving us the opportunity to take stock of our surroundings quickly. Leaving the rucksacks at the col we race up the rather easier North Summit.

The other two tops offer considerably harder climbing. The tortuous routes of ascent, coupled with the bad visibility, make the climbing considerably more difficult. Every crack, every wall that looks quite small from a distance, takes on gigantic proportions when viewed close up. Time is pressing, the day is slowly nearing its end and we have to look around for a place to bivouac. There are plenty of them hereabout and we make ourselves at home on a rock ledge on the West Side of the Aiguille de Blaitièr. The evening is spent brewing tea. Meanwhile, the weather has now improved and we have a clear view down beneath our feet to the Valley of the Arve. Slowly, the darkness creeps along the valley. We sit alone on our lofty perch and listen to the sounds of nightfall. Here and there the thunder of avalanches breaks the stillness of the night. Countless tiny lights glitter in the valley below. This kind of reverie is good for the nerves, which have been badly frayed by the strains of the day. Finally, the cold, gnawing its way through our clothing, drives us into our bivouac sack.

AT 5 O'CLOCK IN the morning we set off climbing again. Descending slightly to a col, we find ourselves at the base of the summit rocks of the Aiguille du Fou. Kuno sets off up it, but I want to bag one of the other intermediate rock needles first, the Aiguille des

The traverse of the Grépon was done on the first day; it was just one section of the three-day undertaking.

Ciseaux, a double-summit needle shaped like an open pair of scissors. The rucksack stays down below, and in my youthful stupidity I do not find it necessary to take a rope along with me. A smooth chimney lands me at the gap between the twin peaks of the Aiguille des Ciseaux, the most westerly of which I have my sights firmly set on. Steep face climbing above a huge drop leads me onto the very edge of the knife-blade arête. The exposure is monstrous. The summit is a real needle—I can actually hold the tip in both hands. I am now on top, but I have given no thought to getting back down. I feel like a mouse who has wandered into a trap. With the utmost care, I down-climb those critical 20 meters, feet on friction only on the very edge of the arête, hardly daring to breathe. I meet up with Kuno again just below the summit of the Aiguille du Fou. The last block of the summit gives us a bit of trouble, and then this slim tower of rock is also behind us. Now, the South West Ridge falls steeply to the next indentation on the ridge. The upper part has to be down-climbed, before the ridge breaks off sharply and the first of the rope slings invites us to abseil down the rest.

WE ARE AT THE COL between the Aiguille du Fou and the Pointe de Lépiney. It is still only early afternoon, but a nice little spot tempts us to take a short rest. Wherever our gaze falls are row upon row of rock needles of a shape found only on the Chamonix granite, a veritable jungle of pinnacles, while behind them, as if to counterbalance the view, lie the white slopes of the Géant and Tacul Glaciers. Tatters of cloud, the harbingers of a storm, lick hungrily up the flanks of the mountains and remind us of the pressing need to set off again. From the col, we have to climb down the North Flank for a bit. The night's frost still lies on the flank; hard névé, the remains of the previous week's storm, covers the slabs. Again, our steel boot rims give excellent service. A long, steep ramp of ice—the only possible route through the sheets of slabs—brings us below the needles of the Pointe de Lépiney and Pointe Chevalier to the notch on the ridge before the Dent du Caiman. Again, the rucksacks are left at the notch and, with a spring in our steps, we climb the very steep cracks and spiral chimneys to the top of Pointe Chevalier. We have to take turns stepping onto the summit, since there is not enough room up there for both of us to stand. While Kuno climbs back down to the notch I clamber up the Pointe de Lépiney which, in direct contrast to Pointe Chevalier, forms a broad, level summit platform breaking off abruptly into steep cliffs at the edges. A particularly impressive

Aiguille du Fou; to the right,
the Dent du Requin, with the
Tour Ronde behind.

and characteristic feature of the climbing on this needle is a two-meter-high, vertical and absolutely smooth step that can only be overcome with the help of a gymnastic layback move. You soon get used to such moves on the granite.

The Dent du Caiman starts with a vertical wall, barred by an 80-meter-high, totally smooth armor of slabs. The only possibility of reaching the summit—300 meters farther up—from this side is first to descend the South West Side for 100 meters to reach the East Ridge, which leads to the top. After a great deal of to-ing and fro-ing we finally believe we have located the right way and make an audacious 100 m abseil into the couloir. Climbing this puts us beneath a 150 m cliff, separating us from the ridge. A diagonal line of juggy edges and cracks leading across smooth sweeps of slabs and a horribly overhanging chimney take us up onto a little platform in the middle of the wall. By now, I am doubting the correctness of our route; the difficulty is simply too great. The climbing is similar to the hardest sections on the Walker Spur; God knows, it is certainly no grade V. Moreover, it all looks very much like new, unclimbed territory. A 20-meter groove pitch, a short traverse left, followed by a strength-sapping series of eel-slick cracks—probably the hardest I have ever climbed on granite—and finally I am standing on the ridge. But progress is blocked by a 30 m high, perfectly smooth wall, devoid of cracks and rugosities, that separates me from the shoulder higher up. It appears we have come in too low. I now have to reverse these hard-won pitches without the benefit of a rope from above and completely unprotected, since there is nowhere to place a piton. By the time we are back in the couloir we have lost valuable time and a great deal of energy better used elsewhere. Slightly to the right of our false line, a series of cracks marks what is probably the right route to take. The climbing is indeed a good grade easier than on the neighboring line. We are held up for a long time by a very loose, ice-filled chimney, in which whole columns of rock sit poised and ready to fall. Finally we are standing at the shoulder, with the ridge sweeping up steeply from ledge to ledge above us. The individual steps in the ridge are very difficult and demand reliable rope-work. . . .

WE HAVE BEEN on the go for eleven hours again today, with no end in sight. Another long row of rock teeth separates us from the Aiguille du Plan below, and to descend from any of these needles is barely possible. Huge sweeps of slabs drop down on both sides of the ridge several hundred meters to the small, yet savagely crevassed hanging glaciers lining the foot of the Aiguilles. Our movements are now lethargic, our senses dulled; we have been worn down by the sheer length of the climbing. We no longer pay particular attention to our surroundings and are just happy when we are able to strike yet another peak off the list. Again the mists close in, making the route-finding even more difficult over terrain that is confusing enough anyway. Then on the way down from the Dent du Caiman we are soaked by hail showers. We push on to the last summit but one, the Dent du Crocodile. Two smooth-faced, stubborn gendarmes stand between us and the main summit structure and force us to make several tiresome detours—traverses onto the North Side, ice-choked cracks and ledges—until a smooth crack leads up onto the ridge again and out onto the exceptionally exposed East Face. Just when we think we have outwitted the first of the gendarmes the way is blocked by a featureless wall; back again the way we came, and try another line. Finally we are at the foot of the summit structure of the Dent du Crocodile. A wall, first vertical then overhanging, rises up above us. We look questioningly at one another, searching for a way round it, but all around us the rock drops away, devoid of holds. Our fingertips are raw and bleeding— understandably so after three days with only rough granite to hold onto. We traverse into a chimney, squeeze up behind huge chockstones, and are soon standing on the summit of the Dent du Crocodile. It had really defended itself with crocodile's teeth. The storm had taken flight again, only a few isolated tatters of cloud still hanging eerily on the slopes of the mountains. Opposite us the ice slopes of the Plan de Sucre plunge down from the teeth of the Requin Ridge into the void. . . .

AT SEVEN O'CLOCK in the evening we are standing on the last of the 15 summits that form the chain of the Chamonix Aiguilles. We had thus accomplished the first complete traverse of the Aiguilles de Chamonix. I suggest a quick climb down to the Requin Hut, 1000 m below; possibly we might still reach it before nightfall. But Kuno indicates that he is not in agreement with this suggestion.

And so we decide to bivouac once more. We arrange ourselves for the night on a roomy slab of rock on the airy ridge. A wonderful sunset is the reward for the day's hardships. The highest spires in the Alps shine in the glow of the evening, while down below the valley nestles in the twilight. From our bivouac ledge we can look down almost vertically to the ice masses of the hanging glacier below. A cold wind blows up from the ice and drives us into our bivouac sack. Our bones are weary, our thoughts still captivated by the route, the greatest of all ridge traverses. I make comparisons with other routes I have done and come to the conclusion that none of them, not even the Gleierschtal Round in the Karwendel, nor even the Jorasses Spur, comes close in terms of endurance and hardship.

The night passes slowly, seemingly without end. In the first light of the new day we crawl out of our damp envelope. Black shadows still lie over the valley, while the Monarch glows bright with the first sunlight. The night frost still cramps our legs and there is

"Here, a bridging maneuver again pays dividends. Mostly, it involves you doing the splits between two rock walls, toes just coming into contact with the rock and hands pressing down flat against the rock, usually at the level of your waist or knees. This is quite a specialized technique but often the only way of climbing such difficult sections."

Hermann Buhl

nothing else for it but to make a fast start. Under the gaze of the Jorasses, we descend to the Requin Hut. Halfway down we meet a few climbers, local guides with their clients. We stroll idly down the Mer de Glace, our gaze fixed on the peaks, where the mists play in the light of the morning sun, and on the ridges, which for a few days had made us forget all worldly things.

Part 2

The Ascent
Nanga Parbat as the Goal

Herman Buhl's route list for 1951 included relatively few "great things." This time obviously was dominated by establishment of his family and by the need to provide for them, earning a living as a mountain guide. In spite of this he did manage to achieve such routes as the first winter ascent of the South Arête of the Grosser Mühlsturzhorn in the Berchtesgaden Alps; the Triglav North Face in the Julian Alps; the Aletschhorn North Wall and Finsteraarhorn North East Buttress in the Bernese Alps; the "Sentinelle Rouge" on the Brenva Face of Mont Blanc, and the North Face of the Dent d'Hérens in the Valais Alps. Buhl was already well known in German-speaking mountaineering circles, but two achievements from the year 1952 would make him famous also throughout Europe: the first solo ascent of the Cassin Route on the North East Face of the Piz-Badile and the eighth ascent of the North Face of the Eiger.

On the Eiger, Buhl and his partner, Sepp Jöchler, were overtaken by bad weather. After spending a third night bivouacking on the icy Eigerwand, Buhl led a rope of nine out of hell. On the top, not just in front of his own partner and the experienced, but badly equipped, Maag brothers from the Allgäu, but also in front of two French parties—including Gaston Rébuffat and Guido Magnone—a despairing Buhl fought his way through the Exit Cracks, which were almost impossible to climb. It was a question of survival. Thanks were due solely to Buhl, who was completely worn out to the point of exhaustion, even unconsciousness, for the fact that the nine men got off the Wall alive. Rébuffat writes the following about this decisive phase in the fight for survival:

> "Then Buhl set to. He was immediately on very difficult terrain. Beneath the snow the rock was covered with a gleaming layer of hard, thick ice, coating everything uniformly. This glazed surface meant that his feet were slipping and his hands sliding off. The cracks were choked, the hand and footholds leveled out, the pitons didn't want to go in, the hammer would knock, make progress, hollow out, become tired, miss, make hardly any impression on the thick ice; one's whole body would start to slip, cling on to one piton, manage to get a firm grip again and then have to start all over again, the gasping breathing stopping for

Hermann Buhl on the Hinterstoisser Traverse of the North Face of the Eiger.

a moment. The hammer would manage to free a foothold, let a snow plaque slip down from a slab, clean off another foothold; the foot would force a crampon tip into the icy glaze, the numb fingers free a crack from its ice and manage to fix in another piton. Buhl gains fifty centimeters, a meter, his feet slip again, everything slides, but the pitons hold. It is bitterly cold, the skies are clear, one's fingers are frozen stiff, feet are numb, muscles stiff . . . clothes are like armor, the rope a rod of iron. But heart and mind will not be put off course. Buhl progresses slowly and, with admirable determination, manages to conquer this section of the Wall. Jöchler catches up and takes over the lead."

Sepp Jöchler, who was standing much closer to the event than Rébuffat, recounts the same episode succinctly: "On the fourth day Hermann gave his all for us on one rope length for four hours. And then at the top he suddenly flipped over and was hanging head down. So naturally I went up to him and had to turn him the right way up, and seeing that he was no longer in a fit state to lead, I had no option but to take over."

Thus Buhl had not only achieved absolute mastery, he had climbed above all the others. In the same way, in 1952, Buhl climbed the South East Buttress of the Tofana di Rozes and was the first to solo climb the Fox-Stenico on the South East Wall of the Cima-d'Ambiéz in the Brenta Group. He also achieved great mixed routes. Yet his ambition drove him still further. Where could he go with all this ability? The Himalaya. Hermann knew his mountaineering history: In 1950 Maurice Herzog and Louis Lachenal had achieved the first eight-thousand-meter summit—Annapurna I. In the same year Rudolf Peters, the first person to climb the North Face of the Grandes Jorasses, had planned a reconnaissance expedition to Makalu. It failed due to insufficient funding.

The German Himalayan Foundation, which carried out the 1937, 1938 and 1939 Nanga Parbat Expeditions before the Second World War, also had plans afoot for further expeditions. A member of the group, Paul Bauer, had become world famous for his "heroic" attempts on the North East Spur of Kanchenjunga in 1929 and 1931. A shorter approach to the East Ridge of Nanga Parbat was being deliberated, along with a more favorable possibility of climbing Rakhiot Peak from the south, from the Rupal side. In the midst of all this musing and planning, a passionate appeal for funds for an expedition to Nanga Parbat penned by "K.M.H." suddenly appeared in the *Süddeutsche Zeitung* on 19 July 1952. "The initiator . . . was, as it transpired a few days later, Dr. Karl Herrligkoffer, a stepbrother

The North Face of the Eiger, covered in snow after an outbreak of bad weather. In similar conditions Hermann Buhl achieved the almost-impossible: he fought his way through the iced-up Exit Crack and led eight mountaineers back to life.

of Willy Merkl, unknown in mountaineering circles and without any other kind of specialist experience," reported Paul Bauer.

Hermann Buhl, who at this time ranked as the top alpinist in the world, was the last person to be invited on the Herrligkoffer Austrian-German Expedition in memory of Willy Merkl. It appeared that the organizers were afraid of Buhl's overwhelming superiority. He was considered to be "difficult to get on with on a personal level." But the Innsbrucker's list of climbing achievements tempted everyone involved who was dreaming of success on Nanga Parbat. It was Hermann Buhl—and he alone—who was the guarantor of success. In addition to this, his longtime climbing partner, Kuno Rainer, was also on the expedition team. It was a strong party. Buhl prepared for the attempt on Nanga Parbat in a way that was typical for him: during a February night in 1953 he achieved the first winter solo of the Salzburg Route on the East Face of the Watzmann. In the same year he made the first winter ascent of the extremely long "Steinkarumrahmung" traverse in the Karwendel. In the spring he climbed the South East Corner of the Fleischbank—twice.

Let us leave it to Buhl to tell us about his eventual route to the Himalaya in the following three journal articles, reporting on climbs on the Tofana Buttress, the North East Face of the Badile, and the night climb of the East Face of the Watzmann.

Storm on the Tofana Buttress

by Hermann Buhl

It was in such 'charabancs' or truck-coaches that the Innsbruckers would make their occasional trips to the Dolomites; here, it is 1949 and they are off to the North Face of the Furchetta. Hermann Buhl is the third from the right.

WE ARE HEADING for Cortina. The Cristallo is still deep in snow, the Tofana still very wintry. It is simply still early in the year and the mountains here do exceed the 3000-meter mark. An old military road takes us up almost right to the start of the route. We have once more found a charitable friend, our fellow club member Walter Fritz, who is only too pleased to take us up in his car, thus making such a route possible for us. After a half-hour drive we are walking up over patches of snow to the foot of the wall. Here, there is not a flake of snow in sight; the wall is dry. Above our heads, the Tofana Buttress rears up steeply. White roofs bar the middle section of the wall; this is the key to the climb. A route of the young generation, climbed in 1944 by the Cortina team of Costantini and Apollonio, and numbering among the most difficult routes in the Dolomites. The first-ascent party reckoned it to be even tougher than the North face of the Western Zinne. " . . . 6 grado superiore, arrampicata effettiva ore 21," it says in *Berti* [translator's note: the "Berti" was the Italian Dolomite guidebook].

We expect to do it in a day, not 21 hours. We have made our preparations, we know where the route goes and we reckon on about 10 to 12 hours' climbing time. We are equipped for extremely severe pitches and have even taken along some etriers and other aid-climbing gear, even though I am usually an opponent of such exaggerated technological equipment. The only thing we leave behind is the bivouac sack, since we do not want to alarm our chauffeur.

At six o'clock in the morning we start up the first pitch. It is already so warm that we debate whether or not to leave our pullovers here as well. All goes well to start with. A series of overhanging cracks splits the wall above us. Where these peter out into blank rock, a rightward traverse leads across to the start of a second crack system, running up diagonally rightward. The rock is smooth and the holds small. My friend Sepp sums up the pitch we have just climbed in one succinct little phrase: "Overhang, peg belay, traverse out onto the wall." Let me introduce my ropemate briefly: fellow club member Sepp Jöchler, a man who is just as accomplished on the rock as he is on the accordion. A winter ascent of the Brunnenkogel

Arête in the Sellrainer Mountains was the first of several trips we made together.

The first of the three bands of roofs now bars the way. This is, however, just a foretaste of the roofs farther up—the overture, if you like. It is, admittedly, pretty big but the juggy rock makes it possible to free climb it. A further pitch lands us below the second roof, not a great deal different from the first. The crack continues and, apart from a brief smooth section that we avoid on the right, does not present any difficulties worthy of mention. It ends at the third roof, and by now we are at the middle belt of roofs that bar passage onto the rest of the wall. On the edge of a large hole leading right into the innards of the mountain, we make our preparations for what is to come. Walter and Rudl Seiwald wanted to do the Normal Route on the Tofana but have now returned; there was probably too much snow for them. They are now lying in the meadow next to the car and following us through their field glasses.

The rock now takes on a brittle character. Beneath the first roof there is a good stance, and I bring Sepp up. An overhanging crack now goes diagonally rightward up into the roof. Only two or three meters farther out in space does the wall finally return to vertical, with the roof cutting across its whole width. We find hardly any pitons in place but peg holes are in plentiful supply. A thin crack on the underside of the roof takes a piton and I clip in a rope sling. Hesitantly, I step into the sling and swing out beneath the roof. I am now hanging under the roof like a fly on a ceiling, feet dangling out over the void. The overhanging wall below me now seems almost easy-angled. I feel around the lip of the roof and finally manage to place an ice piton we had, coincidentally, brought with us. The crack is quite wide and the peg will only hold in a certain position. Another sling is clipped in, and I am now at the outermost edge of the roof, but my feet are still hanging in thin air. I am now finished with bashing in pitons and try to free climb over the roof, but first I need to find something solid for my feet. After another overhang, which I again manage to free climb, I reach a well-deserved stance. Now the desperate struggle begins again for Sepp. He does not have things any easier. As soon as he unclips a carabiner he swings out into thin air and spins like a carousel on his own axis. Several times I see his black mop of hair pop up over the roof, only to disappear again as quickly as it had appeared. Finally, he is standing next to me, gasping for breath.

REDDISH-WHITE mottled rock continues, overhanging all the way up to the second roof. Thin, discontinuous cracks offer the only means of climbing it. A protection peg goes in every ten meters or so. Above me I see a little pulpit and presume it is the belay. I just need to get there, that's all. On the stretch of the last few meters of the 40-meter climbing rope I work my way up a smooth wall: I have got it. But where is the stance? The rock pushes me out so far that I can barely stand upright. A stance in slings makes the job of bringing Sepp up a little easier. Above, a looming groove brings me to beneath the next large roof. It is not as big a span as the first one but makes up for that by dropping away slightly toward the outermost boundary edge. It is split by a wide crack. Nothing goes in the crack; as soon as I stick a peg in it, it falls straight out again. In the farthermost corner of the roof I finally get a "bomber" into a narrow little fissure. Tensioning off the rope, I lean out backwards until I am lying almost horizontally beneath the roof, hands searching around on the lip for a suitable crack. Again, I need a long piton for the next placement. I stick it in the crack, twist it to wedge it in place, give it a couple of blows with the hammer and then go back down for a bit of a rest. Once again, I arch my body out backward and clip in a carabiner and a rope sling. Sepp gives me tension and, with my feet braced in the sling and my body stretched out, I gain the outer edge of the roof. Just a few hard pulls and I have footholds

again. I reach back and pull the ice peg out with my fingers; I can use that one again farther up. Another twenty meters of hard climbing and I am standing on a wide ledge right in the middle of a belt of overhangs. We can hear voices below, getting louder. Someone shouts my name, but it is not one of our companions. We learned later that a group of Cortina climbers had been watching us.

IT IS NOW HALF past three in the afternoon and I reckon on finishing it off easily now. A steeply overhanging chimney juts out above our heads. It does not look particularly inviting, but appearances can be deceptive. Right at the back of the fissure, I climb up on stalactite formations until, after 10 meters, it closes up completely. I have to get out into daylight again, onto the outermost edge of this seriously overhanging chimney. An old, rusty ring peg might have a tale or two to tell; I clip it and review the situation. The rock around me bows out severely. Above, a featureless overhang blocks the way into the continuation chimney. There are no little crevices to be found, not even hairline cracks, that might take a piton. I call for tension and bridge out wide to the edge of the bulge. I can now see the whole of the lower part of the wall right below me. The chimney juts out far beyond the wide ledge below it. I get a few pitons in but none of them

Tofana di Rozes, South Side. The South East Face of the Tofana Buttress—the "Pilastro"—is the prominent, smooth-faced pillar second from the right. Hermann Buhl and Sepp Jöchler climbed it in 1952. They were forced to bivouac and were caught in a storm.

is any use at all. I tie them all together with a sling—that way they might hold—clip a foot loop in and in this way manage to gain about half a meter in height. But that is the limit of my artistry. I try traversing left, but it is all brittle and too off-balance out there. This can't be right. Perhaps the ring peg was placed in error? But this bit is clearly indicated in the route description. Farther over to the left things look better. I lower myself down off the piton onto the ledge; Sepp has to pull me in. After climbing up a short way I try to tension traverse across to easier ground. I am almost there when the pegs rip, depriving me of my last firm hold. All my efforts are in vain. It *has* to go up the chimney. Again I hang there, exactly as before, unable to gain even one centimeter in height. I am starting to doubt my own abilities. This kind of thing has never happened to me before.

Wherever a human being has set his foot, it must surely be possible for another to follow, as long as he has the natural ability to do so—this had always been my theory. "Just leave that bit out and get on with the bit above!" Sepp jokes. I have to go back down to the ledge again and rest. The only thing we can do is carry on up; retreat has been cut off. But how are we going to get over those big roofs? I search for a way out, follow the ledge along, but it peters out everywhere into roofs.

WE TAKE A LOOK at the watch. It is already 6 o'clock in the evening. Time has flown by. We are still hoping to get away without having to bivouac, but this means we need to act fast. Trusting to my better judgment, I decide to have another go at the wall to the left. So as not to lose any more time we leave the pitons, carabiners and rope slings hanging at the overhang in the chimney and pull the ropes through. Ten meters farther left the rock still overhangs badly but at least there are holds. I have to run out a full 30 meters, since there is nowhere to place pitons on this compact rock. My fingers are running out of strength. The climbing is right at the limit of what it is possible to free climb. I painstakingly examine both myself and the moves ahead before tackling each section, to avoid a repeat of what happened to me on the North Face of the Western Zinne. An exposed traverse on tiny holds brings us back into the chimney, above the capping overhang. An abandoned rope sling is hanging there on the wall. We have to leave all our gear behind, since there is no more time to lose. Climbing almost simultaneously, we storm up the easier cracks above. But again the wall looms huge above us. Yellowish-red rock glowers down at us. There seems to be no end in sight. I find myself in a chimney just as darkness falls. Sepp is below on a good stance. A bivouac seems certain. I am happy to swap my cramped and cold crevice for the grassy ledge, where Sepp has already begun making preparations for the bivi. And how glad we are now to have our pullovers, even though the sun had been shining hard all day long. Slowly, the night comes creeping up out of the valleys. In Cortina, the first lights are sparking into life. The

only annoying thing is that we have caused our friends problems by having to bivouac. Their wives will be waiting at home, worrying, and will fear the worst, as women do. Really, they should just drive off home; we can follow on by train tomorrow. But they put comradeship first and do not think of leaving us alone. By means of a flickering candle we signal our position. They answer by flashing their headlights. When we get hungry we reach into the rucksack and stuff a handful of mixed fruit and nuts— bird food, as we call it—into our mouths. So that our comrades should not worry about us, and to show them what good spirits we are in, we yodel and sing at the tops of our voices.

Our howling chorus falls silent only around midnight. In the distance, we can see flashes of lightning—"weather beacons," Sepp reckons, "a good sign." I am of a different opinion. Mountains of gray cloud are piling up over the Pala. Bolts of lightning flash across the dark night sky. We are blinded for several seconds, and then enveloped again by the black night. In the distance, thunder rolls. It is a wonderful natural spectacle; we hope it stays that way! But the mass of black cloud draws ever nearer. From time to time our comrades signal to us with their lights. They have now lit a campfire; probably it had gotten too cold for them. We are beginning to feel it, too. It creeps through our clothing and gnaws at our bones. We huddle close together through the endless hours. It is now 2 o'clock in the morning and the weather is growing more and more worrying. The last windows in the clouds are closed now; there are no more stars to be seen in the sky. The bank of cloud, black and threatening, is getting lower and lower. The summits of the Pelmo and the Antelao are now wearing hoods of cloud. Solitary tatters of mist come chasing across the Falzarego Pass, and from the valleys the mist is rising to form a wall of cloud that intermittently blocks all view of the valley bottoms. We are in for a storm; it is just a question of time. This idle watching and waiting game is hard on the morale and on the nerves. Nearer and nearer the cloud banks grow; mists are descending from our summit; the curtain draws shut. We can feel occasional drops of rain on our faces. No, not rain, snowflakes, falling thicker and thicker. Soon we are stuck in a mad maelstrom of wind-whipped snow. It settles on the ledges and edges, and then melts with its own warmth. Our clothes are unpleasantly damp. We can only hope this weather will not last long. Then we realize that this is the time of year of the legendary *Eismänner,* when it can snow as far down as the lowlands.

SLOWLY, THE GRAY dawn of a new day breaks through the clouds. The occasional peal of thunder can still be heard; not a good sign. A cold wind comes up and parts the clouds. Ghostly swaths of mist chase across the Nuvolau and the Cirque Torri. The cirque is sugar-coated white. The wind hurls plumes of snow across the ridge, the fine drizzle of white crystals pouring down the wall like a cold shower. It is an impressive place, our little bivouac ledge. On every side, yellow walls drop vertically away. It feels like we are on an island in the middle of a foaming, raging sea. We signal again to our comrades down by the car: a lively yodel from Sepp's throat, intended to assure them that we had spent the night well. I am never one for waiting around too long—mostly, things do not get much better. And we need to get off this wall! The rock is still very cold; hand- and footholds are slippery. Snow is still lying on every little ledge. The chimney is not as easy as it was yesterday. Our limbs are still stiff and ache with every move. When I have to flex my ankles they often just turn over; yet after two or three rope lengths things start to get better. The weather seems to have changed for the better, or is this just the calm before the storm? There is even the occasional patch of blue sky visible between the clouds. Then the mists come down again and the whirl of snowflakes begins afresh, but the climbing gets easier and easier. We arrive at the left retaining edge of the face,

Sepp Jöchler, Hermann Buhl's climbing partner on the North Face of the Eiger and on the Tofana Pillar, in the days of the Jungmannschaft.

"Climbing really is the finest sport of all. Of course this is only the case when you are competent and do not overtax yourself beyond what is pleasurable. After the climb, you should feel no trace of tiredness; on the contrary, it is then that you should be really fresh. Then you will have found the correct measure of your abilities."

Hermann Buhl

where we are treated to a picture of tremendous magnificence. The clouds part and suddenly there are pillar upon pillar of rock, rising from the waves of gray, improbably sheer precipices with tatters of mist still nestling between them. A fine veil of mist covers everything, lending the whole picture a special aura. Only a storm can conjure up such ephemeral images. Then suddenly the whole picture is wiped clean—as in a theater—as we are enclosed once again in a uniform gray. The wind increases in strength and the snow grows thicker as we approach the ridge. Another few pitches and we are standing on the crest of the ridge leading up to the summit of the Tofana. Today we can do without that.

ON THE NORTH SIDE everything is covered in deep snow. Our clothes soon stiffen to an icy coat of armor in the freezing northwest wind. We make a rising traverse of the crag-strewn slopes up to the Punta Marietta. The snow here is deep, and to avoid getting too tired we take turns breaking trail. It is a good thing I know the way down; the terrain here tempts you to descend on a straight course, but the pleasant slopes soon break off into impassable rock walls. We keep breaking through and sinking deeply into the rotten snow. The mists part for a brief moment and we use the opportunity to get our bearings, subsequently reaching the notch behind the Punta Marietta direct, without any detours. Coincidence or calculation? We carry on down, trudging and thrashing through the deep, rotten snow, leaving a deep ditch behind us. Wondering how our comrades will receive us, and feeling a little guilty, we run down to meet them. They would all have had good reason to give us both a serious bawling out—and we would have had to accept it—but when they see us they grin broadly and our expressions change in an instant, too. They greet us with warm handshakes and words of congratulation; not a word of reproach passes their lips. "You're a pair of mad dogs!" said Walter. We are very moved by all this comradely behavior and promise them that if they ever want something from us, we will gladly help out any time. Later, when we are all sitting down at "Reatl," Walter says, "You could have said you might have to bivouac, you heroes, you!"

Alone on the North East Face of the Badile

By Hermann Buhl

I KEPT HEARING the name "North East Face of the Badile" again and again. Thus it was not surprising that my burning desire to climb this route, just the once, was getting hotter and hotter. But it just was not happening; something always seemed to interfere with my plans. At the beginning of July 1952 I could wait no longer, and made a definite decision to go and tackle it. Irritated by various incidents and cancellations, I finally decided to set off on my own. As a result of my financial circumstances, it was to be my bicycle that would make the whole trip possible. Although I was advised against it due to the fact that there was too much snow, these warnings went unheeded—nothing more could deter me from my plan.

On a Friday evening—the date is 4 July—I race to catch the evening express train to Landeck. From there I continue by bicycle. At midnight I arrive at the Swiss border and lie down by the side of the road for a few hours' rest. I hadn't gotten a wink of sleep the night before, as I was involved in a rescue call-out, searching for someone missing in Innsbruck's Northern Range. By four o'clock

in the morning I am back in the saddle again, cycling up toward the Maloja Pass. If you know the road through the Engadine you will also know what kind of slog it is to cycle up it. A delivery van gives me a lift for a short way, and I thank the driver by helping him unload his tubs of jam. From Samaden onward I have to rely on my own muscle power again. Midday arrives as I tackle the Maloja Pass in the murderous heat, and then pedal on past the lovely lakes of Sils and Silvaplana inviting me to bathe in their clear, fresh waters. I haven't the time, of course; a long road lies ahead. Now, steep hairpins lead down into the Val Bregaglia. Despite the wind, sweat runs off my body. Down another 1100 m lies Promontogno, the point of departure for the Sciora Hut, its old houses huddling close together on the steep lower slopes of the Bergell Mountains. As I bump my way along its rutted alleyways my gaze is drawn upwards through the scrub and leaves of the copious vegetation, and I stand transfixed—so that is the Piz Badile! The elegant lines of its arêtes and ridges sweep up to the summit, crowned by a shimmering,

The 850-meter North East Face of the Piz Badile in the Bergell Mountains, first climbed in 1937 by Riccardo Cassin, Ginetto Esposito, Vittorio Ratti, Mario Molteni, and Giuseppe Valsecchi (the line of the "Cassin Route" is just right of center). Hermann Buhl was the first to make a solo ascent.

glittering band of cornices. Gloomy and forbidding, its precipices plunge to the valley below.

I SHOULDER MY rucksack and start hiking up into the savagely romantic Bondasca Valley. This hut approach is becoming a real pilgrimage. With pleasure, I let the spray of a roaring waterfall play over my sweat-soaked body. The triple peaks of the Sciora Group fill the head of the valley. Three ridges, flanked by ice gullies, point the way to the summit. Black storm clouds fill the sky, and the summits of the Badile and Cengalo are wreathed in mists. Soon the blessed comfort of a cooling shower sets in. At 7:00 p.m. I reach the Sciora Hut. There are only two other people present, the guardian and a guest from Milan. Sensibly, I say nothing of my plan and in reply to their inquisitive questions, I answer only that I intend to do the Badile Ridge. I set the alarm for two o'clock and settle down to a well-earned rest.

ON WAKING, I NOTICE to my horror that it is already daylight. A glance at the clock—four a.m.! I must have slept through the alarm. In a tearing hurry, I am soon ready to set off. Breakfast is eaten on the move. I traverse across boulder slopes and slabs, finally descending a little to set foot on the expanse of glacier which lies at the foot of the Cengalo and the Badile. Uncer-

tain of the way, I get a little too high up. I want to traverse beneath the cliffs of the Cengalo but a huge crevasse blocks the way, forcing me to make a detour and costing me valuable time. Now the sun rises behind the mountains of the Eastern Bergell and casts its first rays onto the North East Face of the Piz Badile. I am soon following the path again, which is now nice and easy to make out, etched in light and shade. The Wall itself sets a few puzzles for me to solve, but all will become clear when I actually get up there. Along the edge of black and gaping clefts I leave my track and scramble up to the head of the second rocky spur. Another brief pause for thought, a glance at the sky—the weather seems to be holding—and I ready myself for what is to come. The bivi sack and everything else I can do without stays down below. The only things to disappear into my trusty climbing sack are the 30 m length of Perlon line, a few rope slings, carabiners and pitons, my peg hammer, some provisions, and the camera. Then I climb up hard, steep névé to the start of the route, noting that climbing rubbers are not exactly the ideal kind of footwear for such terrain. The sight of these huge sweeps of slabs, on which the eye can barely detect a single feature, briefly gives me cause for concern. I can hear voices coming from the North Ridge, where a rope of three is already at work.

At six o'clock in the morning, I lay hand on rock (the crossing from snow to rock was easy). To begin with, the route goes easily across to the right, crossing stepped terrain on good holds and climbing a seemingly steep section by a chimney pitch—this, too, is quite easy. The first 200 meters of the face are now behind me; it would be nice if it were to continue like this, but I have a feeling. . . . Soon I am standing at the start of the 30-meter corner. I almost missed it! I am already several meters up it before I realize that this is where the difficulties begin, and it would be quite nice to have a carabiner handy. So I down-climb the few meters of the pitch back to the stance. I take everything I might need out of the rucksack, tie the rope around my waist, drape the rope slings, the camera, and ironmongery around my neck and—up I go!

I well remember the pictures in *Alpinisme,* but where *are* all the pitons in this corner? To the right there is a smooth slab with only tiny little rugosities for the feet, while the left wall overhangs the corner itself. A thin crack runs up the back of the corner, while the feet have to search for friction holds on the right. The previous year's rockfall is already making itself unpleasantly noticeable here; the slabs are covered in a fine dust several millimeters thick that fills every crack and almost cancels out the friction of my climbing rubbers. I am soon beneath the capping overhang. A carabiner snaps into the rusty eye of the venerable old piton. A quick test—it holds. I take a little breather, using the peg as a handhold for a short while—it has done its duty—and move on up. The overhang has good holds and is soon climbed. Easier-angled slabs, split by cracks, point a way out left. It seems to be easier ground up here, but the cracks are all full of sand, making the climbing considerably more difficult. Carefully, I push on farther. I am gradually getting closer to a large patch of ice lying on the slabs that seems to block further progress, a relic of the winter snow. Viewed from below, it appeared questionable whether I could climb it. It covers the route for a width of 20 meters, a half-meter-thick layer of hollow ice lying on a smooth base. I have to traverse across its upper edge. Carefully, I hack away the sharp upper edge of the ice; it groans ominously with every hammer blow. It is with relief that I leave the ice and get back onto the safety of the rock and the continuation of the crack line. The rock now becomes a little better and I am out of the line of fire of the falling stones. After an arête the wall goes thrusting up steeply again. I am at the start of the second corner, which rates as an indisputable grade VI and represents one of the major difficulties of the face. This corner is a critical pitch for me. If I find it easy I can continue my ascent with peace of mind, since things will not be getting any more difficult. If not, retreat from here is still a possible option, and would then actually be preferable.

AN OVERHANG now absorbs my attention, running up diagonally leftward. Good holds give me the necessary feeling of security. Where they run out, a short gallery of pitons begins. They do not look very trustworthy and, to judge from the fine patina on them, are probably the pitons used by the first-ascent party. Thereafter, a 30 m high groove, smooth and quite vertical, goes shooting up skyward. The rock, however, is extraordinarily rough so that I am able to climb it "on friction," and it is with particular pleasure that I note here the advantages of my new *Marwa* soles, which are perfect for this kind of climbing. So I wrestle, push and bridge my way up, meter by meter, with the free end of the rope following on behind like a faithful companion. Natural, pure free climbing and technical skill are the only things that help here and I could shout aloud for joy, but I am surrounded by a holy quiet, not a sound disturbs the solemn silence. The valley below still lies in the cool mists of a fresh and dewy morning.

Onward! There is still a goodly portion of the route before me. Huge roofs cap the groove and I

escape out left beneath them, onto a smooth slabby face that is, luckily, endowed with little holds. Now I am not quite clear about the continuation of the route. The description is rather vague here. Everywhere are impending slabs, overlapping like roofing slates and split by thin cracks. I search each of these cracks for pitons. A touch farther away I discover the badly weathered shaft of an old peg. After a bit of hither and thither—it actually looked nastier up here than it really is—I am at the aforementioned piton, my route-finding signpost. After a series of wonderful moves I reach the snowfield in the middle of the face at about eight o'clock. I settle down on the warm rock, take a short breather, and summon up new strength for the hard climbing to come. To the left of the snowfield is the start of the Big Corner, which heralds the beginning of the major difficulties of the wall. Curiosity stops me hanging around for too long; I am really excited about this section of the route. Hechtel compares it to the Schüle-Diem on the Predigtstuhl, but I did that route so long ago that I can no longer judge the accuracy of the comparison. It certainly is very smooth, but with a good deal of bridging and good friction technique I manage to free climb most of it pretty well. The few pitons in place serve briefly as handholds and I climb the whole pitch without protection, although what value this has on a solo ascent like this is questionable. An awkward rope maneuver that takes up both time and energy I would sooner use for climbing, and I am 40 meters up, where a loose overhang bars the way. I find a piton and a carabiner there, French in origin, trademarked "Allain."

I WANT TO TAKE the overhang direct, just as it is, but soon I am hanging from it like a fly on the wall. I am actually above the lip, but there are not any holds to pull over on. I go back down again, take a little rest and start again from the beginning. This time I try to place a piton just above—no easy matter. I hang a foot sling from it, the only one I use on the whole route. There are still 10 meters separating me from the capping roof. I would like to take the piton with me, so I knock in another one farther up and lower myself on the rope down to the overhang. A few heavy blows with the hammer and the ring peg belongs to me again. Then, using the rope, I climb the overhang again. There are two letters engraved on the French carabiner: "L.T." That can only mean Lionel Terray. Delighted and at the same time proud of my find, I carry on up to the roof. Under the roof, however, I can find no trace of the piton for the tension traverse, yet the route has to go out rightward here, and down to the parallel corner. And lo and behold, there, 20 meters lower down, is a ramp-line linking the two corners. Suddenly it dawns on me. I have been hard at work climbing a variation on the route. Now I realize too what the French carabiner meant. But I do not want to go back down and so I try a downward traverse from here into the parallel corner. I hammer another piton in. Carefully, I take a look around the corner: on the right, a smooth slab 10 m wide, with a narrow, finger-width ledge 2 m below it, discontinuous, but offering the only possibility. Carefully, I push myself across rightward, centimeter by centimeter, in a "classic abseil" position. There is nothing at all for the hands. The angle of the slab is so steep that I can only just stay in balance with the aid of the rope. After some ticklish minutes I get some handholds again. I am in the corner. The rope pulls through easily. The climbing is again somewhat easier here, but the sweet taste does not last too long. Again, smaller overhangs bow out above me, but at least they have good holds. Vertical ribs and flakes, behind which the best holds lie hidden, provide a welcome change. The feet are rather worse off; they have to be satisfied with friction holds on the rough slabs. Another roof now puts a stop to all this. From here an exposed traverse left along a horizontal crack leads to the edge of the Big Gully. The first 10 meters are nerve-racking, and no place for the faint-hearted. The

"What an advantage the modern climber has, with the friction afforded by his rubber-soled boots allowing him to climb up easily and athletically, almost as if it were a game."
Hermann Buhl

"There is probably nothing finer than to climb free and unencumbered by equipment, reveling in the gymnastic upward movement, like a Preuss or a Dülfer before you, relying only upon yourself, keeping a sharp eye on things, feeling the rock beneath your feet and fingertips."

Hermann Buhl

holds are tiny, but I think to myself, "They may be small, but they are all mine. . . ."

I AM IN THE BIG GULLY. Occasional stones whirr past me. But this can not disturb my calm. In the bed of the gully, a little bubbling stream makes its way happily down into the abyss. It offers me delicious refreshment, for after hours in the burning sun I am pretty parched. Leaving Cassin's second bivouac on the left, I follow a long sequence of cracks that finally open out into a chimney. . . .

Italian climbers who were on the summit of the Badile on that 6 July 1952, caught sight of Buhl on the North East Face. One of them (S. Bray) photographed him on the upper part of the Face (circled).

A cool breeze wafts down from the summit; it cannot be much farther to climb now. Turning an overhang, I traverse out onto the left-hand containing wall—and there it is: the summit, already visible. There is still a wealth of snow in the gully running up to the ridge. I traverse out left for a rope-length, across an exposed wall on little holds. Again, my gaze is drawn upward—a whole host of people has collected on the summit! I can see only their heads, poking up from behind the cornices, inquisitively following my every move. Of course, it is a rare occurrence to watch a "rope" climbing this face. My rope is snaking its way gently up behind me. After another two abseils I am standing in the bed of the big gully. I artfully manage to avoid the snow and ice by gymnastic moves on loose stuff up a kind of arête. There is still a fair bit to do before the soles of my climbing boots pick their way up the last few meters of the Face.

I reach the summit! I greet the crowd of young Italians with a shout of "Berg Heil!" They answer with "Saluti" and "Bravo." It is 10:30 and I still have the whole day ahead of me. Contentedly, I sit myself down on one of the huge stone blocks on the summit for a well-earned rest. I can read the enthusiasm and astonishment on the faces of the Italians. They introduce themselves, one as Mauri, the other as Ratti. Now I

take notice—their names are familiar to me; they number among the Italian mountaineering elite. I have to dig out my entire Italian vocabulary to answer their many questions. With typically southern temperament they keep expressing their appreciation. Our conversation is very friendly and warm and shows yet again that for mountaineers there are neither frontiers nor nations. We are all possessed of the same ideal: the longing for the heights, the drive to be on top.

OUR COMRADELY get-together lasts about an hour, during which time I hardly find the time to take a look around and treat myself to the view. Chain upon chain of rough-hewn shapes of mountains range along the southern horizon. To the west the blue eye of Lake Como gleams brightly. The hilly landscape of the foothills to the Italian Alps blurs in the haze of the horizon. To the east, the névé peaks of the Bernina Group glitter in the sun, and the knife-edged ice arête of the Bianco Ridge is clearly discernible. Every little piece of this world holds memories for me. The Maloja Pass, the watershed between the Black Sea and the Adriatic, calls across a greeting. The Lakes of Sils and Silvaplana peek out from behind the outlying spurs of the Forno Basin. Far below our feet, in the blue haze, is the Bergell Valley of the Maira with all its lovely little villages:

"There is something elegant, something satisfying about climbing the steepest of faces solo, without all the tiresome ironmongery."
Hermann Buhl

On the summit of the Badile, Hermann Buhl met some climbers from Lecco. They greeted the Innsbrucker cordially and expressed enthusiasm for his audacious solo ascent.

Promontogno, Soglio, Casaccia. The sound of church bells drifts up to our ears; it is midday.

My newly won mountain friends want to take me down to Lecco with them, but I have to explain to them that I have to go down to Promontogno because I have left my bicycle there, and anyway I have to be back in Innsbruck next morning. The goodbyes are heart-felt. My friends from Lecco descend to the south, while my route leads down the Badile Ridge to the north and the foot of the route. My gaze wanders again over the smooth sweeps of rock of the North East Face that lose themselves in the bottomless abyss below. They now seem even more eerie than before, when I was searching for a way up them. I bid the folk farewell and, a little uncertain of the route, keep quite close to the crest of the ridge. Once I am back into the climbing again I descend the ridge without use of the rope. Wonderful, exposed climbing takes me down into the depths. My eye is drawn first left, then right to the steep granite armor of the cliffs flanking the ridge. The rock is heavily lichen-covered in places, in comparison to the North East Face, but the crest of the ridge is also more exposed to the weather. Bit by bit, I progress down the 800-meter ridge, as the walls around me gain in height and steepness. The Cengalo Couloir now soars steeply above me.

The Cengalo itself spreads out its broad bulk above a savage jumble of randomly piled boulders. Its flanks are polished smooth—giant forces have been at work here—and every fissure and ledge is still decorated with a filigree pattern of dazzling white. Meter-thick shields of snow hang on its slabs, poised to fall.

I GLISSADE DOWN a snow slope to arrive at the Sasc Furä spur, a subsidiary of the Ridge, that I follow down farther until I find an appropriate opportunity to descend to the floor of the glacier. The silver blade of the Badile's summit now gleams high above me again and the North East Face once more stands proud and huge as ever. Yet I now see it with different eyes, for now I know its secrets. There is just one more short snowfield to traverse, and then I am back at the rocky spur and my things. I first quench my thirst, then let the sun burn down agreeably on my hide. I have plenty of time; it is still only three in the afternoon. As a cooling wind blows up I get ready for my journey. In high spirits, well pleased with my successful mountain venture, I slide down the heaps of snow, stumble over rubble, stroll over carpets of soft, lush green meadows and stop at every pool to dive into its cool wet waters.

It costs me my last few pennies to reclaim my bicycle. Then it is one quick look back at the Badile, a silent farewell and I swing up into the saddle again.

I now have a proper grind ahead of me: a 20 km slog up to the Maloja Pass, with a height differential of some 1100 meters. Two hours later, at 8 p.m., I am standing at the top of the Pass; 140 km of rural high road lie before me. Hopefully nothing will go wrong with the bike, otherwise I will have to walk home! Once again, the shores of the Upper Engadine Lakes border the road, their surface as calm as a mirror. St. Moritz arrives, its big-town bustle set amid the elemental mountain landscape. I weave my way between rows of parked cars. Slowly the violet colors of evening give way to the impenetrable gray of the twilight hour. The night spreads its black wings over the heights and the low country. I follow the road's monotonous light stripe that loses itself in the dark night ahead. Kilometer by kilometer, my journey slips into the recent past. Hour upon hour, the same rhythm carries me down the valley. At two o'clock I cross the frontier near Martinsbruck. Here, the road becomes more pleasant again. I pedal monotonously on, as if in a dream. My tiredness starts to overwhelm me more and more often now and it is only with a huge effort of will that I can keep myself awake. Several times I find myself coming worryingly

close to the stones and trees at the edge of the road, and it is often only at the last moment that I manage to gain control of the bike and avoid these obstacles. In the east it is gradually getting light. A clear, fresh dawn is breaking. I have 15 km to go to Landeck.

STRAIGHT AS A DIE, slightly downhill, the road follows the bank of the River Inn down to the Pontlatz bridge. The wheels slip easily over the asphalt. Then with a sudden crack I am brought to a violent stop. In a split second I am flying like a leaping salmon in a high arc through the air, to land headfirst on something hard, turn a somersault—and suddenly feel everything wet and cold around me. Still drunk with sleep, I pry my eyes open and see a wide expanse of water before me. "You've fallen in a lake," I think to myself. But very soon I feel the cold of the water and the current and see the opposite bank, and I know where I have landed—in the River Inn! I am standing up to my neck in water, high water. The biting chill of my temporary place of residence very quickly wakes me up. There is my trusty bicycle, too, and my rucksack just about to make a break for freedom, but before the current can carry it away I manage to get a stranglehold. It is quite a struggle to get myself and my fellow accident victims back onto the road. And

"A short time after his marriage he visited me in Bozen with his young wife. He seemed calm and even-tempered, and he asked me for my advice. It was time for him to build an existence that would enable him to provide for a family, he said. Climbing mountains cost money, but did not bring any in. What he was looking for was a job linked to climbing, as an advisor to one of the big sport shops. . . . Finally we ended up at good old 'Daddy' Schuster's, whom I had known for years. On 1 December 1952 Buhl started in his new position at the mountaineering equipment retailer, August Schuster."

Luis Trenker

now I am dripping wet. Battered by the cold, I shake myself like a wet dog. Everything sticks to me. Every movement I make has an unpleasantly clammy and cold outcome. Soon a little lake has formed about my feet and a small stream is running out of my rucksack. It is 4:30 in the morning, not the right time to go for a swim!

And just look at my bicycle! The frame is badly buckled, the forks bent backwards. They can't be bent back into shape here. No more cycling for me now. And not a soul nor a house in sight. My head is hurting now; it has yet another bruise to show. It must have been one of the edging stones that brought my journey to such an abrupt halt. Shouldering the bike, I set off walking. The Bridge of Pontlatz, that historical site, will now be etched much more clearly on my memory than it ever was at school. After several kilometers more I finally come to the first house, the inn "Zum alten Zoll," the old toll-house. After long hours of waiting, during which my clothes slowly dry out again, I board a post bus which takes me to Landeck, where I have to try to fit in with the civilized world once more. . . .

Night Climb

By Hermann Buhl

THE CALENDAR shows 28 February 1953. It is just midday. Laden with rucksack, skis, and ice axe, I weave my way like a slalom ski racer through the milling crowds of people crushed into the main streets of Munich. The high-pressure weather systems of the last few days have made it impossible for me to stay in town any longer. Thanks to the understanding and the allowances made by my boss, himself an enthusiastic mountaineer, I was able to leave my place of work on Friday.

The express train takes me up into the mountains. "Berchtes-gaden—all change!" This little piece of the world has become almost my second home, since the day I found my partner for life here. It is still deep winter up here. A few quick purchases and I push on to the Königssee, leaving my skis behind at the left-luggage office.

The locals there know their business and it is only after buying an "entry ticket" that I am allowed to set foot on the frozen surface of the lake. I have to put up with many a questioning look. "Rucksack, ice axe—going alone towards Bartholomä? Surely he is not hoping to . . . ?" Then, to add to my misfortunes, I meet a neighbor of mine from the

Ramsau. Please don't let my wife find out! An hour later I reach Bartholomä. A furtive glance up at the Watzmann East Face—but it is hard to judge the conditions from here. I satisfy my bear-like hunger at the inn by the lake. A happy group sits at the table opposite me. They look like hunters. They are in the process of discussing the program for the coming evening . . . roast pork, accompanied by a nice big stein of beer, all washed down with a jug of wine. I am served with a bowl of hot soup. Rummaging around for my provisions I can hardly avoid some article of climbing equipment peeking out of my rucksack. And there again are those same questions on the faces of those present: "What are you up to with that ice axe—where's your partner?" And I feel almost obliged to give them the information they want. Instead, I study the route again—the Salzburg Route—in the guidebook. A quick comparison with the real thing; it is still just about light enough outside for that. I stamp the most prominent features on my memory.

I leave Bartholomä at about seven o'clock. The loggers' track ends after only a short while and with it the last traces of human

"Since Hermann could always 'stock up' on his eating, when he was on a climb he never dragged along as much as other people in the way of provisions. . . . He could climb for hours on end without thinking about food and when you were out on the crags with Hermann you had to plan ahead so you didn't die of hunger on the route."

Marcus Schmuck

As one of his hard training climbs for the Nanga Parbat Expedition, Hermann Buhl set out one winter's night in 1953 to make a solo ascent of the 1800-meter-high East Face of the Watzmann by the Salzburg Route (the photo shows the upper reaches of the climb).

existence. Treacherous crusty snow makes every step strenuous; from time to time I sink into it knee-deep. The moon rises from behind the Göll massif, flooding the area with a silver sheen.

The silhouette of the mighty Face rises up over my head. How different it is here now from the summer's noisy bustle of over-enthusiastic people who consider nature merely as a playground. Now only the chamois breaks a trail through the deep snow, and the solemn silence is broken only by the occasional rumble of the avalanches coming down.

I climb up over fresh avalanche cones compressed into hard ice, heading for the farthermost corner of the "Ice Chapel." The first steep pitch lies buried under deep snow. Great walls of ice, hard as concrete and several meters high, have been formed by the masses of snow thundering down the Face with the power of freight trains. I have done well choosing this time—the time when most people are normally sound asleep—to tackle the lower part of the climb, for the night frost is holding the snow together well. Nevertheless, I did make one slight miscalculation—the hard crust of the snow will not support my body weight. The snow has not yet been transformed into hard névé, since the sun touches the slopes of the Face for only a few hours a day. "Crusted" snow, or *harsch,* is what we call this un-

pleasantly brittle intermediate state in the process of névé-formation. However, eventually the hard-packed avalanche tracks do allow me to gain height more swiftly, but only with the aid of crampons since the snow hereabout is rock-hard. Several times the bone-chilling roar of the plunging avalanches causes me to stop and listen. They are coming down the flanks of the Hachel-kopf, which looms monstrous out of the shadows opposite me. . . .

Another easy traverse and I am standing in the Schöllhornkar. Here, too, the deep avalanche-scoured furrows allow me to make fast progress. A dark wall of rock rises steeply above me. I know that the moonlight can play tricks, but even allowing for that it will certainly be no pushover.

A NARROW CREVASSE to cross, a short, steep ice-slope, then suddenly the smooth sheer rock begins. Still standing on the ice, I unstrap my crampons and stuff them into my rucksack; I won't be needing them for a while now. It is approaching 10:00 p.m. My altimeter reads 1400 m; 500 m of the Face behind me already. A very smooth slab almost forces me to make a tedious long detour to get to the start of the Salzburg Route, the hardest of the climbs on the East Face. And on many of the little edges that would otherwise have given a safe support for the cleats of my rubber-soled climbing boots, there just has to be a fine glaze of ice, of course. Everywhere water is trickling down from the walls. The night seems unnaturally mild. The rock is smooth and unfriendly. I try my luck a little to the left, in a kind of groove, but I have to climb the first few meters through drips of chill melt-water. Rusty ring-pegs give me the assurance that I am still on the right track. A steep ramp runs up and to the right. My body casts dark shadows onto the rock, and at times I have to shift over to one side to make out the hand- and footholds right up close to me. Up above on the Face something is moving—falling snow—while ice crashes down the slabs over on the Schöllhorn. Yet I am safe here. I reach a narrow belay ledge, an airy little vantage-point. Above my head a great overhang juts out; two ring pegs peer down and I test their holding power carefully. The rock pushes me sharply outward and the rucksack straps bite into my shoulders. I have to go back to the little platform under the overhang. Using a rope sling I hang the heavy rucksack from the first piton. Without this ballast things go considerably better. A little layback move and the overhang—the crux—is over and done with. I haul the rucksack up and take another look at the *Zeller* guidebook by the light of my pocket torch to make sure of the continuation of the route, for at greater distances the moonlight robs you of the ability to judge correctly

and robs the terrain to be climbed of all perspective and relief.

EVERY POSSIBILITY for retreat is now given careful consideration. The ironmongery and the 40-meter Perlon rope would be sufficient. The exit chimney might hold all manner of surprises still—cascades of ice, snow-balconies and so on—and how will the moves up onto the first terrace be? I avoid a few *verglassed* slabs by climbing out left. A narrow ledge leads out leftward to the arête. There, the rock rises steeply again. The limestone, usually so warm and sunny, is cold and repellent to me now. But the holds are good. Again I have my doubts about the route-finding. A few blind alleys, some on-purpose "variations," then back again. A short traverse with a sling for aid and I am standing at the bottom of the final chimney. A pleasant surprise is waiting for me here, for the route now seems to open out above me. The back of the chimney still holds ice in places, but this hardly interferes with the climbing.

A slabby ramp now runs out leftward to the start of the first terrace. The change from rock to hard snow is abrupt. The Schöllhornkar now lies a long way below me. The gleam of electric light shines up from Bartholomä; the hunters' party is probably reaching its climax by now. The moon has already turned away to

"Buhl had few friends. I would have liked to have extended to him the friendship denied him by his extreme mountaineering contemporaries. They used to wonder why he became a solo climber, even though it was they who had forced him into that tough role."

Reinhold Messner

the south and is climbing now along the Schönfeld Ridge.

A great white patch now runs steeply up to the left; a short interruption and I am standing on the "Giant's Terrace." At various places on the terrace the snow is torn asunder, affording me glimpses down into black chasms. The depth of the snow here might be as much as 10 meters. The terrace gets narrower and narrower, and soon I can look straight down steep snow gullies falling away beneath me. Above me, the wall of snow soars steeply upward. Whole cataracts of ice hang from the wall; they seem to be quite stable. The front points of my twelve-point crampons and the tip of my ice axe offer the only purchase on this precipitous terrain. A short while later I am at the start of the traverse into the Summit Gully.

It is now midnight. Nothing moves; an uncanny silence envelops the Face. An orange revives my dried-out gums. The moon disappears behind the Watzmann Ridge, as dark shadows creep higher and higher up the Face. Eagerly, I set foot onto the Summit Gully. To begin with it looks quite inviting: a steep snow runnel rising almost unbroken to the heights. At first the snow is glass-hard, but it gets worse the farther up I go. I can measure my progress by the neighboring summits; I am at the same height as the Hachelkopf now, and the Watzmannkinder are only a little

way above me. I am moving more slowly now and often have to stop for a short rest break, for the continual trail-breaking through the snow is strenuous work. I reach a little projecting rib. To the right, the wall falls steeply away to the big ledges. This must be where the Kederbacher route joins mine. Everywhere are unreal snow structures—snow mushrooms, balcony-like projections, whole wagon-loads of compressed snow hanging from narrow little ledges, ready to fall. Everything is buried beneath a white mass. Steep snowfields run up to the ridge, covering the rock steps and lending the Face the impression of total exposure.

I TRAVERSE OVER to the right. After the first few meters I am swimming in bottomless powder snow. The conditions have changed swiftly and dramatically. The wall faces slightly north here and does not catch the sun. Delicate snow ridges define the way forward, forming the bridges from one projection to the next. I am almost sorry to destroy these wonderful natural structures. It is almost impossible to make any progress closer to the rocks. Deep hollows have formed between rock and snow and I often have to make tedious detours if I wish to make any headway at all. The summit snowfield of the Hochkönig gleams away to the south east; to the right, the dark pyramid of the Hundstod. I consume my last orange under the shelter of a rock overhang. Here, the creative play of the wind has formed a large pothole-like hollow that provides me with a comfortable little resting-place. This is where the bivouac box ought to be, but it probably lies buried deep beneath the snow. Steep gullies and sharp snow arêtes now point the way up, interspersed with short rock pitches and, for variety's sake, a few grueling traverses.

The summit headwall still rises sheer above me. It lies in shadow and I cannot make out any detailed features. A chimney, completely full of snow, leads up through a steep step. I creep upward on severely overhanging snow formations. The angle increases dramatically. Overhead, so close I can almost touch it, the silhouette of the summit ridge stands out like a white band against the dark night sky. But the Face wasn't going to give in that easily. A short step in the wall—and there before me lies a steep couloir running up to the ridge. I can hardly wait.

I am now standing in the bright light of the moon again. A cold wind has come out to meet me. I rush the last few meters to the summit. There is no handshake, no friends for miles around; no one to whom I can express my feelings. And still it is a splendid moment. Below me lies the dark abyss of the highest face in the Eastern Alps, and farther out the wreath of lights that is Berchtesgaden. It is still only four in the morning. I climb down from the summit a short way, stamp out a little space in the snow, and pull the Perlon bivi bag over my head. In two hours the sun should be up again and I decide to wait it out. I have had enough of sleepwalking, and I am longing for some sun and some warmth. I am not familiar with the descent into the Wimbachgries, so I decide I will traverse the ridge across to the Hocheck.

GRADUALLY, THE SKY to the east gets lighter and I set off again. The ridge does not present any particular difficulties, but it does afford me wonderful views of the Face and I keep retracing my route, meter by meter, as I go. The sun works its beneficial effect on me and I stop on the Middle Summit for a short while to enjoy its warmth to the full. Just a few more cornices and then down the wind-blown spur to the Watzmann House. I am already looking forward to a hot drink of tea. Yet with every step nearer to the hut my disappointment grows. The shutters are closed, the doors are locked. So, despite my hellish thirst, I press on down to the valley. And the descent is a miserable grind.

Nanga Parbat

The 1953 Austro-German "Willy Merkl Memorial" Expedition to Nanga Parbat

The participants in the "1953 Austro-German Willy Merkl Memorial Expedition to Nanga Parbat." Top row from the left: Walter Frauenberger, Kuno Rainer, Peter Aschenbrenner, Karl M. Herrligkoffer, Albert Bitterling, Hermann Buhl (far right). Bottom row from the left: Hans Ertl, Hermann Köllensperger, Otto Kempter, Fritz Aumann.

Karl M. Herrligkoffer, a general practitioner, is a half-brother of Willy Merkl, whose 1934 Nanga Parbat Expedition had failed not least because of its strategic weaknesses. In his own way, Herrligkoffer is also a man driven, possessed, indeed a fanatic. "We have to attempt the Willy Merkl Route once more," Herrligkoffer wrote in his letter to Heinz Baumeister on 10 October 1951. Baumeister, former head of the working party of the State Railway Gymnastics and Sports Club, had provided the lion's share of the funding for Merkl's 1934 Nanga Parbat Expedition.

Although Herrligkoffer himself could not even dream of conquering Nanga Parbat, he wants the "summit victory." Herrligkoffer is not really a mountaineer at all. This fact alone—along with other well-substantiated problems—turns the Himalayan Institute, and in particular Paul Bauer (who had led an unsuccessful expedition to the peak in 1938), against him. The executive committee of the German Alpine Club also refuses to sponsor this "Willy Merkl Memorial Expedition." The reverse is true for the Munich section of the DAV (the German Alpine Club), which strongly supports the expedition in the interests of its own participants. Also supporting the effort is the Austrian Alpine Club, whose renowned mountaineers Frauenberger, Rainer and Buhl are also set to take part.

One must commend Herrligkoffer for his success in enticing a competent team to participate in the expedition. It is also to his credit that he manages—with the help of an illustrious board of trustees made up of personalities from the University of Munich medical faculty as well as from the worlds of politics and economics—to present his mission effectively in the public eye. When Herrligkoffer manages to gain the popular Burgermeister [Lord Mayor] of Munich as Honorary Patron of the undertaking, even the most fervent adversaries do not dare to obstruct the launch of the expedition. Even arch-rival Paul Bauer has to admit, "I would like to show Dr. Herrligkoffer all the recognition he is due for his tenacity. Much of what was done, however, was disapproved of in mountaineering circles and beyond."

The 1953 Austro-German expedition to Nanga Parbat in memory of Willy Merkl comprises: Peter Aschenbrenner, participant in the 1932 and 1934 Nanga Parbat Expeditions, as mountaineering leader;

Fritz Aumann as main camp administrator; Albert Bitterling; Hermann Buhl; Hans Ertl as cameraman for a film financed by Deutsch London Film; Dr. Walter Frauenberger; Otto Kempter; Hermann Köllensperger, and Kuno Rainer.

Of the lads, Kempter and especially Köllensperger are considered to be competent mountaineers. Rainer—not least because of his great routes with Hermann Buhl—enjoys an excellent reputation as a good all-round alpinist.

Although Buhl is superior by far to all the members of the expedition team, he must first fit into the group. If anyone is capable of conquering Nanga Parbat, it is he.

Buhl's diary entries, written in the tent at the high camps and down at base camp, contain the true essence of the man and give us an insight like no other document into the daily expedition routine—at times very wearing—and even into the subsequent division of the team. We discover quite a lot about the lack of organization on the part of the leadership, and about the bigotry of a few dilettantes, who first try to stop the brilliant Buhl at base camp and who then want to monopolize him after his success. The narrow-minded way in which they try to force Buhl into the yoke of their group mentality is material for psychologists.

It is a good thing that Buhl is not a man who would let himself be forced into anything.

First Expedition Diary:
17 April—2 June 1953
(Extracts)

The preparations and hurdles piled up even faster towards the end! The date for departure was postponed for two weeks, as the ship was not ready to sail until 18.4. Lucky—otherwise we'd never have finished the preparation. Two weeks of strenuous packing work—most of the equipment arrived right at the end.

13.4.: Luggage goes to Genoa, but still not certain of entry. . . . 16.4. visas and entry permit arrive from the Pakistani Consulate during the night. Afternoon—went shopping. Evening—lecture by Hans Ertl, at the same time farewell to Munich.

17.4.: 12.00 hours departure on the Rome Express First Class from Munich—lots of cheering and enthusiasm. Reception in Kufstein, and

"Hermann Buhl's book with the terrible descriptions of falling and the self-torment of fighting one's way up some snowy mountain . . . No, that could not give any fuel to my desire for a better life."

Reinhard Karl

again in Innsbruck, from the club and relatives. Generl leaves me here.

18.4.: Arrive 4 a.m. in Genoa, short sight-seeing tour of town, midday on board the "Victoria," of the Lloyd Triestino shipping company; only its second journey. Reception by delegation from the C.A.I. [Italian Alpine Club].

14.00 hours depart Genoa, happy moment. Kuno, Hermann [Köllensperger], Otto, and I in one cabin, Walter and Karl in one and Albert, Fritz, and Hans in another. We travel 1st Class.

We eat as much as we are able and want. Eight to ten courses per meal. . . . Develop good appetites. Sea is smooth as ice. . . . We pass the Island Gargano at 6 p.m. Very tired. Slept brilliantly.

5.5.: Arrive 10 a.m. in Rawalpindi. Hotel Flashman, have to go to bed straight away, due to tonsillitis. Caught on the journey. 50 hours on the train. Sweat cure, four penicillin injections and tablets. Can hardly lie down, let alone sleep. Can't eat, just drink tea.

6.5.: Arrive airport 9 a.m. With the second party to Gilgit in a "Dakota." Terribly hot to start with. Wonderful flight, just short of the Himalayan foothills. Fly past Nanga—partially hidden by cloud. Then down to Gilgit. 1+ hours flight. Great reception from the people and the authorities. . . . Invited out for the evening. Folk dancing. Throat already better.

8.5.: Ceremonial handing over of the Pakistani flag to Mayor of Gilgit. 3 p.m., 5 jeeps set off to Talichi with 5 Sahibs, a few Hunzas, and equipment. Wild journey along steep mountain slopes and huge ravines. Road just wide enough for the jeep. To the left often a drop of 100 meters down into the riverbed. Daring drivers. Countryside brilliant, wild and romantic. Wonderful views through deep-cut valleys to ice-covered mountains. Confluence of Gilgit and Indus, then farther in the darkness, completely mad. Arrive Talichi 8 p.m.

9.5.: Wonderful view from Talichi to Nanga Parbat forty kilometers away; very impressive. In the north Rakaposhi. Tedious negotiations with the porters who have already been waiting here for two days and who want to carry less but be paid more. In total there are 265 porters at our disposal. Messenger to Gilgit—Karl is to come at once.

10.5.: Negotiations continue. . . . Karl, Ertl, and Köllensperger arrive in the afternoon. Jeeps don't drive any more. A private employer promises to drive four times a day. But many things are promised here. Situation not favorable—but not hopeless. . . . We finally come to an agreement thanks to the language skills of Mr. Knips [advisor to the ambassador at the German Embassy in Karachi, who joins the expedition for his four weeks' holiday]. A rate is agreed for a normal load of 20 kilograms; anything over that has to be paid for separately. Because of a lack of coolies [porters] everyone has to make two carries. In the meantime mule convoy has set off from Gilgit. 80 loads are in Talichi. These will be dispatched in the evening.

11.5.: At 6 a.m. Walter and I leave Talichi for the Rakhiot Bridge with six Hunzas. It starts to get interesting as the valley bends. The road has subsided in parts but is undergoing improvements. Steep drop to the Indus, which flows out in roaring cascades.

Reach Rakhiot Bridge at 8:30 a.m. Steep ascent on the far side of the left-hand slopes of the Rakhiot ravine. Seems to take forever. Terribly barren—only rocks and boulders, right and left terrific ravines. At about 2800 meters the path turns off right up to Tato. Here we see the first greenery and the first trees. . . .

12.5.: Set out 5 a.m. Wonderful path through pine woods, completely, wildly romantic, reminds me of our Karwendel. First view of Nanga. Fairy-tale meadows, really fantastically beautiful. Temporary Camp in a moraine hollow at the edge of the woods.

At 12 o'clock the dispatching of the coolies begins. Wild chaos, wild shouting. A large tent and two normal tents are pitched. Approximate height 3700 meters. Scenery fantastic, just like at home.

Nanga Parbat. Left of center, Rakhiot Peak, next to it Nanga Parbat South East Summit. Right of center, the main summit. The route of ascent ran diagonally left beneath Rakhiot Peak, through the ice fall of the Rakhiot Glacier with Camps 2 to 4.

"The first impression at the exit from the South Wall was the greatest moment on Nanga Parbat for me. We talked about Buhl and followed his path with our eyes, up and then down again."

Reinhold Messner

17.5.: Went with a rope ladder to Base Camp in the morning, in bad shape. Weather oppressive, rain, back in the afternoon. Peter [Aschenbrenner] already here but without Sherpas. It took him six days to get here from Munich, dressed in a suit, wearing shoes and carrying a small suitcase.

Now the expedition gains momentum. A large tent is pitched. Great importance is placed upon the cooking. Base Camp catering standards must be maintained. Peter complains about a great deal of the equipment; tents not OK, sleeping bags too small. Things missing in the catering department: such as butter, vinegar, *rollmöps*.

18.5.: Everyone is assigned an orderly. Nobody is allowed to do a great deal now; that is what the orderly is for. Nor are we allowed to carry very much any more. Just a rucksack and personal equipment, no crates or ropes. In the evening 60 porters arrive from Tato. Bad weather, it rains and snows. Slept well.

24.5. (Whitsun): Base Camp set up, large tent pitched, everything unpacked, weather good.

30.5. Base Camp

3:30 a.m. set off from Camp 1 with Kuno, Otto, and Hermann for Camp 2. Weather beautiful, very cold, temperature at 3 a.m. minus 8 degrees. Slept very well. Snow really hard, progress quickly. Path marked out with little flags. In the uppermost third, deep powder; broke trail up the final steep gully almost alone, tunnelled through the snow, up to my chest in it. Wonderfully fit. 8 a.m. reach the plateau of Camp 2, 5200 meters. All in the shade up to now. Kuno and I search for suitable place for a camp. Terribly hot. Return after two hours with a satisfactory result. Bad headache—due to the dazzling sun.

In the afternoon descend again in terrible heat, really exhausting slog. Reach Camp 1 at 4:30. Ertl there. Post has arrived, first post since Karachi. Two letters from Generl. Emotional barometer rises suddenly, headache gone.

Ertl says Walter will reach Camp 1 today in order to climb to Camp 2 the next day with Otto and Hermann and six porters. Therefore Kuno and I descend to Base Camp for a rest day. Halfway down we meet porters with news for Kuno. Walter is not coming after all, thus Kuno has to go to Camp 2 tomorrow with the porters. Kuno is not happy and goes back to Camp 1. I go down [to Base Camp] in order to climb back up to Camp 1 at night if necessary. Every five minutes the instructions are reversed. Because I tell him what has happened, Walter then does climb up to Camp 1 in order to relieve Kuno. But now he [Kuno] does not want to come back either.

31.5. Base Camp

. . . Peter, who is out hunting, comes back in the afternoon, asks about Kuno and then lays into me because everyone is doing exactly as he pleases. If we don't want to obey the orders we should go on our own. . . .

As Peter says nothing to me about going up, I ask him again. As my altimeter is broken and we only have one between four, as opposed to Base Camp where there are four altimeters, I would like to swap mine, also on the wishes of the others. After asking several times and being told we could manage with one, I eventually get Albert's. I don't even want to mention the map—although there are five of those at Base Camp.

As I set off Peter tells me not to be such an egoist. I don't really understand and ask why. He finally says it's because of the altimeter. It's all too much for me so I give it back to him and leave. Peter calls me and then comes after me. Gives me the altimeter back and tells me not to be so childish, he had put himself out for me, and after all they were not dependent on me, and could manage without me, whereupon I leave. It takes me 50 minutes to get to Camp 1, it is snowing heavily again. Walter is waiting for me up there.

There were quarrels between the mountaineering leader of the Nanga Parbat expedition, the experienced Peter Aschenbrenner (center), and Hermann Buhl (to his left). This possibly could be explained by the age difference (the "generation problem").

Second Expedition Diary:
3 June—2 July 1953
(Extracts)

3.6. Camp 2

Did not sleep well, bad headache in the morning, not hungry, just drank tea with *schnapps*, ten minutes' storm around the camp in the morning. Kuno and Otto prepare the route ahead, but cannot see anything and come back at midday. I busy myself with cooking, but headache no better so descend alone. . . .

On the steep section I see Albert with eight porters, make tracks towards them. Suddenly a slab of snow with us all on it breaks off. I am able to dig myself out, but the porters, all roped together(!), roll down like a ball. Avalanche soon comes to a halt. Porters very frightened.

Hunza porters descending
from Camp 3 to Camp 2 on
Nanga Parbat (1953)

Take the loads to a safe place away on the left and carry on down with Albert. . . . See Walter at Camp 1, then on down to Base Camp. Headache gone, feel wonderful again, really hungry.

Karl examines me in the evening. Blood pressure normal, pulse 65, everything OK. Just because of the altitude, not yet well enough acclimatized. News from Everest; 600 meters below the summit. Heavy snowfall in the evening.

6.6. Camp 1

Advance watches by one hour, local time, I like that. Set off at 5 a.m. with Hermann and six porters for Camp 2. As we cross the glacier basin, giant avalanches come down from the summit plateau and cover us in spindrift; ran until I couldn't get my breath anymore, felt as if my lungs were being ripped out. A second one comes down from the left straightaway; just as strong, fills the whole basin, so that the tents in Camp 1 wobble, and moves on directly above us, so that we are almost unable to breathe; we look like snowmen.

Otherwise everything goes off without incident until Camp 2, yet during the whole ascent I don't recover from all the running. Use the stepladder at Camp 2. Nobody in the camp, everyone is breaking trail to Camp 3. Hermann stays, I go back down again with the porters. . . .

7.6. Camp 1

Slept well last night. Set off for Camp 2 at 4 a.m. with twelve porters. Weather wonderful, very good trail, crusty *harsch* snow, very cold. No avalanches, nevertheless Ertl spent the whole morning on the lookout for them. Reach Camp 2 at half eight [7:30], nobody here again, everyone preparing the route up to Camp 3, but Otto knows that I am supposed to relieve him. So I climb back down again with the porters to Camp 1. Reach the camp at half eleven [10:30].

Start of a period of good weather, but they are all still asleep at Base Camp. It does not seem to bother them very much, they don't even keep to the agreed transmission times, haven't got time, don't even go to Camp 1 and Peter just laughs at everything.

Impossible orders are coming through from Base Camp. The porters bring up the food much too late, we only get it at 8 p.m. Three of the good porters have to stay at Base Camp as servants, although we have too few porters. . . . Only now do they send to Gilgit for fifteen additional Hunzas, who won't get here for ten to fourteen days. . . .

8.6. Camp 1

Continue with porters to Camp 2. This time there are only seven; five are ill, or don't want to climb. . . . Weather very good, trail wonderfully hard. In good shape.

Reach Camp 2 at 9. Hermann [Köllensperger] is only just waking up. Otto went down to Base Camp the previous evening, Kuno climbs down with me today.

I stay with the porters at Camp 1. The porters who are ill don't arrive from Base Camp until 8:30 a.m. It seems as if everyone down at Base Camp wants to sabotage the whole affair. Karl is even treating the porters who are ill like dogs. . . .

9.6. Camp 1

Slept well. This time all twelve porters go with me to Camp 2 and Albert comes with me. My "Leica" is broken, don't get a replacement even though there are two or three Leica housings at Base Camp. I'm told I can't take photographs and that Peter is the "Leica" specialist! Reach Camp 2 in the early morning. I stay at the camp and Albert climbs down to 1 with the porters. Six Hunzas stay here. . . .

10.6. Camp 2

Slept well. Get up 3:30 a.m., very cold. Hermann and I go ahead to prepare the route. In good shape . . . in spite of the fact that I have a full rucksack. Hermann goes ahead while I prepare the ice so the porters can walk on it. An hour later Walter follows with the porters. After catching Hermann up I prepare the path up to Camp 3. . . .

I leave my rucksack at about 6200 meters. It is only 7:30 a.m. I don't want to wait and the Southern Chongra Peak appears to be close, so I set off on my way there. Quite a slog to the foot of the mountain. I cross on the southwest side and climb up from the west. Had to break trail the whole way, very strenuous. Reach the summit (6450 m) at 11:30. My first six-thousander. Wonderful view of Nanga, steep drops to the south. In good shape, yodeled like never before. Then climbed down again, broke through into a crevasse, but all very harmless. Terrible slog in the midday heat to Camp 3. Arrive at 1:30. . . .

12.6. Camp 3

Get up 3:30 a.m., very cold, weather good. At 5 set off for Camp 4, beneath Rakhiot Peak. There is something odd about the first steep slope so I take the lead. Suddenly I see Walter right down below on

"It was the walk of a man possessed by an idea into a seemingly certain destruction, an enormous undertaking which appeared to go against the grain of 'mountaineering sense' and which had virtually no chance of success. . . . Yet in spite of this Buhl was the first man to stand on the summit of Nanga Parbat, the summit that had been fought for so hard."

Reinhold Messner

Hermann Buhl climbs the summit needle of Rakhiot Peak.

the glacier. Suspect he has slipped off the slope and as I do not want to wait, I climb down to him. His hat has fallen off. This little interlude costs us half an hour.

I take my rucksack and go up again. Am in good shape. Deep slopes with powder snow. . . . Bitterly cold. Cold feet, in spite of good boots with insoles. Take short break in the first of the sun's rays. Two to four breaths with each step, really terribly strenuous. . . . Long traverse beneath a crevasse until we can cross it. Short maneuver on a vertical snow wall. Then a very steep slope, traverse across to the foot of Rakhiot Peak. Longer break, then up to the ridge. Lunch about 12 o'clock, 6700 m.

Weather deteriorates, fog everywhere, very hot. Broke trail all the way up to here, extremely arduous. . . . Climb back down in the footsteps. Reach Camp 3 rather shattered at 2 o'clock. Three porters were up there, without Hermann. Cooked and slept in the afternoon. Weather continues to worsen.

19.6. Camp 3

Set off with Otto, Hermann, and porters to Camp 4. New snow, but easy walking. In very good shape. Hermann descends with the porters, Otto and I stay. I dig a cave in the slope and then pitch the tent in it while Otto cooks. Light snowfall, a little windy. Very cold in the snow cave, a real draft coming from the doorway. Temperature always between -10 and -20 degrees or below. Everything frozen and full of hoar-frost.

21.6. Camp 4

High winds during the night. Entrance under a meter of windblown snow, tent no longer visible at all. Set off at 8:30 with a 100 m rope up the Rakhiot ice wall. Stretched it out with other bits of gear at the bottom, but still 30 m short of the bergschrund. Traverse behind the Rakhiot Shoulder prepared; smooth ice. . . . Cut many steps, weather good but windy.

Then a diagonal traverse up brittle snow to Rakhiot Peak. Strong wind and cold. Climbed the last needle, IV, without gloves; just like being at home. First seven thousander, 7070 m. Otto stayed down below.

Over the summit, down the other side without rope. Wonderful view to Silbersattel and Nanga, particularly the South Face above the fog.

Climbed down to Moor's Head, left snow shovel behind. Mist whipping up above the ridge. Traverse back to Rakhiot Face. Send Otto back to cook something while I cut a ladder of steps down the Face. Three porters, Hermann, and Kuno are at the Camp. I arrive at 7 o'clock but no food is ready yet. There are two tents in the hollow.

Tomorrow we are supposed to go to Camp 5. I'm already looking forward to it.

22.6. Camp 4

Snowing in the morning; a real pea-souper. Porters all ill, it looks like a morgue in there. Hopeless situation. I suggest we take some provisions and cooking equipment to Camp 5 and make a depot there. Everyone laughs at me. So I take a load of tinned food and a rubber mattress, about 10 to 12 kg and start to climb the Rakhiot Face. Seriously hard slog.

Up on the shoulder I put everything down and go over to the traverse and fix a rope. Fairly worn out, I slide down the face on the rope. When I reach the bottom there is not anything to drink let alone anything to eat. Only in the evening do we get something.

There is no petrol left so we have to cook with Esbit [solid fuel tablets]. Terrible stink and smoke, can't stand it in the cave anymore.

23.6. Camp 4

Took a sleeping tablet, slept well, but headache in the morning. Kuno and Hermann climb down with the porters. It's impossible to cook with Esbit. You'd starve doing it. Otto is still lying in his sleeping bag. I climb down to get petrol. Hard slog. Reach Camp 3 at midday. Kuno in a bad way. Wonderful here. Everything to eat. So I eat all afternoon. Slept well at night.

24.6. Camp 3

9 a.m. set off for Camp 4 with four porters. One turns back right at the start. Trailbreaking through very deep snow, not in good shape. Otto also in bad shape, goes down to 3 with one of the porters. Two stay at 4.

I stay in the tent because of the high winds. Terrible camp, always windy. Disastrous battle with the cooker. I've got water by 7 p.m. and the porter's shouting at me so I have to give it to him. It's hopeless, the cooker goes out numerous times, the storm matches won't light, the candle goes out numerous times. By 9 p.m. I finally have some lukewarm water to drink and then crawl into my sleeping bag hungry. Slept well.

25.6. Camp 4

Get up at 7:30 a.m. Blowing a gale all night and it continues. Start cooking. At 9 a.m. one of the porters arrives. I tell him he should add some snow to the water already in the pan, instead of which he throws away the water that was already boiling. . . . I have to start boiling water again from scratch. In an hour there's a bowl of tea ready. . . . Eventually at 11 a.m. we are in a position to set off. . . .

Meanwhile the wind has picked up again. I set off with one porter. I'm not good on my feet. The wind is too strong, and we haven't enough desire. We turn back, fetch one of them out from the tent and climb down. We meet Hermann with three porters en route. Midday in Camp 3. Ate and drank well again—almost too much. It is sunny and warm here. . . .

26.6. Camp 3

At 5:30 a.m. Albert, Hans, and Peter go up to Camps 4 and 5 with porters. Walter comes up at 8. At 11 a.m. Hermann and Otto still in their sleeping bags.

Great disappointment, in the afternoon the porters come back again, they won't carry on to Camp 5. Peter returns. Hans and Albert stay at 4. Weather good in the morning, foggy in the afternoon. Monsoon already forecast for the 28th in Rawalpindi. Hardly slept all night, heavy snow.

27.6. Camp 3

Initially good weather but soon turns to thick fog and snowfall, monsoon has arrived here. Set off at 7 a.m., Otto and I go ahead without loads, then Walter and Hermann and three porters with our personal effects. Have to break trail. Snow gets deeper and deeper. Feel terrible, can't breathe, probably the weather.

Reach Camp 4 at 11, snowing heavily. Camp was moved a little lower down yesterday. Hans and Albert climb down to 3 with the porters. Hans declares the Camp hopeless for the time being, Albert doesn't want to know any more. It snows extremely heavily all day; typical monsoon weather, a little on the warm side. It clears up at night, full moon, summit clear; most of all I would have liked to carry on up. Slept well.

28.6. Camp 4

Wake up at 6. Otto and Herman have no will to go on. Camp meeting with Walter. I want to get up as high as possible, bivouac in a snow cave and go for the summit the next day. The three porters agree to carry my things.

Clear at first but soon begins to snow. Don't set off until 11. I go first and break trail, in very good form. As for the other three—an absolute funeral procession, already very combat-weary. There are continuous small avalanches coming down the flanks of the mountain. We make very slow progress; lots of snow.

Reach the shoulder at 4. Lengthen the rope on the traverse. Cut steps in a few places, anchor a rope with ice axes and tension it off. Hermann falls ten meters, I am able to hold him on the rope. A rubber mattress flies down but we are able to retrieve it. The weather gets worse, it's 6 p.m.

Half an hour before the Moor's Head, Otto says, "I suggest we turn

> "Hermann Buhl's solitary summit bid, an unparalleled achievement in the history of alpinism, is a triumph of will and courage and is the crowning glory of all the previous efforts and sacrifices made on Nanga Parbat."
>
> Karl M. Herrligkoffer

back." I don't want to force the issue, I've had enough; I would have had an unrestrained will to go on. I take my rucksack and lead the way back down. Reach camp as darkness starts to fall. Cook for over an hour in the tent. Clears up at night again, summit visible. Slept well.

29.6. Camp 4

The snow continues; it's coming down thick and fast. We decide to go down, possibly for the last time. That's it, I've had enough. Everything is packed up. . . . Set off at 1 o'clock, snow above our knees, zero visibility; almost step out over the cornice on one occasion. High risk of avalanches, every steep slope is going down. Leave everything, and climb down in the path of the avalanche. Extremely painstaking, snow up to midriffs, dig a channel.

Reach Camp 3 at 4 p.m. Ate well. Cleared up again in the evening, slept wonderfully well.

30.6. Camp 3

Rest day, good weather, everything OK. Sorted out the post. Order from Base Camp: bring everything down, Peter is leaving. Only Hermann goes down as he does not feel well. Several calls from Base Camp, telling us to come down.

Great atmosphere here, mad desire to go on.

1.7. Camp 4

Set off for Camp 4 at 6 a.m., Walter, Hans and I with three porters. Otto stays at Camp 3 for another day. He does not feel very well and wants to rest up for another day and follow on with Madi the next day. Wonderful weather, no clouds as far as you can see, haze in the valley, best indication of a lasting period of good weather. Minus 20 degrees in the morning, deep snow, difficult to break trail.

Three walkie-talkie calls with Base Camp. Order to retreat; we should rest and then follow new orders for attack. Do not say what those orders are. We don't even consider climbing down, we've never been in such good shape.

Aschenbrenner still at Base Camp. He's still officially the mountaineering leader, although he handed the task over to Walter days ago. Conversations with a very agitated Ertl end with the message "kiss my arse," and we continue. Ertl makes us aware that they will have cause to thank us one day. . . . Midday at Camp 4. Totally snowed up, first have to dig everything out, very arduous. Then Hans and I each take a 100 m rope and climb up the Rakhiot Face with them, fix them on the traverse to the Moor's Head and climb down again, while Walter busies himself with the porters, fitting crampons, etc. Back at Camp 4 again at 7 p.m. Slept well all night.

2.7. Camp 4

Hans wakes very early; very cold but clear. Weather wonderful. Walkie-talkie conversation with Base Camp. They ask for Walter. Once again they order us to retreat to Base Camp. Walter makes them aware of their mistake and after much discussion we get the reply from below, "Well, get on with it then, you have our blessing."

In the afternoon Kempter comes up from Camp 3 with Madi. We set off together, I go ahead with some more rope to fix on the Rakhiot Flank. Have to break trail and cut another ladder of steps up the Flank. Very hard work!

Hans carries the film equipment. Walter has the porters on the rope. They are going very well. Otto brings up the rear. We have to put in some more pitons on the Rakhiot Traverse, fix ice axe anchors for the porters and cut steps, and after everyone has seconded the traverse, I cross knee-deep in snow to the Moor's Head. Prepare the route farther ahead to the deepest notch, 6900 m, with a "snow roller," but the porters won't go any farther and I have to go back. Hans would have liked to go to the summit with me, he's in really good shape, but he leaves the opportunity to Otto. Porters go back down, descending to Camp 4 with Walter and Hans, as there is only one tent up here.

We pitch the tent and begin to cook as night falls. Wonderful sunset. Retire at 8 p.m., Otto follows an hour later. Can't sleep. Wind returns and presses violently on the tent. Anchor it more securely with ice axes and ski poles. Alarm not working properly, keep looking at the time. I get up at one in the morning.

Hermann Buhl recorded the summit approach in his diary as far as the Bazhin Gap. The entries end abruptly with the words "Enormous cornice, really hard, steep rock ridge." There are various essays by Hermann Buhl about the forty-one hours spent alone during the ascent, reaching the summit, bivouacking, the descent and about being reunited with his friends Hans Ertl and Walter Frauenberger in Camp 5. We have chosen the following one because it seems the most authentic to us, as it contains typical Buhl vocabulary.

Nanga Parbat 1953. On the left, P.7530 (South East Summit); to the right, the Silberzacken; between them the Silbersattel.

"On this path between life and death, the lonely wanderer is accompanied and protected by the hard life that he himself has lived. His body and his will have not learned how to give up, as long as there is the slightest spark to keep the motor turning."

Kurt Maix

The Summit Push

by Hermann Buhl

3 July 1953

OTTO IS STILL LYING buried in his sleeping bag. He seems to be sleeping well and I don't disturb him in spite of crashing around making tea, getting dressed, and packing the rucksack. We're due to set off at 2 a.m. I remind Otto of this several times, but he says it's too early and tells me that I had said three o'clock yesterday, whereupon I remind him that we will be glad of every minute today. I inform him that I will set off at 2, come what may. So I proceed to pack the rucksack just for myself initially. It is already a bit heavy. After I have asked him to get up again, Otto actually does get out of his nice warm cocoon. Thinking to myself that I will have to prepare the route ahead anyway, and he'll easily catch me up, and therefore I do not have to carry everything myself, I leave a few bits and pieces for him. Thus I also pack Kuno's bacon, which is intended as hill food, provisions for the summit, in Otto's rucksack too.

At 2:30 I set out into the great wide open. It is a clear starry night, and the crescent moon is shining down and casting silvery light over the ridge rising up before me. I put on all the clothes available including my overtrousers this time. Deep, brittle *harsch* snow makes progress difficult; the route continues round beneath gigantic cornice formations and I soon notice that the dimensions are deceptive; it is no longer like the Western Alps, this really is the Himalaya. I reach the ridge again via a hard strip of *firn* snow. The crest of the ridge has been packed down hard by the wind, and I put on my crampons again so that I do not have to pay so much attention to not slipping. The ridge rises steeply upward in wonderful steep surges. To my right giant *firn* slopes broken by ice barriers fall away to the plateau above Camp 2; to my left dark shadows line the path; beyond them my glance disappears into the bottomless depths. Sharp knife-edges of *firn* snow and cornice galleries alternate with traverses across steep slopes. A sharp wind blows up from the south and forces me onto the Rakhiot side. I take my first break at the start of the traverse to the

Silbersattel. It is 5 a.m. and behind the peaks of the Karakorum the golden sun is rising. The first rays of light shine down upon me and I am greeted by a sea of peaks, ice mountains with the steepness of the Dolomites, all around. K2, Masherbrum, Rakaposhi, the Mustagh Tower, all those mountains which I know only from books are now just opposite me, almost tangible. There's a fine haze in the valleys, the best weather indicator. I enjoy the morning sunshine while I have my second breakfast.

Otto is still way behind, almost an hour, but he'll soon catch me up. After a short while I set off again on the traverse up to the Silbersattel. The *firn* snow is getting hard and in some places even pure ice is visible. Once again the distance is deceptive; the rocks of the Silberzacken just will not get any nearer. Finally, after two hours I am standing on the Silbersattel at the start of the great high *firn*-field. I've always dreamed of this moment and now I take it for granted. My altimeter registers 7400 m.

Up to now conditions have been good, and I'm not feeling the altitude particularly, two breaths per step. Another short break, then I continue. The high *firn* stretches out for three kilometers, flat at first, then rising gently and finally climbing steeply up to the subsidiary summit, with a difference in altitude of 500 m. The hard *firn* snow has been plowed up wildly by the raging winds up here. Meter-high wind tunnels have made furrows right through the summit plateau and greatly hinder my progress; it is like climbing a continuous flight of steps. The 7500-meter mark is like a frontier to me. All at once my body becomes limp, my lungs cannot get enough air, and each step requires enormous energy. The breaks are becoming more frequent and progress more and more strenuous, and I am painfully aware of how thin the air is.

OTTO DOESN'T SEEM to be finding it any easier, for only after quite a time do I notice out on the Silbersattel a figure up against the horizon, moving slowly closer and then stopping, and, finally, falling horizontal. The spot does not move any more. Otto has given up. The distance between us was simply too great. With my mouth watering and my stomach rumbling I think of the bacon in Otto's rucksack, the treat that I've now lost. I have got some dried fruit and "Neapolitans" wafer biscuits with me but they are so dry that they get stuck in my throat. By now the sun is really burning hot and the air is extremely dry, and there's not a breath of air moving at all, all of which contributes to making my limbs grow weaker. After each break I really have to force myself to get up, otherwise I would just

"A lonely fighting man in the merciless sun of the never-ending firn-field beneath the summit; half in a dream, deceived by hallucinations, engaged in a tormented battle through the massed defenses of the final, sheer, and extremely difficult towers of the summit ridge."
Hugo and Luis Vigl

stop where I was. The steep swing up to the subsidiary summit just does not get any closer, although I've already been on the go for hours. My calculations of reaching the summit by midday won't come to anything.

I steer a path right to the edge of the plateau where it plunges down onto the South Face, hoping to get a cool breeze from the south, but here, too, the air is still. My rucksack is pressing down on my shoulders; I am tormented by hunger but can't get any of the dry food down. If only I had the bacon. I leave my rucksack behind at the start of the steep rise up to the summit, in the hope that I might make faster and easier progress; I will surely be back by the evening. I wrap my anorak around me and put the summit flag, my gloves, and the flask of coca tea in the chest pocket, together with some Pervitin [a stimulant] and Padutin to prevent frostbite, and take the ice axe too. Now progress is a little easier and the breaks not as frequent; with determined energy I make tracks beneath the subsidiary summit and toward the right, to a gap between the subsidiary summit and the Diamir Gap. That is farther than it seems, too. I am already beginning to doubt whether I will find the energy to carry on, although I am sure of the subsidiary summit at least. Even though it is not an eight-thousander it would still be a

first ascent, and at any rate I have the Pervitin with me, although I would use this only in an absolute emergency. Less than 100 m below the subsidiary summit I reach the aforementioned gap.

The cliff breaks away to the Bazhin Gap, 7812 m, in steep ledges. Over scree-covered ledges and projections, across snow and ice, I cross the rocks to the gap with great anticipation; I scramble from one projection to the next and always with the questioning glance—will it be possible to continue? Although I am used to extreme climbs and have often mastered these alone, I feel that in these conditions extreme climbing is just not possible. Yet eventually I climb down a steep gully and manage to get across to the Bazhin Gap.

It is already 2 in the afternoon and 300 m still separate me from the main summit. These 300 m would be nothing in the Alps, yet here it seems like another mountain to climb. I almost fail to see myself making it. In addition to this, these 300 m contain the most difficult section of the whole ascent. A steep rock ridge, covered with towers; vertical, sharp-edged upthrusts of granite with sharp cornices and covered in snow, extremely exposed. Cornice galleries and steep *firn* slopes rise up to the shoulder.

I REMEMBER THE Pervitin. It is tempting, and would give me renewed strength, new drive, but no, the effect only lasts for six to seven hours, then it's over and the side effects kick in, and that could have disastrous consequences. Where would I be in six or seven hours? On the descent, at best here at the Bazhin Gap again, that wouldn't be enough. I fight a real battle with myself and then, finally, because of the summit and in spite of the possible dangerous consequences, I take two Pervitin tablets.

A giant cornice hangs out from the Bazhin Gap toward the south. A steep *firn* ridge rises up to the start of the rocks. It's a bit easier now. The rocks get steeper. It is an extremely reckless undertaking. Because of the icy rocks I am often forced to take a different line, sometimes on the snow that is sticking to the rocks, sometimes on the rocks themselves. I can often see right onto the South Side through the gap that has formed between the snow and the rock. The flanks of the mountain drop away 1000 m sheer from the ridge on each side. Never in my life have I seen such a precipice as this South Face of Nanga. I work my way along from one steep section to the next, each individual ledge representing an interim target. And when I see the summit pop up far above me I can hardly comprehend that I am to go up it. At the end of this rock ridge, which is a straight grade IV and V in parts,

one bold, vertical pillar stands in the way. I immediately see that it would be impossible to climb it. The vertical rock is still swathed in snow, so I need to climb round to the right of it. The rock is very brittle and demands extreme caution. At the end, an overhanging 10 m wall that stretches out above the whole tower bars my entrance to a gully that would lead back to the ridge. Thus I am forced to traverse a small slope and later to climb a vertical-to-overhanging crack, and only by using my last reserves of energy am I able to work my way up the last few meters to the ridge.

THE LAST STEEPER section before the shoulder is a very steep, long *firn* slope. It does not cause a problem but is very strenuous, and at 6 p.m. I finally reach the shoulder, at about 8060 m. Occasional little rises and pinnacles—some rock, some ice—lead up to the foot of the summit formation, yet it is neither the "mown field" nor the "motorway" suitable for anything from a handcart to an eight-cylinder car, as it was once suggested. This section, too, demands extreme energy and stamina. I feel I have reached the end of my capabilities; the last upsweep to the summit seems to be beyond my strength. As a mountaineer I know that it all depends on the summit, but in reality it could be just any other summit in my local mountains. I'm not really

On the Silver Plateau; right of center the subsidiary summit of Nanga Parbat; to the left and below it the Bazhin Gap; above it the shoulder (8070 m) and on the far left the main summit of Nanga Parbat.

"Hermann Buhl's solo summit bid has become . . . a legend. According to all the rules of common sense he should not have been able to return from this journey."

Kurt Maix

conscious of the fact that we are talking about Nanga Parbat here, an unclimbed eight-thousander; about a mountain from which seven expeditions have already had to retreat empty-handed, and that has already cost so many lives.

The last mouthful of coca tea from the flask picks me up again, and I traverse across to the North Face; rough, steep blocks lead up to the summit, another 100 m still.

Every step is a challenge. I have left my ski poles behind, so I crawl on all fours, heading for the highest point. The snow-covering rises two meters above

The world-famous Nanga Parbat summit photo: Hermann Buhl's ice axe with the Tyrolean flag; in the center the Silver Plateau, to the left the Silberzacken and in the background the mountains of the Karakorum.

the rock, I am on the highest point, on Nanga Parbat, 8125 m. I am not conscious of the significance of the moment; I do not feel the joy of victory, do not feel like a champion, I am just glad to be up here and to have all the hard work behind me for the time being. Going down will be easier.

I take a small flag out of my anorak, the Tyrolean flag, tie it round the ice axe, take a photo and put it back in my anorak. Then I take out the flag of our host country, tie it to the ice axe, ram the axe into the summit snow and take a few documentary photos, looking down to Rakhiot Peak, across to the subsidiary summit, the plateau and the Silbersattel. A quick look down to the Rupal valley, where the setting sun casts far into the countryside the mighty shadow of this mountain on which I am standing. A glance at the panorama, my eyes cast far out over to the Himalaya, the Karakorum, Pamirs and to the Hindu Kush in the west, and in the south to the Indian Plain, to Kashmir. It is seven o'clock in the evening; the sun is just disappearing on the horizon and it immediately goes noticeably cold, but the mountains are still pleasantly warm from the day's sun.

WITH RENEWED VIGOR I descend the pile of boulders again; I jump easily from stone to stone as if some transformation had taken place within me. I actually wanted to bivouac on the shoulder, but as I now feel stronger again I decide to make the most of the daylight, and continue my descent as long as I can still see. I might even make it to the Bazhin Gap. The ridge seems too difficult and dangerous for a descent, so I want to try to get down on the flank opposite the Diamir Face. From the shoulder I now climb straight down the vertical *firn* flank in order to lose as much height as possible. I have left the axe at the summit so the only aids to balance are the two ski poles— a bad replacement. And that one small mistake in the equipment department could almost have been the death of me. I am standing in the middle of the *firn* flank when suddenly my right crampon comes away from my boot and is lost. I just manage to get hold of the crampon but the frame for attaching it has gone. I have not got another with me, either, so the crampon is useless. I am left standing on one crampon on the hard snow slope like a stork on one leg, supported by ski-poles and without the faintest idea of how I can get off the slope. With the utmost caution I finally manage to reach rocky ground again. Here I continue my descent, but then the night takes me in her claws. I am at an altitude of about 8000 m, 150 m below the summit. There is no sense in continuing in the darkness, yet I cannot spend the night where I am, either. Some

"If the news that Everest, the world's highest mountain, had been conquered flew around the whole world, occasioning the greatest admiration, then the victory over Nanga Parbat that followed almost immediately triggered no less enthusiasm. Buhl's name was on everyone's lips, the whole world over."
Hugo and Luis Vigl

distance away I can make out the outline of a boulder; I try to reach it and succeed. True, it is a little wobbly but I can stand on it quite well. With my body leaning against a slabby wall that inclines 50 to 60 degrees, a good boulder for my right hand to hold onto and my ski poles in my left hand, I am able to spend the night here quite well. The thought of bivouacking at 8000 m with no equipment, no sleeping bag, no survival bag, no rope, not even a rucksack, doesn't seem particularly strange to me at all; I take it for granted. After all my boots are warm and lined with felt, so it won't be too easy to get frostbite. My rucksack with the thick sweater and spare clothing is down on the plateau, but I can spend the night like this dressed just in my thin sweater. I've spent many a night in unfavorable conditions in temperatures of minus 20 degrees. The moon will be out at midnight, and I can think about continuing my descent. As a precaution, to aid my circulation I take a few Padutin tablets.

It is nine in the evening. The final shimmer of the old day is dying out in the west. It does me good to rest, even if I am standing upright. The time passes relatively quickly and considerably better than I had imagined. With the exception of a few short gusts that whirl around the summit, the air is generally still. The starry sky above me is immaculate. The Milky Way passes over me and in the north, the Plow. I doze for a while, nod off from time to time and pull myself upright again. Then I am shaken again by a bout of shivering; everything is bearable, it is just my feet that are slowly becoming numb, because I cannot move them around enough. Only really late, at about 2 a.m., does the moon come out; it is only a really small crescent and doesn't have much strength. It is right above the summit, and wonderfully illuminates the slopes of the north and subsidiary summits below me; its light also reaches the Bazhin Gap, but does not make it as far as I am. The flank is still covered in dark shadows as before; that means I just have to wait until daylight breaks, when all the time it is getting colder.

4 July 1953

THE HORIZON HAS long since had a strip of light, yet the stars do not want to move from the sky; it is still twilight and too dark to climb. At about 4 a.m., as soon as I am able to see a little bit again, I set off. My feet are numb, my boots frozen stiff, the rubber soles iced up, so I have doubly to pay attention. I cross into a gully, want to traverse this, then because of the brittleness of the rock I go back and come down the gully instead. Only farther down do I traverse out of it. I have to think extremely carefully about every footstep; even when the terrain is not too steep, a small slip could be fatal. If your foot slips even once in the snow, it is momentarily so strenuous that it takes minutes to recover. Crossing steep snowfields and slabs, I reach another gully and continue to climb down through this. At the end there is a 10 m high overhanging section with a crack running through it, a difficult bit of climbing that completely takes my breath away. I have to rockclimb right to the last move, then I am standing on a rock-hard snowfield that runs down from the Bazhin Gap. This time I want to go back via the Diamir Gap, as there will be less altitude difference to overcome than if I use the other route, as on my ascent. A long horizontal traverse leads me to the rocks beneath the Diamir Gap. It is very strenuous. My right crampon keeps falling off; I have merely tied it on with string, and to keep putting it back on while on this steep terrain is really exhausting. At lunchtime I finally reach the rocks and dive into a giant snow hole.

THE SUN IS BURNING down mercilessly, and I fall into a half-slumber. But thirst and hunger soon wake me. I am totally dehydrated and can think of nothing but getting something to drink. Here and there I hear voices

above me, possibly my friends with a flask of tea, but no, nothing; it takes all my strength to pull myself together and continue the descent. Now there is a 30 m climb up to the Diamir Gap. Supporting myself on the ski poles, I drag myself from one rock to the next; every step is a hurdle. It seems strange to me that I was fit enough to make it to the summit yesterday. Everywhere I can see signs of human presence: cairns, familiar territory, but I know full well that I am the first person to be here; it is all new land.

At last I had reached the Diamir Gap. The great plateau was ahead of me once more. I searched up and down the snowy surface; perhaps Otto would be sitting there somewhere, waiting for me with tea. What would I give for a drink? I can no longer swallow or talk, even less shout. Only blood and spittle come from my mouth. Going down is a little easier now, but soon I have to cross to the right. I want to get to my rucksack—I know it contains something edible, and hunger is tormenting me just as much as thirst. That is probably the reason that I feel so weak, too. The traverse is never-ending. I just keep stumbling around even more in the channels cut by the wind. Finally I have to climb up and back down again as I do not find the rucksack straight away; it must be hidden somewhere in the wind channels.

Then I fall over next to it. I

Hermann Buhl returns to Camp 5—after becoming the first man to climb Nanga Parbat and after spending a night bivouacking standing up at 8000 m—41 hours after leaving the Camp.

Buhl, who had "aged" several years, at Camp 5 after his return from the summit of Nanga Parbat

simply cannot force down dried fruit, and wafer biscuits even less, so I just make a broth from the Dextro-Energen and snow. It tastes good and is wonderfully refreshing. The snow makes me even thirstier, but it helps for the moment and then I just have to keep repeating it. After a longer break I feel better again. Out on the Silbersattel I see two dots. I could shout with joy; now someone is coming up, I can hear their voices too, someone calls "Hermann," but then I realize that they are rocks on Chongra Peak that rises up behind. It is a bitter disappointment. I set off again subdued. This realization happens frequently. Then I hear voices, hear my name really clearly—hallucinations. What on earth has happened to Otto? He ought to come up and have a look. I cannot understand that nobody is coming up to meet me; have they already given up on me?

The breaks get more and more frequent, the pauses longer and longer. It's always all right to begin with—20 m, 30 m—then it starts all over again. Two to three steps, ten to twenty breaths and so on until I cannot carry on at all, and then a longer break, and the game starts all over again. I am at the lowest point of the plateau; I could despair in the wind channels. The descent to the Silbersattel goes on forever. Three more Pervitin, now that's almost it, but I will be at the tent in a few hours anyway. If it works at all, if I've got any reserves left at all.

I REACH THE SILBERSATTEL at 6:30, look down to the individual Camps; nothing is stirring down there, they are all empty, only at the foot of the ridge in front of the Moor's Head are there two men. That gives me a new will to go on, and I carry on down again. As if strengthened again by secret powers, it is much easier to go down now. With leisurely steps I climb down the ridge in my old tracks. When I get nearer I can see that it is Walter and Hans.

Our reunion is indescribable. Both of them are very moved. They had almost written me off,

and now here I am coming down with the summit, hoarse and unable to speak. Hans gets me something to drink straightaway and then they see to my right foot, which is in a really bad way. The three of us spend the night in the little storm tent at Camp 5. My mind is still very active. For a long time I talk about my route, my solo climb to the summit. I tell them about the unspeakable efforts, how it was only my iron will which enabled me to carry on step by step, about the difficult ridge to the summit, the sunset and the wonderful long-distance view, about the bivouac and the hallucinations on the way down. And only now that I am once again among friends and safe do I begin to realize what I have achieved, that Nanga Parbat has been conquered. . . . Only after many hours, when I notice that both my friends are already asleep, do I try to get to sleep myself . . . .

A new day dawns, just as bright and clear as all the days before. We equip ourselves for the descent. We greet the glistening snow crest of the summit, our summit, one final time. Feeling melancholy we bid farewell to this mountain that means such a lot to us.

Days later, as I am lying outside my tent at the foot of the mountain at Base Camp tending to my wounded foot, I often look up to both peaks, 4000 m higher,

Hermann Buhl on 5 July 1953 during the descent between Camp 2 and Camp 3 on Nanga Parbat

Buhl—completely contented after his return from the great mountain.

behind which I know the high *firn* to be, rising up against the sky like a white seam, and let the hours up there pass through my mind's eye. And it is as if I have been in a dream, a dream that one cannot experience—intangible and yet real.

THE STAR

In those days, Buhl's solo ascent stood as the most outstanding success thus far achieved on an 8000-meter peak. Even though the expedition leader [Herrligkoffer] tried to mobilize both the team members and the general public against the lone climber, through his trick of referring to a "communal performance," it was Buhl—not Herrligkoffer—who was the star.

After Nanga Parbat—in spite or because of the amputations to

From the moment of his triumph on Nanga Parbat, Buhl became a mountaineering star. The photograph shows the more mature and "stylish" Buhl as he appeared post-1953.

his right foot—Buhl continued to train as consistently hard as he had before for his return to the big walls. He soon regained his old form, but lecture tours, squabbles with the expedition leader and, not least, the commitments which fame had brought put the brakes on his continued rise.

In 1955-56 Buhl once again found the form he had enjoyed during his great years as an alpine climber. Cured of the pathos of thoughts of conquest and the warlike language of victory by Herrligkoffer's publications, Buhl climbed the hardest alpine faces. It was not enough for him. He wanted to return to the highest mountains of the world. He had to see Nanga Parbat, his mountain, one more time.

With his trip to Broad Peak, Buhl was to achieve more than just a success on a second eight-thousander. He also was able to realize his idea of a small expedition to the high mountains of the world, and he again succeeded where his detractor Herrligkoffer had failed, despite the latter's enormous organization and the help of several of Buhl's former friends. Without Buhl, Herrligkoffer was revealed in his true light: an organizer, dependent on the skills of top-flight alpinists. Buhl's feeling of vindication was tempered, however, by the rivalry that existed between Buhl and that excellent mountaineer Marcus Schmuck, who obviously viewed the Broad Peak expedition as his opportunity to emerge from Buhl's shadow.

Buhl did not have any foreboding that his life's breath would be extinguished in a few days and that he would die. He did not give himself any rest.

On Broad Peak, the friendship between Hermann Buhl and Kurt Diemberger grew. Although basically very different in character, they became a very strong team; two climbers united by similar ideas, mutual respect, and the desire to discover the secrets of the mountains.

Although Diemberger and Buhl did not reach the summit of Chogolisa, the climb they made was a work of genius. It pointed the way to the future. For the next 40 years, Diemberger was to return again and again, captivated by the Chogolisa area.

Part 3

The Star and the Death
From the Challenge of Broad Peak to the End

After becoming the first to climb Nanga Parbat, Hermann Buhl was destined to become a star. In the most daring style imaginable at the time, climbing solo from the last high camp situated at over 6900 meters, he had reached the summit without oxygen and without preparatory work on the route. In doing this Buhl had achieved something that in those days had seemed impossible. Only his strength of will and the stimulant Pervitin brought him back down again to the land of the living.

Upon their return to Base Camp, Buhl, Ertl, and Frauenberger were met with an atmosphere of inhuman coldness and neutral objectivity. The seeds of mistrust had already been sown. Hermann Buhl's achievements were not celebrated. His outstanding individual contribution was seen as a natural part of the team's success, a success that Herrligkoffer wished to exploit. This becomes particularly clear when as the leader of the expedition, Herrligkoffer says to the camera crews of the *"Wochenschau"* news program at Munich-Riem airport, "Together with you, we are all very pleased that we have at long last managed (that the extraordinary initiative shown by our man Buhl has managed) to conquer the Fateful Mountain of the Germans and thus to fulfill the last wishes of Willy Merkl and those others whose lives were claimed by Nanga Parbat."

One needs to watch this film in order to see how hard it was for Herrligkoffer even to mention Buhl's name!

Buhl's longtime editor and writing-collaborator Kurt Maix is right when, in the preface to *Nanga Parbat Pilgrimage,* he writes: "One forgets that Hermann Buhl was initially one of the favorites in the race for the great mountain. We only remember how Hermann Buhl, together with the whole summit team, became an outsider. That this outsider then won the race, as was expected of him as the favorite, seemed to annoy the organizers. The favorite was shown none of the recognition due for such an outstanding achievement as he had accomplished it as an outsider, a curious fallacy of terms. From this narrow-mindedness grew all the evil. . . . A little more understanding for the size of this achievement and the character of this solitary individual would have saved everything; it would have

"He had no idea . . . that he was playing into the dangerous action zone of calculating managers with a need for recognition. He was powerless in the face of slander and misjudgment. Trust was extremely important to Buhl, and unfortunately he usually represented the voice of justice with criticism that was too honest."

Hugo and Luis Vigl

Hermann Buhl and Hans Ertl (right) immediately after their return from Karachi. Thanks to Ertl's vehement efforts, the expedition leadership gave the green light for a summit attempt—and thus for the success on Nanga Parbat.

Hermann Buhl (left) had become an international climbing star; here he is seen relaxing with Guido Magnone (center) and Paul Keller.

nipped these differences of opinion in the bud. Everyone would have had something to gain from this. Yet it happened that something extraordinary was accorded hardly even an ordinary measure of respect. People did not consider that this individual, on his own initiative and being responsible even to the bounds of destruction, had trodden the very fine line between life and death. What had he achieved? He had stood on our shoulders and only needed to reach for the crown. . . . "

The battle between Buhl, Ertl, and Frauenberger on the one hand, and Herrligkoffer and his loyal followers on the other, had already begun to roll at the foot of the great mountain. It may be that Buhl was egged-on by Ertl, who was the driving force behind the success—it was only his vehement "No" to a retreat that managed to get the green light from the mountaineering leader, Peter Aschenbrenner, for the summit attempt. Ertl would have made Buhl see, even more clearly than he did already, that it was Buhl, and Buhl alone, who was to be thanked for the expedition being able to return home successful. The more Herrligkoffer tried to diminish Buhl's success at home, the more the latter went on about the amateur expedition leadership.

It was just a question of time before all of Buhl's pent-up aggressions surfaced. "When Herrligkoffer said to me, when talking about my summit bid at a press conference in Lahore in the presence of the Consul Mr. Knips, 'Shut your mouth, it's got nothing to do with you,' I knew what I thought of this man. At the time I had wanted only to correct a mistake in the report." (Buhl)

Hermann Buhl protested and rebelled against Herrligkoffer's "authentic" publications, which he claimed were not "genuine." And with his lectures, Buhl no longer kept to former agreements. He was no longer concerned about who gave the lectures on Nanga Parbat, or where and when they took place. What annoyed him was that Herrligkoffer praised Kuno Rainer to the heavens. And Rainer, in return, "betrayed" his old climbing partner Buhl in exchange for inclusion in the 1954 Broad Peak Expedition, also led by Herrligkoffer.

In the meantime, Buhl had become so famous that he no longer reacted to such intrigue and regimentation, which seemed narrowminded to him. With pictures from Hans Ertl's Expedition film—exhibition material—he held successful lectures on an international level. The applause of a large audience gave him more self-confidence. The battle, spurred on by a long, cryptic, remarkably well-researched article by Jürgen Thorwald entitled "Fight for Nanga Parbat" in the magazine *Quick* (here, once again, Herrligkoffer suspects Ertl has been involved), leads to the setting up of an arbitration tribunal and, as this is unsuccessful, to a battle in court which drags on into 1954.

This all signifies stress, pressure, and even disappointment for Buhl. Nevertheless his career curve climbs steeply upward. In Austria he is named Sportsman of the Year and he is honored in both Italy and England. He is now a star and recognized on the street. Admired, envied and even hated, he gets to know a new world, and not a very pleasant one. As every "Great Star" discovers, the "wannabes" all start to have a go at him, cocking their legs like dogs to pee on his trousers. Buhl is a sensitive man, and not the kind of unshakable character to be left undisturbed by all this. It eats into him and prevents him from exploiting his creative potential to the full.

Buhl's answer to this dilemma is to go climbing! After a first few cautious attempts—hampered by the amputations on his right foot, Buhl initially finds climbing hard—he is soon tackling difficult routes again: the South Arête of the Great Mühlsturzhorn, the Eisenstecken Route on the South Face of the Mugonispitze, the Fox-Arête on the Campanile Basso. In 1955 he does the East Face of the Grand Capucin, the Direct West Face of the Aiguille Noire, and the second solo ascent of the South East Corner of the Fleischbank.

Between 1954 and 1957 Hermann Buhl achieved some great routes, for example the South East Corner of the Fleischbank (right of center) in the Wilder Kaiser.

In 1956 Buhl achieves the first solo ascents of the Auckenthaler Route on the North Face of the Laliderer-Spitze, the second solo of the Gervasutti Couloir on Mont Blanc du Tacul and . . . the West Face of the Petit Dru. Hermann is once again "The old Buhl." In the mountains he can be "himself." High above the abyss of tarnished human nature he forgets envy and resentment.

It is now, and not just at the moment of achieving his second eight-thousand-meter peak, Broad Peak, that he is in the truest sense of the words, "at the top." He is—indisputably—the greatest mountaineer in the world. That he does not return home from the Karakorum Expedition in 1957, that he can no longer experience the love and respect of all those who like him, and that he can no longer see his millions of admirers, is tragic for *them*. He is no more. He becomes a legend in their memory.

Would the number of enemies, those who envied him, have continued to increase had he still been alive? We think not; nevertheless it is not too far from the mark to suspect that in the summer of 1957, there were those who were happy about Hermann Buhl's failure to return.

Before following Buhl on the Karakorum Expedition through his diaries, we include here an article he wrote on one of the 1956 climbs that took him away from the squabbling over Nanga Parbat and back into the restorative arms of his beloved Alps.

The West Face of the Dru

by Hermann Buhl

"**EXPEDITION INTO** the vertical!"—this is what the first ascent party called their undertaking on the Dru. "The changing face of Alpine climbing?"—this is what they wrote after their successful ascent of the West Face.

And everyone paid attention, for the impossible had been done! Of course, people did wonder whether the difficulties and the dangers on this face were so great that they really were beyond comparison with any other route in the Alps. Had the young generation of elite French mountaineers really ushered in a new era of alpinism? Were they so far ahead of what had gone before?

We were owed an answer to all these questions. This was not a matter of one isolated incident; it was more a *Prix des Nations,* a battle of *materiel* hitherto unknown in the world of alpine climbing. And the French had fired the first shots.

Many attempts had been made prior to the first ascent. The route had been pushed to a point high on the face before by Parisian climber Guido Magnone, a man who until just a few years earlier had known nothing about the mountains. Magnone finally devoted himself heart and soul to

this wall, and with three companions forced a route through the huge sweeps of rock and the overhangs of the West Face. The climbers were on that awesome wall for seven days, traversing out from the middle of the face onto the North Flank, using expansion bolts to work their way upward to terrain that was again climbable, and from there launching a second attempt to reach the summit. The motto of the undertaking was "At any price!"

Thus it was that they used hundreds of meters of rope, dozens of pegs and wooden wedges of every description, a stack of rope slings, and a 40-meter metal ladder that still hangs on the exit pitch of the face even today!

It really was an "expedition" into the vertical! Doubts were expressed as to the possibility of repeating the climb. Was it even worth all the effort? But the thirst for action, the lust for adventure, and perhaps even a measure of inquisitiveness drew certain climbers to this face.

Nor would the wall leave me in peace until I had found my own answers to all of these questions.

That night the *föhn* wind was blowing hard. The gale-force southerly wind was flattening the

Like Hermann Buhl before him in 1953, Reinhold Messner also was able to admire the view from the summit of Nanga Parbat (in 1970, after the first ascent of the Rupal Face, and again in 1978 after the first complete solo ascent from Base Camp to summit, the year in which this photograph was taken) across to the false summit, down to the Silberplateau and the Silbersattel and beyond to Chongra Peak.

Arriving in Gilgit after his summit success on Nanga Parbat, Hermann Buhl was presented with a garland of flowers by the locals.

The frostbite which Hermann Buhl suffered during his enforced bivouac at 8000 meters on Nanga Parbat meant he had to undergo amputations to his right foot. One of the first routes he climbed after this was a solo ascent of the Grosser Trichter (right of center) on the West Face of the Hohen Gall in the Berchtesgaden Alps.

On 4 July 1955, two years after his first ascent of Nanga Parbat, Hermann Buhl and Luis Vigl climbed the East Face of Monte Rosa.

Like Paul Preuss 40 years before him, Hermann Buhl was a master on loose rock. Here, one of Buhl's climbing partners follows him up a pitch in the Dolomites.

Generl Buhl, photographed by Hermann in 1956 on the Moore Spur of the Brenva Face of Mont Blanc.

Hermann Buhl in 1955 on the East Face of the Grand Capucin (Mont Blanc region)

The Bonatti Route on the East Face of the Grand Capucin. In 1955, four years after the first ascent, it was still held in high regard.

The 400-meter-high East Face of the Grand Capucin; the Bonatti Route takes a line slightly left of center.

Facing page:
In 1956 Hermann Buhl and Marcus Schmuck made the sixth ascent of the West Face of the Petit Dru (center of picture), completing the climb in just one and one-half days.

Camp 1 on Broad Peak, 1957

"We wanted to climb it by the Buhl Route. Thus it was that, exactly 25 years after Hermann Buhl, I had the chance to follow him to his last summit. . . . From a mountaineering-history aspect, Broad Peak was of great interest to me. In 1957 Buhl, Schmuck, Diemberger, and Wintersteller applied 'alpine style' to an eight-thousander for the first time and were largely successful in realizing their aims."
Reinhold Messner

Broad Peak (8047 m) in the Karakorum was first climbed on 9 July 1957 by Marcus Schmuck, Fritz Wintersteller, Kurt Diemberger, and Hermann Buhl without the help of high-altitude porters and without using bottled oxygen.

Kurt Diemberger, "the Academic" (accorded the title of "expedition doctor" by Buhl) gives Buhl an injection against frostbite damage. © Kurt Diemberger

In 1957 Camp 2 on Broad Peak was dug into a little cornice.

Above Camp 2, the "Cornice Camp" on the West Face of Broad Peak in 1957.

A splendid atmosphere, a glorious view. Camp 3 (1957) on the West Flank
of Broad Peak.

Hermann Buhl during his ascent of Broad Peak, with Chogolisa in the background. In spite of the frostbite which hampered his performance on the summit day, his overall life energy was unabated. ". . . I still want to do excursions, perhaps climb a six-or seven-thousand meter peak," he wrote home after the ascent. © Kurt Diemberger.

On the summit day, Hermann Buhl takes a short rest on the icy cold West
Flank of Broad Peak. Behind Buhl is the Savoia Range. © Kurt Diemberger

View from the notch (7800 m)
between the Middle Summit
and the false summit of Broad
Peak across the sea of peaks
of the Sinkiang.

With his success on Broad Peak, Hermann Buhl became the first non-Sherpa to have climbed two eight-thousand-meter peaks. © Kurt Diemberger

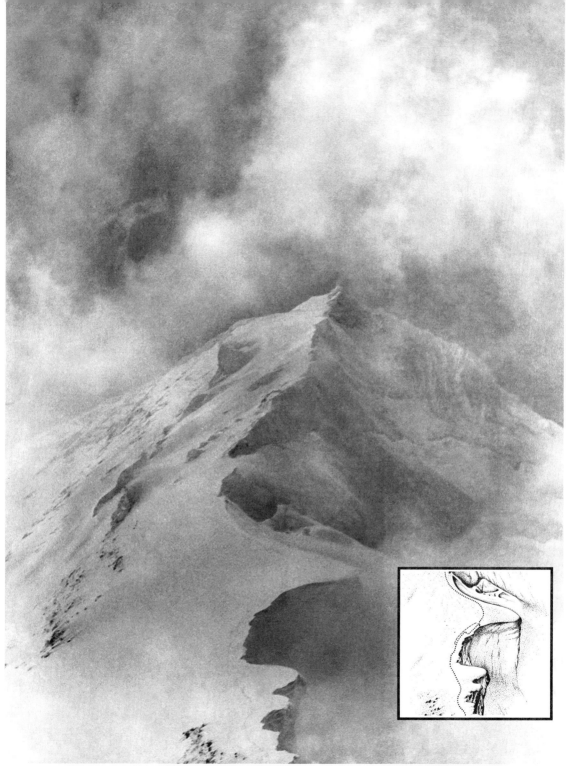

On the South East Ridge of Chogolisa, Hermann Buhl's last tracks lead to the edge of a fresh break in the cornice. © Kurt Diemberger (From *The Kurt Diemberger Omnibus,* 1999)

Working on his portable typewriter, Hermann Buhl drafts
the sections of his report on
the Karakorum Expedition of
the Austrian Alpine Club 1957
to publication standard.

*"'This has been the finest
day for me since I have
been on this expedition,'
says Hermann, 'I always
imagined something like
this; a 7000er in three
days, not in three
weeks . . .'"*

Kurt Diemberger

Chogolisa. The two peaks
of the summit plateau are
7654 m (left) and 7665 m
(right) high.

A special edition of postage stamps was issued on the occasion of the successful 1978 Austrian Nanga Parbat Expedition to commemorate Buhl's first ascent.

Gasherbrum Base Camp 1997 with Chogolisa in the background on the right.

"Exactly 40 years after Buhl's disappearance on Chogolisa, about 100 climbers gathered on the Abruzzi Glacier in a communal act of remembrance for this unique personality. Although the development of high-altitude mountaineering has again moved away from the small, self-contained expedition—the dinosaur has awakened!—Buhl still remains unforgotten by the young mountaineers."

Extract from a letter to Horst Höfler from Reinhold Messner

On 27 June 1997 Reinhold Messner organized a celebratory gathering at the foot of Chogolisa to commemorate the 40th anniversary of Hermann Buhl's death.

bushes against the ground as I set off on the walk up to the foot of the Drus with my friend Marcus Schmuck, with whom I had shared many a hard-won battle in the mountains. A waterfall, the first real obstacle, seemed to be trying to physically beat us back and to prevent us from gaining access to the foot of the face. We had both driven through the night in order to meet up in Chamonix at the prearranged time, and had left that world-famous mountaineering village, nestling at the foot of Mont Blanc, at eleven o'clock the same evening. Now, at the foot of the Drus, we waited for morning to come. The dark outline of the mountain raised a warning finger into the starstrewn night sky. It was up there that my thoughts lay; on those rocky flanks that seemed almost to be collapsing down upon our heads.

What would the coming day bring? I had to be back in Chamonix the following evening! Marcus seemed oblivious to such concerns; he slept the sleep of the just, as if the wall up there was of no concern to him at all. But he was terribly tired from the drive and had hardly been able to follow the little approach path, stumbling around behind me like a sleepwalker.

The last meal before one meets the executioner is always a delicious affair. Like Max and Moritz, each with a piece of fried chicken clutched in his greasy fingers, we

attempted to ascertain the exact anatomical structure of the animal we were feasting on.

The first rays of sun greeted us on the rocks bounding the ice couloir that cuts through the face like a deep, open wound. To our left, things were getting lively and from time to time the fusillade of stones hummed down over the black ice. We were moving together, still unroped, and the little patch of snow at the foot of the face sank deeper and deeper and diminished in size rapidly. As always on such big routes we had reduced our equipment to the minimum. I am of the same opinion as Rigele on this matter: "Better to starve and freeze than carry huge loads!" We were still able to avoid the stonefall crashing down at short intervals from the loose cliffs of the "Flammes de Pierre" and crossed the Dru Couloir at a run before picking our way with the utmost care—like walking on egg shells—up the cracked and loose rocks to the terrace. The rock hereabout seemed to have been smashed to bits by some giant fist. A fine layer of dust lay on every little ledge; every knob of rock, every edge was smashed flat, rounded off, and any attempt to hammer a piton into a crack caused whole blocks to part company with the mountain. Above us the cliff reared up abruptly, overhanging, a huge precipice with a massive depression clearly marking the place where a fresh rockfall had occurred. Our route

"It was barely believable how Hermann mastered the smooth, holdless overhangs. Like a spider scuttling up a smooth wall he stood on the vertical face, and just like the spider, it was impossible to see how he did it."

Marcus Schmuck

went right through this scene of destruction. Right up to below the huge roofs blocking the passage to the upper part of the face, the rock had been torn apart as if by a mighty grinding machine. On the left-hand edge of this zone of rockfall, cracks and grooves led upward in a thin, dark line— the route of the first ascent party.

THE DIFFICULTIES now began. To outward appearances, the gear was almost always the same: double ropes, a few pegs and two wooden wedges, maybe a few slings and etriers more than on other routes. But within ourselves we were ready for anything, mentally prepared for the most extreme tests that the medium of rock could place in our way. We now began to see the occasional signs of previous retreats. How many climbers might have sat up here searching for a way up and out of their dilemma? Maybe even asking themselves the question—not entirely unjustified—what all this was meant to achieve? Many had gone back down from this point perhaps not too disappointed, for this was the West Face of the Dru after all. And those who chose the route to the summit—one can count the parties on the fingers of one hand—remained prisoners of this terrible mountain for a good four days!

OUR CONVERSATION had become more and more tight-

lipped. "This face gives me the creeps," I was thinking to myself. We got out the route description and read about a second bivouac somewhere around here, but it was only 8 o'clock in the morning, which was a very comforting thought. A good third of the face already lay behind us, but now it was a case of making that leap of difficulty into upper grade VI territory. Smooth cracks, featureless grooves sometimes choked with ice, an overhang beneath which the rope became jammed solid— with me hanging on the Vignes Crack, of all places, the crux of the route! And that was only the first hard pitch! It does not differ considerably from the other exceptionally severe pitches on the route, maybe a bit more strenuous, though. We avoided the really featureless sections wherever possible and, once over one of the many roofs, felt just like a pedestrian who has managed to weave through the traffic and reach the safety of the zebra crossing just in time. But it was certainly all climbable, and wherever the holds ran out we found a peg. Then, however, a belt of huge roofs blocked the back of the groove. We puzzled over the best route to take. Over to the right, a thin crack split a smooth, roof-capped slab. Three pitons pointed the way across and for the first time we were forced to use our etriers. Unfortunately, as soon as you tried to

Climbing quickly, Hermann Buhl crosses the Dru Couloir. The risk of stonefall here is extreme.

stand upright in the stirrup loops your head hit a protruding section of roof! We were starting to get a bit anxious again about what the next few meters would bring and peered around an arête—very cautiously, as if there might have been some carnivorous beast lying there in wait for us! But what we could see was nothing but eel-smooth slabs of rock with a very fine crack shooting up through them, as if put there on purpose, and disappearing into nothing. The route description here says only that it is "artificiel." So yet again we had to trust ourselves to the insecure holds provided by pegs, wooden wedges and etrier rungs.

The crack got wider and wider; the pitons just wandered about inside it, the wooden wedges were rotten, and the few rope slings in place were also either rotting away or had snapped and could barely be used at all. And when I looked down at my rope-mate, he was leaning casually against the rock and seemed to be asleep! "I completely understand the need for a midday snooze, but not here, Marcus! Can't you find yourself a more comfortable spot?" Whereupon Marcus pulled himself together again. But the sun was burning down so beautifully and after two days without sleep—it was understandable.

The rock now grew incredibly compact, terribly smooth, and completely featureless. Handholds and footholds were now a thing of the past. Then the crack ended abruptly. Damned cheek!

Away to the left I could see a narrow little ledge; that was where I had to aim, but how was I to get across the smooth intervening section? As usual in such situations the rope would hardly pull through and there I hung, on the smallest finger holds, anxiously watching the distance back to the last piton getting bigger and bigger. In such situations you have a think about it all and make a quick judgment about the reliability of the peg and wedge placements; over there, they were all poking too far out of the cracks and did little to inspire confidence. But then before you know it you are at the belay, not even knowing how you got across to it. You get to experience moments like these over and over again on really hard sections. They always remind me of the crux of the North Face of the Western Zinne. You think you are on easier ground and you can easily let yourself be completely fooled by the climbing.

The wall, of course, still had plenty of surprises in store for us . . . a wide chimney, totally wet; a smooth, greasy slab with water splashing down it. We greeted the latter with pleasure at first, but by the time we had quenched our thirst our clothes were soaked through and heavy as lead. Then we were standing at

Hermann Buhl free-climbing above the zone of terraces on the West Face of the Dru.

the source of the water, a steep snow gully, and thinking that the hardest bit was now behind us. But the climb had tricked us again, and the following overhang seemed to want to be even bigger and harder than its predecessor. There were a few wooden wedges in place, with just their tips biting into the rock and obviously hammered in from below, but they had held the weight of our predecessors, so . . . I clipped in the first carabiner. The rope sling was tatty and frayed and stretched alarmingly as I tried my weight on it, but it held! I decided to trust myself completely to the wedge, swung out into mid-air and stepped up into the etrier, way up above the terraces. I was accustomed to such exposure in the Dolomites but not on the rock faces of the Western Alps. I tried several times to haul myself over the lip of that monster overhang but was repulsed again and again by a smooth, holdless slab above. With my strength now gone, I slumped back onto the wooden wedge, the one upon which I had placed all my trust . . . it pulled, and went winging down toward my companion! When climbing I often have an aversion to using my hammer, but such thoughts would have been inappropriate here, and as soon as I had a decent wedge in above to replace the old one I realized I should have used it earlier. A roomy stance soon appeared above me, a wide terrace with a light covering of snow, described in the guide as the third or fourth bivouac ledge.

IT WAS ONLY 3 IN the afternoon, but we felt we had now deserved a rest. The sun had really dried us out, our stomachs were growling like caged dogs, and we were feeling a little tired. But we had the right stuff for each: lemonade for the parched throat, a bit of fruit and a few peanuts for the stomach, and room enough to stretch our legs on the broad, sun-warmed platform. We let the whole grandeur of our surroundings wash over us; it was an incredibly impressive sight. Our gaze swept right across sheer swaths of rock, up and down, back and forth, but could find no point of reference, finally coming to rest on the boulders at the foot of the Dru. Above us, the wall still loomed huge. A single slab of rock, scoured smooth, led up to the black roofs perched like a balcony and guarding the lower section of the Face. The laws of gravity seemed not to exist here. The reddish-yellow hues hinted at even more compact rock to come.

TO THE LEFT, THIS monstrous slab of rock abutted another sheer precipice that overhung and led out at an obtuse angle onto the North Face. At the point where these two gigantic rock faces met there was a corner with a thin crack in the back. The corner overhung our stance fearsomely, and instead of the little ledges at regular intervals one would have wished for, the rock displayed a series of little right-angled protuberances. Taking stock of the corner, up which we would soon have to climb, we suddenly became aware of something moving. Yes, there was no doubt about it, up there something was stirring—another party of climbers. Their progress was barely discernible; the second was moving at a snail's pace, but he was moving. We had a worm's eye view of the seat of his trousers! Over in the Couloir I could see tracks and now tried to confirm the suspicions I had had that morning. It was hardly surprising, really; I had met up with two other ropes on the East Face of the Grand Capucin, three on the North Face of Eiger. This kind of thing always seemed to happen to me on big routes. We were a little worried that this pair might actually seriously hold us up. In view of the limited time we had available this would have been very inconvenient. But then they identified themselves as acquaintances of mine, two of them, whom I had met last year on the Aiguille Noire and on the Capucin. It was Siegfried Löw from Salzburg and Jörg Lehne from Traunstein, both of them good climbers. We relaxed again. They had started up the route a day earlier than we had, which was why we were only now able to get a view of them.

Now it was our turn to get moving again. There was nowhere at all to bivouac up there, so we had to get up beyond the corner system that the route description said would take eight hours. I set off up an extremely strenuous crack to reach the top of a pillar at the foot of the huge corner. The rock pushed me out backward, my rucksack pressed into my back. I managed to get the rucksack off with a series of unusual contortions, but the crack was still hard work even without it. I then had to switch back to "artificial mode" and trust myself again to questionable existing wooden wedges. We soon realized we had too little equipment with us, and the pegs that we had, especially the two wooden wedges, were guarded as jealously as any treasure trove. I had been experimenting with two rope slings and a couple of carabiners for a while, with the distance between me and the last point of protection through which the rope ran growing all the time. The double ropes ran through a total of only five carabiners but this did at least mean they ran smoothly. I was slowly beginning to develop cramps in my arms. They had had to take most of the weight today, since footholds were non-existent. Finally I took a belay hanging in slings and brought Marcus up. Swapping over belays is always one of those complicated and dangerous maneuvers. One of you is supposed

"The way Hermann Buhl tackled that overhanging, holdless corner—it was a crafty game of chance played with gravity—was a feat unlikely to be repeated by anyone so soon. I had to push myself to the limit just to follow the pitch."

Marcus Schmuck

Buhl on the tension traverse below the capping belt of roofs on the upper section of the West Face of the Dru.

to make room for the other, but he is always caught up in a tangle of ropes, slings, pitons, and carabiners, yet still has to belay the other while all the time making sure that he does not unclip the wrong sling, especially not the one he is hanging on!

It was now becoming imperative that we get out of this corner system fast, for the sun was soon going to disappear behind the foothills of Mont Blanc. There was one more pitch ahead of me, just like the previous one, but I now had the bit between my teeth. All I had to do was switch off my thoughts and my nerves and things went considerably better. The sweep of slabs still loomed large above my head, but a tricky little traverse brought me out to the right onto a kind of slabby roof set at an angle of about 80 degrees. With the help of a tension traverse I managed to climb along the lower edge of the roof to reach a little platform. The stance was perched on the wall like a swallow's nest. The exposure left nothing to be desired. Marcus followed really quickly, and while he was coming up the slab the rock grew redder and redder in color, becoming darker and darker until the whole mountain seemed to glow like a huge burning torch.

ONLY 50 METERS away and at the same level as we were was the big platform on the North Face, the "Niche," an ice field scooped

out of the North Face like the imprint of a huge thumb. Years ago I stood over there, but back then I could not imagine that one day I would be climbing these terrifying sweeps of slabs. I just sneaked a shy look across and down.

At this point the face has a little blemish. The first ascentionists had forced an exit route onto the North Face with the aid of expansion bolts, returning a second time to complete the upper section of the wall to the summit. Now, however, these bolts and the fixed ropes anchored to them have become unusable. The rope is weathered and some of the pegs and bolts are hanging loose. The Face has now removed the blemish. Anyone wishing to climb the West Face of the Dru needs to be aware that there are only two possibilities here: either you retreat or you battle on through to the top.

The snowfields of Mont Blanc glowed in the last shimmer of the evening sun; the Chamonix Aiguilles rose darkly against the paling sky, and down in the valley the first lights were flashing and sparkling. How often had I experienced moments like this, seen the same picture; yet it was always like a new experience. A prominent rock tower on the "Flammes de Pierre" that we had christened "the Penguin" due to its shape now lay far below us, and this allowed us to gauge the true size of the Face. When we had set off it had risen high above us. We were able to use it to estimate our progress.

We sat in silence on a narrow pulpit of rock surrounded by sheer precipices, nibbled at our meager provisions, and tried to catch up on some of the sleep we had missed over the last few days. Our feet were very painful. Climbing in big boots—and in my case in new ones, about one size too big—on the smallest of footholds is dreadfully tiring. We had now been climbing for over 15 hours and 800 meters of the face lay behind us. Normally one would have reckoned on two to three days. Then there was the ascent from Chamonix to be added. We had left the town 21 hours ago and had not allowed ourselves any kind of longer break. Little wonder, then, that our feet were sore. There was another reason for our haste, too. We not only had to be back in Chamonix tomorrow evening, but the weather was also a little too uncertain for us. Today it was fine and it would certainly hold tomorrow, too, but whether it would remain so for long was very questionable with this keen south wind blowing.

IN MY DREAMS, Marcus now took over the lead and stayed about a pitch ahead of me all the way.

We had to cuddle up really close to get the bivi sack over us. Marcus was lying on the outermost edge of the platform, held in place only by the sack and the rope, and with half of his body hanging out over the Nant Blanc Glacier. For my part, I had to press my nose flat against the rock and had only a sharp-edged boulder for a pillow. At 6 o'clock in the morning we began the day's work with a few squares of chocolate clenched between our teeth.

The climbing now became pleasant again. In fact, the description even referred to sections of III and IV, which meant that we no longer had to use artificial means to make progress. Marcus was a bit surprised at the grading, of course, but when you have done a lot of climbing around the Mont Blanc region you gradually get to know the local customs and soon realize that a "French IV" would be at least grade V in Germany. The upper limit here is also around the VI mark, but it would seem that as yet there is no level of difficulty that would warrant "French VI." To the uninitiated, the grading system used on the West Face of the Dru might appear to be rather peculiar but in time you do come to grips with it. Good nerves and the appropriate technical ability are more important here than etriers.

We were making rapid progress, since the terrain was once more exactly to our tastes. Although there were still massive roofs to be negotiated, the rock was so covered in holds that you

"I have shared a rope with many people, but never with anyone who was so focused on the job as Hermann Buhl."

Marcus Schmuck

The West Face of the Petit Dru (the wall to the left of the prominent pillar) was climbed by Hermann Buhl and Marcus Schmuck in 1956. This, the sixth ascent, was accomplished in the record time of one and a half days.

only really needed the pitons for moral support, and the few that were in place were quite sufficient. We could hear the voices of our comrades again; they must have bivouacked two pitches above us. Finally, a steep ramp brought us to the arête between the West and North Faces and back onto easier ground again. Below us an old, frayed and tattered metal ladder was still hanging, bearing mute testimony to the days of the first ascent. Looking at it you could not help asking yourself the question—had it really been strictly necessary?

Just a few steps around the rib were enough and we were soon confronted by totally different conditions. Ice-choked cracks and verglassed slabs, snow-covered ledges, and glazed rock replaced the vertical walls. There was more and more ice around, forcing us to put our crampons on. Meanwhile, we had caught up with our friends and were now climbing together, first up a tight icy chimney cutting through the upper part of the gloomy North Face, until the West Face fell away completely and we stepped out into the bright sunlight just below the summit of the Petit Dru.

IT WAS STILL ONLY midday and the weather was holding as it had promised to do that morning, so we were able to enjoy our time on the summit to the full. A feeling of contentment was mixed with the visual impression of a splendid panoramic view—an unforgettable finale. I said hello to all of them, to all my old acquaintances—the Jorasses, with their terrific North Face; the Chamonix Aiguilles, a Dolomitic landscape with the character of the Western Alps; Mont Blanc du Tacul and the Capucin; the Dent du Géant; even the Peuterey Ridge and the North Face of the Aiguille Blanche were poking their heads up in greeting; and last but not least Mont Blanc itself, bathed as ever in the eternal light of its snow slopes. There were countless memories connecting me to all these mountains. I loved them because they had given me so much that is beautiful. Yet now, below our feet, a wall broke away that was so huge, so unbelievably steep that we might have had cause to doubt had we not seen clearly the tracks we had made rising up from the void.

It was only now that the pleasure of our achievement broke through and we were proud of our success. Who would not have been? To be sure, we had been well prepared, yet we had not set off on the climb under the best conditions. A feeling of duty and the weather conditions had rather forced the issue. But it had not demanded our last reserves.

I will admit that I know of nicer routes on the granite, and that it is not always pure pleasure, but the West Face of the Dru is one you just have to have done. It dominates the Valley of Chamonix even more than Mont Blanc itself. It is the uncrowned king of its domain and the Chamonix mountain guides are mighty proud of it. We had not come here to rob it of its reputation; we merely wished to get to know it, yet it would seem that our way of doing things was not about to impress the locals! Should we perhaps have done them a favor and bivouacked intentionally?

THERE WILL BE climbers who come here and do this Face in a single day. Maybe it will even be soloed. That is the way things go. Time waits for no man; it marches on with rapid steps, never pausing, not even in the mountains. Yet if we pause a while and look back, then all these deeds are no more remarkable than those of a man such as Preuss, who climbed the Guglia solo by a route that is even today graded V, free-climbing sections previously tamed by a series of pitons. Or Dülfer, for whom even the steepest of the Kaiser faces held no fears and who was the first to solo the overhanging Dülfer Crack on the Fleischbank, a pitch that again bristles with pegs nowadays. Or Comici, who found a way up the smooth bastion of the North Face of the Grosse Zinne—a route that, by today's standards, is still an extremely difficult undertaking—and when accused of indulging in

nothing more than acrobatics, promptly soloed the route.

I think of the mountains of my homeland, of the massive precipices of the Laliderer Walls. Here, too, there is a route climbed recently that pushes the boundaries of what is humanly possible. With the Laliderer North Corner, Hias Rebitsch has established a line that I would describe as the purest form of sixth-grade climbing. The Laliderer Corner is to the Eastern Alps what the Petit Dru is to the Western Alps. In each case, however, the type of climbing is very different. The latter is powerful, athletic, an artificial tour-de-force with the word "artificial" writ large. The former is elegant, acrobatic, requiring the utmost in skill and commitment, "un escalade libre" in the truest sense of the term.

One could level the accusation against each of these men [Magnone and Rebitsch] that "this is not mountaineering, this is pure sport climbing." But let us instead see what the future brings. And above all let us guard against accusing the young men of tomorrow in the same way, because perhaps by then the Alps will have become unfashionable and one will be concerned only with the Big Walls of the Himalaya. A generation of climbers will arrive who smile at our present-day deeds, but let them smile. The mountains are not an adventure playground; they are too mighty for that. They

"This route [the North Corner of the Laliderer] had only been climbed nine or ten times, and only by German and Austrian teams. The best proof of its difficulty is the fact that there had been at least as many failures on it as there had been successful attempts and that up to that point no foreign parties—not even that first-class French climber Rébuffat—had been able to do it."

Hermann Buhl

merely tolerate our presence with dignity, as we buzz around them like flies, scrambling up and down them with awe-struck reverence. A sea-change in the world of alpine mountaineering? Yes or no? Represented by the West Face of the Dru? Whatever, for us it was an experience, a ray of light in the gray monotony of everyday life, a demonstration of the affirmation of life!

Broad Peak

Karakorum Expedition of the Austrian Alpine Club 1957

The overall leadership of the Austrian Karakorum Expedition of 1957 fell to Marcus Schmuck. Hermann Buhl was the mountaineering leader. Buhl's seven-part report about the preparations and the running of the expedition leading to the first ascent of Broad Peak would be—in conjunction with his diary notes—worthy of a book on its own. For reasons of space we are able to publish only extracts here. We have had to restrict ourselves to the descriptions of the essential phases of the trip. But even this summarized version is a pleasure for the reader. It is apparent that the language of the man—who is now 32 years old—has gained in strength. How intensely he has worked on himself and on the idea of mountaineering!

HERMANN BUHL'S REPORT
(Extracts)

8 APRIL 1957, RAWALPINDI

Before success, the gods made sweat and toil. I would much prefer now to be sitting outside in the fresh air, following the colorful comings and goings of the locals, listening to the birds singing or the palms rustling, or enjoying the splendid colorful array of the varied flora. Instead of which I am sitting in a dark room and hammering out impressions on my typewriter. At first I found it very hard to create some kind of order from the chaos of the last days and weeks. Unpleasant experiences merge together with pleasant ones, disappointments interchange with surprises. Shouting jubilantly to the high heavens, then worried half to death—this was how we were tossed around from one mood to another. And that was merely with the idea of it all. We wanted to go to the Himalaya! When I saw Nanga Parbat for the last time, I secretly hoped that I would be allowed to see this mountain once more. The idea would not let go of me. I drew up the plan for a Karakorum Expedition—Mustagh Tower—but the French and the English beat me to it. They were faster! Or were they better organizers?. . .

Then I wanted to go to Broad Peak. I had been able to see the Karakorum so well from Nanga Parbat. Yet this idea had for the moment receded again, as my best friends [the Vigl brothers] were

This Broad Peak photo taken by Günther Oskar Dyhrenfurth was used by the Karakorum Expedition of the Austrian Alpine Club in 1957 as a postcard. (The three high camps are marked I, II and III).

unable to take part for professional reasons. Then I thought of Marcus Schmuck. He had not yet had any Himalayan experience, but he was a brilliant organizer and a first-rate mountaineer. . . . Fritz Wintersteller, one of Marcus' friends, and Kurt Diemberger—still remarkably young for this kind of undertaking, yet he had already made a name for himself as an ice-climber—were the other participants. Thus the team had been decided and each of us had his area of responsibility. . . .

My connections from the Nanga Parbat expedition were of course very helpful for this trip. Yet all the preparatory work had dimensions that, in all honesty, became too much for me, for whenever resistance surfaced, I was obliged to jump in and sort things out. Thus my correspondence alone numbered over a thousand letters. I was pleasantly surprised at the cooperation that was shown to me again and again. The most unpleasant thing about the preparations was the time pressure. Because of the Suez crisis all the equipment not only had to be prepared during a timespan of three months, but also loaded onto the ship within that time. [The sea voyage to Karachi lasted considerably longer due to the enforced diversion around the continent of Africa.] As usual, reporters often asked me about my preparation. In answer to this I could only say that my training this time consists of sitting night after night—often until 2 in the morning—at my typewriter writing to firms. Or driving around in a car like a madman from one corner of Austria or Bavaria to the other, in order to address people personally. But it was successful!

Then, however, the heavens did seem to cloud over. We were not to receive permission to climb Broad Peak [solely that for Masherbrum]. That meant missing out on an eight-thousander. I did not consider this to be too tragic, and thought to myself that although Masherbrum was 200 m lower, it would possibly be more interesting from a mountaineering point of view. But these 200 meters had far-reaching consequences: they caused the finances to be brought into question. What on earth could be done in order to reach that magical figure of 8000?

Then it came to me. At the time of the Nanga Parbat climb I had received a gold medal from the Pakistani governor, the first such award in the country. Would this perhaps be able to help us out of our predicament? Perhaps we would be granted an audience with the Pakistani premier. Perhaps our envoy—who was already working like a Trojan—would be able to manage it? And indeed he actually did manage it! . . .

A few days later all the equipment, a total weight of 1000 kilograms, was loaded onto the *Asia,* accompanied by Diemberger and Wintersteller. . . . They had survived the race; we had to keep it up for another four weeks in order to find the remaining funding and sort out equipment, arrangements with newspapers, etc. My plans for a joint skiing holiday with my wife that I had wanted to do for the sake of both of our healths, were shelved. . . . In any case, on 29 March 1957 I was standing at Munich-Riem airport with a plane ticket for Karachi in my pocket, in order to say a brief hello to Marcus on his stopover and to inform him that we would meet in Rome the next day. I still had important purchases to take care of.

A day later, at almost the same time, I was standing at the airport again, this time with my wife, my daughter Kriemhild, and a few good friends and acquaintances. Things were beginning to get serious! . . .

25 MAY, BASE CAMP GODWIN-AUSTEN GLACIER
about 4900 m
First reconnaissance

For fourteen days now our Base Camp has been standing at the foot of the West Spur of Broad Peak, which, with its three summits, counts as one of the last eight-thousanders as yet unclimbed. . . . There are only the five of us left: Marcus, Fritz, Kurt, and I as well as our accompanying officer [Quader Saeed], who has proved to be a really good and useful fellow. The porters have gone and our two post runners, who left us with letters two weeks ago, still have not returned from their long journey. . . .

We had recruited about 80 porters. . . . Liligo, the first camp site situated behind the snout of the Baltoro Glacier, was reached in a pleasant mood, but on the next day new snow was already making progress more difficult.

In Urdokas, the critical point of the whole operation, everything seemed to be going well and without any porters' strikes. Yet the following day the porters suddenly—as if they had come up with the idea overnight—demanded snow goggles. We had only 25 pairs with us so we were unable to provide them for everyone. After that we wanted to arrange a shuttle system with 25 porters, but they would not agree to that. After a lot of to-ing and fro-ing we paid three rupees compensation to those who had not been given goggles, and the others got their snow glasses. We were surprised to see that,

"Above me Hermann is already addressing himself to the precipice. He is already tackling a difficult crack pitch. 'It's much easier off to the side!' I shout to him. But Hermann is already up it. I am amazed: Yes, this is the famous Hermann Buhl. . . ."

Kurt Diemberger

following this, everyone was wearing glasses of some sort, the majority of which were of Italian or German origin. After a considerable delay we set off again. . . .

One evening the sky was really clear, and the distinctive ice cover of Masherbrum shone down unrealistically high and bold over us. . . . I weighed up in detail the Baltoro side of this mountain, that even experts consider to be almost hopeless. I must honestly confess that this mountain absolutely fascinated me and I would have liked more than anything to climb it right there and then. . . .

The porters' monotonous "Schabasch," meaning that they were at rest, droned on behind us. We had left Udokas three days ago and were on a one-day walk to Concordia. . . . There the tension that had been weighing down on the expedition because of the bad weather and conditions suddenly erupted. The porters unilaterally declared that this was to be our Base Camp. They maintained that Base Camp was always set up three days after leaving Udokas, and that since they had now been on the move for three days, this was where Base Camp had to be. Yet they did not take into account the fact that the stages we had completed each day were not representative of the usual daily stages.

We tried to maintain a small group of porters by offering better conditions and thus arrived at the 24 who were prepared to carry on. . . . We had to reach the foot of Broad Peak. Concordia remained on our right; I turned left to the Godwin-Austen Glacier and at three in the afternoon had reached a little moraine valley with large boulders. Here we would wait for the porters.

A good hour later they arrived cursing and swearing about the length of this section and we kept hearing the word "Askole." So they, too, wanted to abandon us the next day and return to Askole even though two-thirds of the loads were 15 km away and the usual place for Base Camp was still 10 km distant.

We tried really hard to cheer up the porters again. Four hours we spent with them, in driving snow in sub-zero temperatures. We constantly made them tea, built them a shelter for the night and even gave them some of our meager rations, but the next day they disappeared without a word. We let them go. There were still about 40 loads that needed to be carried up to Base Camp. Toward evening a figure slowly approached our campsite. It was Kurt. He said that Marcus and two porters were behind him. All the others had cleared off and gone back to Askole. . . . Now we knew what we were up against, and that made us even more determined.

The next day Fritz and I went off to look for a site to establish a proper Base Camp. Kurt and Marcus hurried back, and in the evening, five heavily laden men [the two climbers, the two porters and the liaison officer] came up from below.

The following day saw all seven sauntering off down the valley and, each of us loaded up with weights of 30 kg and over, climbing back up the same way again. . . . One evening—Friday, 10 May—a wonderful Base Camp has been set up in a moraine hollow. A boulder, protected by a tent roof, serves as a cooking area. Linked with roofs of blue, orange, and green, the tents stand in a row next to each other. And just next to them the ice masses of the Godwin-Austen Glacier roll onwards to Concordia.

We appear to be ready.

But the weather is bad. The snowstorm is sweeping around our tents, driving the airborne snow into each and every little furrow and crevice.

Days like this are hopeless. You hardly dare to creep out of your sleeping bag. You try to eat but even in the cooking area the gale force wind is whistling around. You creep back into the tent and write or read a little, formulate plans. Or you take your guitar in hand and sing.

A few days later we climb up to the Godwin-Austen Glacier and steer a course toward the foot of our spur. High up on the left is an enormous overhanging glacier. It looks too threatening to me. I do not feel like moving around beneath it. Thus we take a line up a steep snow slope on the right of a separating spur, on top of which lies the hard-packed snow of an old avalanche. We easily gain height here. . . .

At about 5800 meters we have reached a small projecting ridge that rises out of the equally steep flank. It is the only suitable camp site far and wide. We have had enough for today. We are all flagging a bit after 900 meters of load-carrying and trail-breaking. Descending is easy. You just sit on the seat of your pants and half an hour later you reach the Godwin-Austen Glacier again. . . . The best moment is always when we reach Base Camp and our Captain presses a cup of hot tea into our hands, and immediately after that calls to tell us dinner is ready. . . .

It takes us three hours to do the stretch from Camp 1 to Camp 2, three hours for a height gain of 600 meters. . . . We enjoy the atmosphere and the warmth, and look over to K2, down to the glacier that stretches out like a river, across to neighboring summits in the west

Setting off for the Baltoro Glacier. Three days after leaving Urdokas the porters decided to strike. Some 24 remained with the expedition for one more day, after which the four mountaineers, the liaison officer and the two remaining porters had to drag the remaining 40 loads to Base Camp.

where storms are breaking, and up to the dark rocks of the summit area of Broad Peak, the focus of our desires. Fritz prepares a delicious meal of potato pancakes and tea, but at the same time he makes so much that we are hardly able to move afterward. We had intended to go for an evening stroll, up to the plateau and on to the so-called "Knee" above the clean-swept ice flank.

On the plateau a cold wind is whistling. On the far side, somewhat lower down, is Camp 3 from the 1954 Herrligkoffer expedition, the first attempt on Broad Peak. Now the two routes continue jointly [as far as the 7000 m point, where the earlier expedition turned back]. . . . Soon we make a pleasant discovery. "There are ropes hanging here," I call to Fritz, "loads of them." Yet then they disappear into the snow and beneath the ice covering. We climb for a good hundred meters over the plateau and suddenly come upon a frozen scrap of material at a little knob of rock. We dig down and find a tent with provisions and rope supplies from the earlier expedition. . . .

Today [25 May 1957] the preparations are made for a serious attempt. . . . In the afternoon Marcus makes a pleasing discovery. Far away we can see two dots coming towards us over the Godwin-Austen Glacier. It can only be our two porters with the mail. We are already looking forward to it, but our disappointment is huge. There is no post from home for any of us.

We quickly see to the mail so that the runners can be on their way again. During this time the weather gets better and better, the atmosphere calmer and calmer, until a harmonious evening sweeps over this positively arctic highland scenery and, one by one, we all disappear into our tents. . . .

My dear Generl,

As the mail runners are leaving Base Camp again tomorrow, I would like to send you this report. We are climbing up tomorrow, and if we are lucky we will be able to tell you of our successful summit bid in the next report. Apart from that we are all in good form, if a little wild-looking with proper beards. We feel well. Sometimes all the snow gets on our nerves. There isn't even a small patch of green to be seen, so our thoughts often wander homeward, where it is now spring and where we could go skiing or even climbing in shorts and enjoy the warmth.

Darling Generl, the post takes a particularly long time to get to us here. We have not heard anything from you yet. But everything has to sort itself out first.

Herman Buhl fixing ropes between Camp 2 and Camp 3. The 1957 Expedition incorporated the ropes of the 1954 Broad Peak Expedition, found under the ice, in its own fixed rope constructions. © Kurt Diemberger

And take heart, everything will work out again and then seeing each other again will be so much more beautiful! . . . Say a big hello to everyone at home for me, especially the children, Mama and Franzl. Lots of love and kisses to you and the children,

Your loving Hermann and Papi!

Hermann Buhl's sixth report, entitled "A bold push," describes the summit attempt between 26 and 31 May 1957. On the evening of 28 May, in Camp 3, Buhl writes, "I must confess, I do not sense the same excitement, enthusiasm or anticipation as in the days leading up to my route to the summit of Nanga Parbat."

At 6 a.m. on 29 May they leave the camp and head for the summit ridge: ". . . Initially an endlessly long, interminably tedious steep slope. I've got no energy left. I have over-exerted myself during the past few days. Or is it hunger? I did not have enough breakfast and am very sensitive in this respect. Fritz is in top form and for the most part it is he who breaks trail. The last 100 m to the gap is a steep ice slope. I am amazed at how safely Fritz masters it and still manages to cut steps. He is also very confident on the rocks that follow and is at last standing at the gap, perhaps 7900 meters high. To be honest, today I do not really have the desire to carry on or to stand on the summit. . . ."

However, Buhl does force himself to climb up to the gap, where Marcus Schmuck is waiting for him, while Fritz Wintersteller and Kurt Diemberger have already set off up the summit ridge. "Tired, I drag myself along behind Marcus. 50 m higher Fritz and Kurt are working their way over a very steep snow slope. . . . Marcus and I are at about the same height as the middle summit, about 8000 m, as Fritz and Kurt . . . reach a point that from our perspective appears to be the summit. It is six in the evening. I call and tell them to come down immediately. Otherwise it will be night. We have not even set up for a bivouac, as we have left the rucksacks below the gap. But they follow the advice and we hurry to get out of the difficulties and down from the gap."

Due to bad visibility—fog is drawing in and it has started to snow—we are not sure whether Fritz Wintersteller and Kurt Diemberger did actually reach the highest point of Broad Peak on that 29 May 1957. Because of this uncertainty the four mountaineers leave equipment and provisions in the high-camp tents in order to make a further summit bid after a few days recuperation at Base Camp.

Hermann Buhl sorting out the post at Broad Peak Base Camp in 1957. © Kurt Diemberger

A SECOND ATTEMPT—AND SUCCESS
1 JUNE, BASE CAMP

We are not in bad shape. But Kurt still has to hold a surgery, when everyone comes to him with his little ailments. Fingertips, nose, split lips; my and Marcus' toes have been affected a bit by the bitter frost. For me it's my "Nanga Parbat toes" again, but it is not too bad, they just feel a little bit woolly.

In the evening before we go to sleep, we tune our little travel radio into the frequency for Karachi and are able, as we did yesterday, to enjoy two wonderful hours of European music: Kurt Edelhagen's orchestra, Puccini, Léhar, and many others. We almost feel as if we are at home.

8 JUNE 1957, CAMP 3

Everything has been well prepared for the morning. Our breakfast, a kind of porridge, is kept in one Thermos flask and there are two other flasks containing tea. Two plastic bottles filled with tea for use en route are stashed in our sleeping bags so they do not contain lumps of ice in the morning. . . .

"When do we set off tomorrow?" Marcus calls over. "At daybreak; or we can go earlier, there's a good moon tonight!" I call back. "Yes, fine, how about 3:30, OK? Don't anyone dare set off any earlier without me!" comes the call from a neighboring tent. "OK, I'll get up at 2 then," I add, then everyone tries to get to sleep.

I have to get up once in the night. The moon is really bright, you can see almost as well as in daylight. The moon is waxing. Icy cold, the many formidable mountains stand in a circle around us. I would like best of all to set off right now. I know how essential time reserves can be. "Marcus," I call cautiously into the neighboring tent, "Marcus, it's really light, do you think we should go now?" But there is no reply. He doesn't feel like it. So I try to get back to sleep.

9 JUNE 1957, WHITSUNDAY

I wake up again at one and look at my watch every quarter of an hour. At 2 a.m. the cold is really noticeable. Everything is silent, nothing is moving. I wait until 2:30, but then it is high time to move. It takes a whole box of storm matches until I finally get a candle to light, and by that time I've almost suffocated in the tent and am having a coughing fit, and tear open the tent entrance as quickly as possible.

Outside it is now dark; the moon has disappeared. It is awkward getting dressed in the little tent. Above all it takes a lot of effort to get your trousers tucked into your boots. Then the overtrousers, gaiters, two jumpers, an anorak, and then finally you are in a position to have breakfast. We have to wait a bit until the others are finished with their share of the porridge, then it's our turn. It is all still wonderfully warm and tastes delicious.

Meanwhile, Marcus has already left the tent and Fritz follows straight after him. We finish eating and then at 3:30 as agreed, we, too, set off. As we shut the tent we cast a final glance at the thermometer—minus 20 degrees. For the time being we are warm; just our hands are cold in spite of the thick leather and wool gloves. Stupidly I left them outside the sleeping bag overnight. . . .

Above the rock boulders of Camp 3 we can see Marcus' and Fritz's dark silhouettes. Actually I am a bit annoyed; we had agreed to set off together. But Marcus and Fritz always do it like that. They never wait and just set off ahead. Normally that doesn't matter, but at 7000 m and more, it is difficult enough to make up the time difference even when it is only a quarter of an hour.

The conditions are similar to the previous time, and while we climb in a rhythm of two breaths per step the day slowly dawns over the mountain summit. The sun coats the highest summits in a golden armor. My hands are icy cold, but in contrast my feet have not yet begun to feel the cold.

Then the snow gets deeper. It is light powder and wind-blown drifted snow. It takes us hours to catch up with Fritz and Marcus, and take over the trail-breaking from them. Meanwhile my feet have gone icy cold, but I do not take time to massage them and continue—one, two, one, two—in order not to lose the rhythm. . . .

Sometimes the snow is quite hard and we make good progress, then we sink in again up to our knees. But if you closely examine the surface of the snow you can recognize the hard slabs. From time to time Kurt takes over from me and we make quite good progress. Another steep slope, a traverse, then we step out into the bright sunlight.

It is gone eight o'clock. High time I took my boots off. My feet are completely numb again. It has got colder too; I imagine the temperature must have dropped to about minus 30 degrees. . . . Each of us works on his feet in the warmth of the sun in order to bring them back to life. My right foot is suffering the most; the cold has not affected my left foot at all. After about half an hour our feet have thawed out again and we rub them with cream to protect them from the frost. Then we have a little something to eat.

"My dears!

On Whitsunday my entire team was able to reach the summit of Broad Peak. We have now reached Base Camp again safely. I stood on the summit at sunset; it was a wonderful feeling.

All my love
Your Hermann"

Hermann Buhl in the gap between the middle and the subsidiary summits of Broad Peak. The Main Summit can be seen immediately next to Buhl on the right. © Kurt Diemberger

Marcus and Fritz are ready to set off again and continue to prepare the track, while Kurt and I sit barefoot in the sun massaging our toes. Then we too have to set off again. This time it is considerably easier than the last time, although my body gradually feels overcome by a heavy tiredness. Is it the cold that has such an negative effect?

We reach the steep ice slope again and Kurt suggests I should leave my rucksack at the bottom like Marcus. But I'm not really bothered about that. It is good to take hold of the fixed rope on the last 30 rocky meters up to the gap, and at 1:30 p.m. we reach the gap between the middle and the main summit.

My altimeter registers 7800 m exactly. I am overcome by a tiredness that would be known as midday tiredness in normal regions. I lie down and would dearly love to go to sleep but Kurt passes me all sort of things to eat from the rucksack. Sweets, dried fruit, hazelnuts, but none of it tastes any good and I have to force myself to get something down. Not even a swig from the flask tastes any good. Fritz and Marcus are still ahead and have already set off up the ridge. . . .

Kurt and I set off at half past two. Kurt is having a good day today. He goes ahead, and I am not unhappy about letting him "tow" me, as they say at home in cycling circles. . . . By 5 we have reached a projection on the ridge beneath the subsidiary summit. "Hermann, do you mind if I go ahead a little faster, or else I won't make it to the summit?" Kurt asks me. I agree that in this condition I am a burden to him, and I've got nothing against it. He, the young tiger, will not sacrifice an eight-thousander on my account. I must admit honestly that all my ambition has deserted me. My eight-thousander is Nanga Parbat, and what I experienced there could never be repeated anyway. I sit down intending to wait until the others return from the summit. Fritz and Marcus have just reached their goal. Two little dots on a slim *firn* edge. My feet are really getting the better of me; they are already numb again.

Just by chance I happen to notice how quickly Kurt is getting up the last rise leading up to the subsidiary summit. This spurs me on again and, after all, so I think to myself, we did—the whole team—all want to stand on the summit. It is already late. Past five o'clock; will there be enough time to do it? I'll give it a go. After all we have a good companion this time, the moon.

On the subsidiary summit Fritz and Marcus come towards me. When I ask how far it is to go to the summit, they tell me a good hour. But we are all past the stage of being able to talk very much. "I'll try to

On the summit of Broad Peak (8047 m). In the center left is the subsidiary summit, on the right the middle summit. In the background left is K2, the second highest mountain on earth. © Kurt Diemberger

get as far as I can," I say and continue. A few short, hard upward pulls, then comes the long traverse over the horizontal ridge up to the main summit. Now in the evening hours it is better and I get along much faster. Half-way up I meet Kurt who is just returning from the summit. When I tell him that I still want to go up he walks with me.

The sun is setting slowly on the horizon; there are already black shadows on the glaciers. To the north one can see as far as Sinkiang, a mountain landscape with brown patches bordering directly onto white snowfields. The northern Gasherbrum glacier stretches out down in the depths. I hurry in order to reach the summit before the sun finally sets, and step out strongly. I am amazed at how easy I am now finding it, and at 7 in the evening—it is Whitsunday—we are standing on the Summit of Broad Peak (8047 m), more than 3000 m above the Godwin-Austen Glacier.

It is a solemn moment. The sun is glowing red and hanging just above the horizon. Chogolisa, Gasherbrum IV, and K2 are lit up in the dying light, and from minute to minute the dark shadows wander higher and higher, gradually extinguishing the light over the surrounding summits. As this happens the really high ones begin to burn; the whole horizon has turned red. Gasherbrum IV and Chogolisa are no longer white, they are positively glowing. Finally they too are extinguished and only our summit remains floodlit by the sunlight. . . .

It is half past seven and as we follow the ridge to the subsidiary summit, the last shimmer of the dying day lights up the snow surfaces. Dusk greets us on the subsidiary summit, but by then the

"Dear Hermann,

I congratulate to you and your team on your success and best wishes for the next couple of eight-thousanders!!! . . . Wishing you lots more luck until we next meet.

Yours,
Hias Rebitsch"

Herman Buhl, his features marked by the exertion of climbing Broad Peak, which he achieved thanks only to his enormous strength of will. © Kurt Diemberger (From *The Endless Knot—K2, Mountain of Dreams and Destiny,* 1991)

moon is already lighting the way down for us—except when it disappears behind the subsidiary summit or the steep ridge. On the steep sections and in places where the ridge is interrupted by rocks, we belay ourselves with the rope. Then from the gap it is down the steep ice flank, using a few ropes which have been tied together, and finally we are standing on the snow.

The descent in the brittle *harsch* snow is a painstaking one, and in spite of the moonlight we have to be very careful not to take a wrong step. Concordia is shining silver and the Biarchedi Glacier flowing down to the Baltoro looks like tinsel. Our eyes search desperately for the boulders and tents that we must surely reach soon. Our feet carry our bodies very reluctantly now, and our bones are hurting. At long last the first boulder and the outlines of the tents. It is past midnight when we fasten the tents behind us. We do not eat or drink; we just want to rest and get straight into our sleeping bags. Again, just like the last time, we fall into a deathlike slumber. . . .

Broad Peak has been climbed, and by the most idealistic, shortest route. Without high porters, by all four participants, what more could we ask for? We can allow ourselves to feel pleased and that we do. And in order to make our happiness complete, the next day the mail runners arrive with a bundle of post for each of us from back home. Each of us retires and hides his bearded face behind a letter.

It is already summer at home, but here it is still "winter." Suddenly we notice how icy the surroundings are, even if water is now flowing. The ice needles of the Godwin-Austen Glacier are still there, our tents are still standing on snow, and where there is no snow, there are stones and boulders but no greenery. So you really look forward to seeing the first green and imagine how you will spend your days. Swimming, sunbathing, enjoying yourself, and then a little bit of climbing too. That is how it has to be.

The Death—
the Myth Lives On...

14 JUNE 1957, BASE CAMP

An extract from Hermann Buhl's last letter home:

... maybe you could sort something out with Luis, that he drives you down to the "boot" of southern Italy, to Brindisi or further down, then it wouldn't be too far to fly over or take the boat across. I think Cairo would certainly interest him, too. That's my suggestion. Then the whole thing would not be so expensive. . . . I definitely want to make a stopover in Cairo this time and meet you somewhere there. . . . Kriemhild could easily stay with her granny in Ramsau and Silvia could go with Ingrid to the same place she went last year. I am sure they would be happy to take them for one or two weeks. Then you'd have a break too and it would be a nice end to the expedition for me. . . .

If Ingrid really has started walking now I can well imagine what's going on; she is going to be the same little bundle of energy as Silvia and Kriemhild. I'm really looking forward to seeing the three of them. Three little tots waiting for me!

Between 17 and 19 June 1957, Kurt Diemberger and Hermann Buhl clear Camps 2 and 3 on Broad Peak. On their return to Base Camp they learn from Quader Saeed that Marcus Schmuck and Fritz Wintersteller have already left (on 17 June) for a three- to four-day trip to the Savoia Glacier region.

20 JUNE, BASE CAMP

During the night Kurt wakes me with a mug of tea and says he is leaving for Chogolisa at midday. At 9 o'clock Marcus and Fritz return. Apparently they had got to over 7400 m on Savoia Peak.

Fritz wants to know where Kurt is going. Quader had already told Fritz that morning that it was not right to leave us to clear the camps, while they went off climbing without our knowledge—to a mountain we had always talked about climbing together.

At 5 o'clock in the morning of 21 June 1957, Hermann Buhl followed Kurt Diemberger (who had set off the previous day), across the Upper Baltoro Glacier. "In the evening we had discovered a splendid site for a Base Camp, on the lateral moraines close to the huge ice-falls of Chogolisa, and pitched the tent. Above us soared the

"With (the death of) Hermann Buhl another star in the mountaineering firmament was extinguished, such as have burned so brightly throughout all the epochs of mountaineering. . . . They are the sleepwalkers treading the boundaries of the possible, the obsessive mountaineers who are gifted and decisive enough to dare again and again to reach for the holds beyond the highpoints which have thus far been achieved."

Fritz Schmitt

monstrous roof of Chogolisa—nothing but ice and snow as far as the eye could see. It was still a long way to the top, but Hermann thought it was possible to climb the mountain in three days. . . . " (Diemberger)

On 22 June the two men make a reconnaissance of the mountain to an altitude of 5500 m. The following morning the weather is bad. Rest day. In the early hours of 24 June, Buhl and Diemberger begin their ascent. Both of them are in exceptionally good shape; carrying heavy rucksacks, they climb until evening. Hermann breaks trail for the whole of the five-kilometer stretch to the Kaberi Col (6360 m).

On 25 June, despite knee-deep powder snow, the two climbers carry their "portable high camp" (Diemberger) up to a little shoulder on the South East Ridge at 6700 m. On 26 June a savage snow storm rages. Buhl and Diemberger sit it out, tentbound. In the evening the weather clears and they gear up for the summit.

Diemberger recounts: "Then comes the 27th of June. The weather is splendid. . . . We are full of joy and make swift upward progress. It may be about 7 o'clock as we reach the top of the ridge. We are now over seven thousand meters high and before us lies the main summit, seemingly improbably close. But before we can tackle it we have to descend the heavily corniced summit ridge to get to a notch at 7000 meters—the hardest part. Thanks to Hermann, who leads the difficult traverse at an amazing pace and with his customary technique and skill, we are soon afterward standing in the notch on the ridge. We laugh; it is 9 o'clock in the morning, the most difficult half of the route lies behind us, while up ahead just 650 meters of easy scrambling lead to the summit . . . ! For all our optimism we had never expected this. We could be up there by midday!"

The South East Ridge of Chogolisa. Buhl and Diemberger pitched their tent at 6700 m as a top camp for their summit bid. To the right of this point is the top of the ridge (7150 m). The 7300-meter mark is the point at which the two climbers turned back. At about 7200 m the cornice collapsed beneath Hermann Buhl. © Kurt Diemberger

One of the last photos of Hermann Buhl. To the left is K2, with Broad Peak to the right. © Kurt Diemberger

THE LAST TRACKS IN THE SNOW

Buhl and Diemberger untie from the rope, rest, eat, and drink. The sun burns down, the sky is blue and Hermann says that for him this is the finest day of this expedition. When the pair starts climbing again, Buhl carries the rope.

Suddenly clouds begin to close in from the south. At an altitude of between 7200 and 7300 meters the two climbers are fogged in, and a little later (Diemberger continues)

"... there is the most savage wind one could imagine. Taking turns to break trail we battle on higher and higher. Visibility becomes worse and worse. At the 7300-meter mark, Hermann turns round and shouts that we ought to turn back immediately; the wind is blowing away our tracks behind us, and with visibility like this we could easily stray out onto the cornices. He is right; we never even thought of that. Hermann had been leading the last bit, so I am in the lead on the descent. Due to the avalanche danger we maintain a distance of 10 to 15 meters from each other.

"Although the only thing we can still see of our tracks are the holes made by our axes—and even these become ever more seldom—we get down to around 7200 meters all right. Then suddenly—shortly beforehand I had discovered a hole in the snow made by an ice axe—the snow surface starts vibrating. It is like a hammer blow and for a moment I have the feeling that the ground is sinking away beneath me. Horrified, I leap to the right onto the steep slope and go down about another 10 or 15 meters,

"Hermann Buhl is missing, yet he remains alive through the great mountains, through his stories, through his friends—and even more so through his desire to push himself to the last."

Reinhold Messner

Hermann Buhl on the traverse of the summit ridge on Chogolisa. At this point Buhl and Diemberger were still roped up. At the gap beyond the top of the ridge they untied from the rope and Hermann Buhl put it in his rucksack. The arrow marks the point at which the cornice broke under Buhl's weight as he stepped on it. © Kurt Diemberger (From *The Kurt Diemburger Omnibus,* 1999)

all the while with the image in my head of the curled lip of the cornice and the little pieces detaching themselves from it.

"Why, oh why?

"I turn to face Hermann, but behind me there is a little hump that I cannot see over. When Hermann does not arrive I suddenly get this eerie feeling and gasp my way back up the slope. . . . Hermann has disappeared. Then I see his tracks; they lead right to the edge of a fresh break in the cornice. Hermann . . . fallen to his death?

"Somehow I get myself back down to the gap and from there climb back up to the top of the ridge. From here I must surely have a view over onto the North Face, if the weather clears. It clears. Not for long, but now I can see with a terrible clarity that up there, Hermann, about ten, fifteen meters behind me, has strayed off my tracks where they bend round a little and has carried on walking straight on—right out onto the lip of the cornice. And then—after a fall of at least 300, probably 500 meters . . . somewhere down there, under the extensive mass of snow debris of an avalanche, Hermann now lies."

Kurt Diemberger fights his way back down the ridge, bivouacs at 5500 meters and then drags himself down into the Broad Peak Base Camp. Straight away, Marcus Schmuck and Fritz Wintersteller set off with Diemberger on a search attempt. It is in vain. On 30 June 1957 they report back to a snowblind Kurt, who has remained behind at the foot of Chogolisa, that—from a height of 5700 meters— despite the good Zeiss binoculars, they discovered nothing and were able to establish only that further avalanches had thundered down into the big cwm below the snow flank. "To climb up into the cwm below the flank would, however, be impossible due to the avalanche danger." (Diemberger)

The expedition leaves the Baltoro region, returns to Skardu and finally goes home. Without Buhl.

In 1958 the first ascent of Chogolisa is made by the Japanese climbers M. Fujihira and K. Hirai (the expedition leader is Takio Kuwabara). They find Buhl's and Diemberger's tent and salvage Buhl's last diary, then entrust it to the care of Walter Bonatti who, together with Carlo Mauri, has just climbed Gasherbrum IV. It finds its way back, via Kurt Diemberger, to Generl Buhl. One of the last entries reads as follows:

"24 June: . . . Set off at 3:30 with tent, etc. Light snowfall; weather nothing special; in good shape; 7:30 at 5500 m depot. With gear from depot—rucksack approx. 25 kg weight—on over spur in knee-deep snow; broke trail to Kaberi Saddle; established camp at 6360 m about 5 pm; marked everything with flags."

Diemberger comments, "For all those who had imagined a weak Hermann Buhl on Chogolisa, these facts . . . speak a clear language. His days on Chogolisa brought true fulfillment for him once again. Unlike the closing phases of the Broad Peak expedition, he again felt like the Hermann Buhl of old."

Yes, this was the Buhl of old; the young, 32-year-old, top-class mountaineer. Had he survived he would have continued to influence the sport of mountaineering right up to the present day.

"With his ascent of Broad Peak Hermann Buhl has shown the young climbers a new way—they will follow it. The example of Hermann Buhl, it will remain."

Kurt Diemberger

Appendices

Appendix One
The "Original" Hermann Buhl

In this book by and about Buhl, we have tried (almost) exclusively to publish Hermann Buhl's original texts. We have not included chapters from *Nanga Parbat Pilgrimage* or chapters from the so-called new editions of this alpine bestseller, not even when we are dealing with descriptions of one or another of Buhl's most significant climbs and expeditions. If, however, sentences in the "original" Buhl—his diaries, journals, essays, and articles—are identical to those in Kurt Maix's "edited" version found in *Nanga Parbat . . .*, then that is because Maix—to his credit—left countless parts of the original manuscript as they were.

Even though it has been said again and again that Hermann Buhl wrote his book entirely on his own, with Kurt Maix serving solely as his editor, this is not true. Nevertheless it *is* true that Hermann wrote the *original* text for *Nanga Parbat Pilgrimage* himself, often writing into the small hours, and then the next morning reading to his "Generl" the text that he had spent many "lonely hours in front of the typewriter" producing. We regret that Buhl's original manuscript has been lost. It is a real tragedy that this document is no longer available.

How much "Maix" there is in the first Buhl book becomes clear, however, in the chapter "Straight on up—The Laliderer Wall," for example. Reading this text, you would think that these are serious, educated men at work, and not two top young climbers from North Tyrol: "On the easily recognizable, white scored slabs of the Gully Traverse we could just make out two tiny dots—a party climbing. What an undertaking, to pit oneself against Nature just in the very place where she is at her most savage! The other climbers move on like ridiculous little toys, and yet they were human beings—possessed by the same inner urge as ourselves. And if a layman were to ask them what they were doing, they would give the answer Norman-Neruda gave half a century ago: 'Because we like it!'"

Could it be that Kurt Maix liked to read a little of himself in his Buhl?

When he did the Laliderer Direct, Hermann Buhl was an up-and-coming 22-year-old—someone who wanted to climb the wall and then leave the summit to go off with his friend Luis Vigl to a stag night on the Hallerangeralm. And early the next morning Luis had

Kurt Maix, center; Generl Buhl, left; Luis Vigl, right. Maix not only edited Nanga Parbat Pilgrimage but also rewrote some parts and added completely new chapters not included in Hermann Buhl's original manuscript.

"I met Hermann Buhl in Oberreintal. He introduced a new style there: climbing several routes in one day. Those were routes such as Gelbes U., Schobergrat, and the North Face of the Lower-Schüsselkar Tower."

Hermann Huber

to go to early Mass in Hall because he felt a duty toward his mother. We do not seriously think that, in his wild climbing years, Buhl would think of Norman-Neruda, the Swedish-born rock climber of the previous century.

Another example: in the *Nanga Parbat Pilgrimage* chapter "A Lesson from Death," the facts simply do not add up. The entry in Buhl's climbing diary about "Scharnitzspitze—South West Wall" says that Hermann Buhl and Sepp Fuchs formed one party and Herbert Eberharter and Herta Maier the other, and that Franz Hermann—who Buhl knew, and who the other three probably knew as well—had fallen 250 meters to his death. In *Nanga Parbat Pilgrimage* it says that Herbert Eberharter and Ferry Theyermann were planning to do the "Direct" and that Sepp Fuchs and Hermann Buhl would do the Kadner Route. The text gives the impression that Buhl and Fuchs did not know the solo climber: "Odd to see a man on his own, up here. We wondered what he wanted . . . at that moment a mop of hair appeared below us in the chimney. Could it be another party? But we immediately recognized the solitary climber, who had approached the foot of the climb in such hesitating fashion. . . . He climbed past us and went up more quickly than we, being alone. Soon he was out of sight."

One last example: the first attempt at the South West Face of the Marmolata in winter. Hermann Buhl writes about this in a letter to Walther Flaig:

> "After I had climbed up a rope length into the gully, we discussed what we had to do. Kuno could see what the weather was doing much better from where he was, and he advised me to turn back. I would have loved so much to carry on climbing up the gully; I was really tempted by the route that opened out ahead of me. Yet the gully overhanging us was unsettling. So I abseiled down to Kuno, leaving behind the pitons I had hammered in. The Rosengarten was by now already covered in heavy cloud; it could even be snowing down there. The mist was swirling about over the Ombretta Pass beneath us. The air was completely hazy, the sky black. I was made to think of the sudden change in weather on the South Face of the Schüsselkar. We could not afford to let ourselves be surprised by the weather up here. The most sensible thing was to get down to the cirque quickly. The last thing we wanted was for the rescue services to have to get us down off the wall, worse still the Italians, given how expensive they are. It was just a pity that we had dragged all the provisions and bivouacking equipment up here. We had to take it down with us again. We suspected the weather really might turn and that we would

not get back again before the summer. So once again we had to deny ourselves this pleasure. I had got used to the disappointments by now. At 17:00 hours we prepared to descend. It had already started snowing lightly. Our surroundings looked like a laundry room. We removed everything apart from the pitons and rope slings. At 20:00 hours, after 300 m of abseiling, we were standing once more on the safe ground of the Ombretta Pass."

In *Nanga Parbat Pilgrimage* the following version is printed:

"The gully pushed me remorselessly outwards. I felt like a spider as I hung with my hands and feet on the same level, maintained there by nothing but friction, in a series of acrobatic exercises, 400 meters above the floor. I reached a small belaying spike and wanted Kuno to come up to me, but he insisted on a withdrawal, pointing to the imminent break in the weather; and he was right. It was essential to get down as quickly as possible . . . over the Pala a massive cloud came rushing at us, driven by a howling gale; in shape and color appropriate to the end of the world. By the time we were ready to go on down, the mists were already creeping over the Ombretta Pass. We joined the two 40-meter ropes, safeguarded ourselves with the belaying rope, and down we went into the depths—sheer acrobatics in space under the Big Top of the sky and with no safety-net below. . . . The gale whipped the ropes out from the rock in a great loop and it began to snow. We were thankful to the core that we had decided to turn back in time. At half past eight, in pitch darkness, we were back at our skis at the morning's starting point."

What a difference, even though the facts tally—the threatening change in weather and the withdrawal that this caused. And what a difference, too, between the version in this new book [using Buhl's original materials] and that in *Nanga Parbat Pilgrimage*.

We could find many examples of how Kurt Maix had not only edited but also in parts re-written or even written from scratch. Maix goes so far as to admit this himself in a letter to Generl Buhl dated 6 December 1958: "I respected those people and mountaineers who were fond of this lovable and sensitive Hermann Buhl. I was proud to be able to edit his work, and I carried out this task carefully without wanting to suppress him. But I removed everything that might be harmful to him and rewrote certain parts. I protected Hermann—from himself and from the evil world—as I

> "I cannot get rid of the feeling that Hermann would like to climb alone for as long as possible, until I ask him for the rope. But under the Great Corner, which is graded a straight V, even he thinks it appropriate that we belay."
>
> Martin Schliessler

had always done. Thus I chose to change whole chapters and even to write some of them anew from my own perspective."

We do not want to diminish the credit due to Kurt Maix for Hermann Buhl's bestseller. Maix and Buhl were friends. It is true that the style of language used by this Viennese journalist, a style of gushing with emotion, was an expression of the times that carried on throughout the fifties, and which people loved to hear and read. But it was not the language of Buhl's inner world. The romanticism and heroism of Maix's language was what he had learned as a reporter with the newspaper *Völkischen Beobachter*. It was not Hermann Buhl's way of thinking. Even when reporting romantic events, Buhl remained objective, almost sober, and never slipped into pathos.

Anyone who hopes to understand Hermann Buhl must therefore read him in the "original"!

Appendix Two
Hermann Buhl's Route List

(Extracts)

1940

Kalkkögel: Nördliche Schlicker Zinne, Steingrubenkogel-West Face (Gipfelstürmerweg), Kleine Ochsenwand West Face (Gipfelstürmerweg).

Karwendel: Grubreisen Südturm South Arête (Auckenthaler Crack), Vorderes Brandjoch South Arête, Kaskarspitze South Arête.

Stubai Alps: Ruderhofspitze, Zuckerhütl.

Wetterstein: Öfelekopf South West Arête, Scharnitzspitze South West Face, Schüsselkarspitze South Face (Spindlerweg).

Wilder Kaiser: Predigtstuhl Main Summit West Face ("Dülfer-Westwandl"), Hintere Goinger Halt North Arête, Fleischbank Herrweg.

Zillertal Alps: Olperer.

1941

Kalkkögel: Kleine Ochsenwand West Face (Gipfelstürmerweg).

Karwendel: Grubreisen South Tower South Arête (Auckenthaler Crack), Vorderes Brandjoch South Arête, Martinswand South Face Crack.

Stubai Alps: Wildes Hinterbergl, Längentaler Weisser Kogel, Lisenser Fernerkogel.

Wetterstein: Scharnitzspitze South Face (Hannemann Route), Scharnitzspitze South West Face.

Wilder Kaiser: Predigtstuhl North Arête, Zettenkaiser East Face.

Zillertal Alps: Traverse of the Hornspitzen, Grosser Möseler Firndreieck, Zsigmondyspitze South West Arête.

1942

Kalkkögel: Riepenwand North West Face, Riepenwand West Face (3rd ascent; Hermann Buhl's first grade VI route), Riepenwand North West Corner (8th ascent), Kleine Ochsenwand, Direct North Buttress, Kleine Ochsenwand West Face (Schmidhuber-Lang Route).

Karwendel: Grubreisen South Tower South Arête (Auckenthaler Crack), Kumpfkarspitze East Face (Frenademetz Route), Laliderer

Spitze North Face (Auckenthaler Route, 7th ascent), Praxmarer-karspitze North Face (Auckenthaler-Schmidhuber Route, 2nd ascent).

Wetterstein: Schüsselkarspitze South Face (Spindler Route, 2nd winter ascent), Schüsselkarspitze South Corner, Schüsselkarspitze South Face (Herzog-Fiechtl Route, 1st solo ascent), Schüsselkarspitze South East Face, Schüsselkarspitze Direct South Face, Schüsselkarspitze East Face, Musterstein South Buttress, Öfelekopf South Buttress.

Wilder Kaiser: Fleischbank South East Face, Fleischbank East Face (Dülfer Route), Predigtstuhl Middle Summit West Corner.

1943

Berchtesgaden Alps: Grosses Mühlsturzhorn, Direct South Arête.
Kalkkögel: Riepenwand, Direct North West Face.
Wilder Kaiser: Maukspitze West Face (1st ascent), Vordere Karlspitze East Face (3rd winter ascent), Fleischbank Dülfer Crack, Fleischbank South East Face, Leuchsturm, Old South Face, Maukspitze Spengler Chimney, Predigtstuhl North Summit West Face (Schüle-Diem Corner), Totenkirchl Westwand (Dülfer Route, probably 1st free ascent).

1944

Kalkkögel: Nordeck North Face (Laichner-Fischer Route), Grosse Ochsenwand, North East Arête Direct ("Kalte Kante," 3rd ascent), Kleine Ochsenwand North Buttress ("Himmel und Erde"), Kleine Ochsenwand North East Face (9th ascent).
Wetterstein: Schüsselkarspitze East Face.
Wilder Kaiser: Predigtstuhl Middle Summit West Face.

1945

Karwendel: Grubreisen South Tower South Arête (Auckenthaler Crack), Grosser Solstein, Old North Face, Kleiner Solstein, Old North Face, Martinswand South Face Crack (2nd solo ascent), Hechenberg, Direct South Face (Auckenthaler Route).
Wetterstein: Schüsselkarspitze-South Face (Herzog-Fiechtl Route), Scharnitzspitze South West Arête.

1946

Dolomites: Grosse Zinne (Cima Grande) North Face.
Karwendel: Laliderer Wand North Face (Schmid-Krebs Route).
Ötztaler Alps: Seekarlesschneid North West Buttress (1st ascent).

Rofan: Rofanturm West Arête (1st ascent).

Stubai Alps: Goldkappl South Face (2nd ascent).

Wetterstein: Oberreintalschrofen South Buttress (1st ascent).

Wilder Kaiser: Totenkirchl West Face (Peters-Eidenschink Route).

1947

Karwendel: Speckkarspitze–North West Corner, Direct West Face ("Buhl-Durchschlag," 1st ascent), Laliderer Spitze, Direct North Face (1st complete ascent), Kleiner Lafatscher North Buttress (2nd ascent), Lamsen Hütten Tower, Direct North Face (1st ascent), Lamsen Hütten Tower North East Arête ("Gelbe Kante" [Yellow Edge], 1st ascent), Rotwandlspitze East Summit, Direct North Face (1st ascent), "Gipfelstürmernadel" South Arête (1st ascent).

Stubai Alps: Schrandele, Schrankogel, Ruderhofspitze, Pflerscher Tribulaun.

Rofan: Rofanspitze East Face (Rebitsch-Spiegl Crack, 2nd ascent), Rofanspitze North West Corner ("Buhl-Roof," 1st ascent), Sagzahn-East Face Roof Groove (1st ascent).

Wilder Kaiser: Predigtstuhl North Summit West Face (Fiechtl-Weinberger Route), Fleischbank East Face (Aschenbrenner-Lucke Route), Fleischbank South East Corner, Bauernpredigtstuhl West Face (Lucke-Strobl Crack).

Zillertal Alps: Hochfeiler North Face, Grosser Möseler North West Face.

1948

Kalkkögel: Nordeck, Direct North East Face (1st solo ascent).

Karwendel: Laliderer Spitze North Arête (1st winter ascent), Grosser Solstein North Buttress (1st solo ascent).

Mont Blanc range: Aiguille de Triolet North Face (5th ascent), Grands Charmoz North Face.

Wetterstein: Oberreintaldom North Face (Schliessler Route, 5th ascent), Unterer Berggeistturm North Arête (2nd ascent), Schüsselkarspitze, Direct South Face (1st winter ascent).

Wilder Kaiser: Fleischbank East Face (Dülfer Route, 1st winter solo ascent), Maukspitze West Face (1st winter ascent).

1949

Dolomites: Rotwand–South West Face (2nd ascent of the Eisenstecken Route), Piz de Ciavázes–South Face (Micheluzzi Route with 1st ascent of the Direct Finish to the "Gamsband"), Furchetta North East Face, Auckenthaler Route (5th ascent), Marmolata South Buttress.

Kalkkögel: Grosse Ochsenwand, Direct North East Arête ("Kalte Kante," 1st winter ascent).

Mont Blanc range: Aiguille Blanche North Face (2nd ascent) and Peuterey Ridge, Aiguille Noire South Arête.

Wetterstein: Oberer Schüsselkarturm North Face (4th ascent).

1950

Bernina range: Piz Bernina (Bianco Ridge, ascent and descent).

Dolomites: Civetta North West Face (Solleder Route), Marmolata South West Face (1st winter ascent), Western Zinne (Cima Ouest) North Face, Tofana di Rozes South Face (Stösser Route), Cima Canali West Face (1st ascent of the "Buhl Crack").

Mont Blanc range: Petit Dru North Face (4th ascent of the "Allain Crack"), Grandes Jorasses North Face ("Walker Spur," 7th ascent), first complete traverse of the Aiguilles de Chamonix.

Ortler range: Königspitze North Face.

Valais Alps: Breithorn North Face (Young Rib), Zinalrothorn East Face (3rd ascent of the Roch Route).

Wilder Kaiser: Fleischbank South East Corner (1st winter ascent).

1951

Berchtesgaden Alps: Grosses Mühlsturzhorn, Direct South Arête (1st winter ascent).

Bernese Alps: Aletschhorn North Face, Finsteraarhorn North East Rib.

Julian Alps: Triglav North Face.

Mont Blanc range: Mont Blanc Brenva Face ("Sentinelle Rouge").

Valais Alps: Dent d'Hérens North Face.

Zillertal Alps: Schrammacher North West Face (1st winter ascent), Fusstein North Arête (1st winter ascent), Sagwand North Buttress.

1952

Bergell: Piz Badile North East Face (1st solo ascent).

Bernese Alps: Eiger North Face (8th ascent).

Brenta: Cima-d'Ambiéz South East Face (Fox-Stenico Route, 1st solo ascent).

Dolomites: Tofana di Rozes South East Buttress ("Pilastro," 4th ascent), Einser North Buttress ("Weg der Jugend"), Zwölfer North Arête (Schranzhofer Route).

Valais Alps: Zinalrothorn, Direct East Face, Dent d'Hérens North Face, Täschhorn-Dom traverse, Weisshorn Schalli Ridge.

Wetterstein: Schüsselkarspitze South Corner (solo).

1953

Berchtesgaden Alps: Watzmann East Face, Salzburger Route (1st winter solo ascent).

Dauphine: Meije traverse.

Karwendel: Steinkar integrale (1st winter ascent).

Stubai Alps: Pflerscher Tribulaun South Face (2nd ascent).

Wilder Kaiser: Fleischbank South East Corner (twice), Fleischbank East Face (Aschenbrenner-Lucke Route), Fleischbank East Face (Dülfer Route, solo).

Zillertal Alps: Hochferner North Face (twice).

Kashmir Himalaya: South Chongra Peak (6450 m), Rakhiot Peak (7070 m, with summit needle), Nanga Parbat (8125 m, 1st ascent).

1954

Berchtesgaden Alps: Rotpalfen Crack, Schärtenspitze West Ridge (solo), Hoher Göll West Face (Grosser Trichter, solo), Hoher Göll West Face (Kleiner Trichter), Kleines Mühlsturzhorn, Old South Face, Grosses Mühlsturzhorn–South Corner (3rd ascent).

Brenta: Paganella, Direct South Face.

Chiemgau Alps: Kampenwand West Summit South Face ("Die Gelbe").

Dolomites: First Sella Tower West Arête, Piz de Ciavázes South West Corner.

1955

Allgäu Alps: Himmelhorn Rädler Arête.

Berchtesgaden Alps: Kleines Mühlsturzhorn South West Face (2nd ascent), Wartstein Arête, Third Watzmannkind, Direct South Arête, Berchtesgadener Hochthron South Face Buttress.

Brenta: Campanile Basso South East Arête (Fox Arête, 4th ascent).

Dolomites: Mugonispitze South Face (Eisenstecken Route, 3rd ascent), Zwölfer North Arête (solo), Kleinste Zinne (Cima Piccolo) South East Face (Cassin Route).

Mont Blanc range: Grand Capucin East Face (10th ascent), Aiguille Noire, Direct West Face (15th ascent), Dent du Géant South Face.

Valais Alps: Monte Rosa East Face.

Wetterstein: Schüsselkarspitze, Direct South Face, Partenkirchener Dreitorspitze West Arête (solo).

Wilder Kaiser: Predigtstuhl North Summit, Direct West Face (10th ascent), Fleischbank South East Corner (2nd solo ascent).

1956

Berchtesgaden Alps: Watzmann East Face, Salzburger Route (solo), Berchtesgadener Route, Hochsäul South Face (3rd ascent).

Bernina: Piz Palü.

Dachstein: Däumling East Arête, Grosse Bischofsmütze South East Arête (2nd ascent), Grosse Bischofsmütze Direct North Face (with new variation start).

Hohe Tauern: Grossglockner.

Karwendel: Laliderer Spitze North Face (Auckenthaler Route 1st solo ascent), Laliderer Wand North Face (Dibona Route), Laliderer Wand North Corner (9th ascent), Laliderer Spitze North Arête (solo), Spritzkarspitze North East Face ("Schiefer Riss").

Mont Blanc: Petit Dru West Face (6th ascent), Mont Blanc du Tacul, Gervasutti Couloir (2nd solo ascent), Aiguille du Moine East Face (Contamine Route, 3rd ascent and 1st solo), Aiguille du Midi South Face (Rébuffat Route, 4th ascent and 1st solo), Aiguille des Pèlerins South West Arête (1st complete ascent/descent), Mont Blanc Brenva Face (Moore Spur).

Ortler group: Ortler, Königspitze.

Ötztaler Alps: Wildspitze.

Wilder Kaiser: Vordere Karlspitze East Face.

1957

Broad Peak (8047 m, 1st ascent).

Appendix Three
Sources

The primary source material used in the compilation of this book included Hermann Buhl's climbing diaries, expedition logbooks and reports, lecture notes, letters and personal notes. Use was also made of the notes taken by Reinhold Messner and Horst Höfler during conversations with Eugenie Buhl, Kriemhild Lornsen-Buhl, Silvia Bögl, Luis Vigl, and Hermann Köllensperger, and those made during the 103rd episode of the ORF TV programme "Land der Berge." Further primary sources included documents held by the Archiv des Deutschen Instituts für Auslandsforschung (The Archive of the German Institute for Foreign Research).

Appendix Four
Bibliography

Aufmuth, U.: *Lebenshunger. Die Sucht nach Abenteuer.* Walter Verlag, Zürich and Düsseldorf, 1996.

Bauer, P.: *Das Ringen um den Nanga Parbat 1856–1953. Hundert Jahre bergsteigerischer Geschichte.* Süddeutscher Verlag, München 1955 (*The Siege of Nanga Parbat,* 1856–1953. Hart-Davis, London 1956).

Bechtold, F.: *Deutsche am Nanga Parbat. Der Angriff 1934.* Bruckmann Verlag, München 1935 (*Nanga Parbat Adventure.* Murray, London 1935; Dutton, New York 1936).

Buhl, H.: *Nanga Parbat Pilgrimage.* The Mountaineers Books, Seattle 1998.

———: *Achttausend drüber und drunter.* Commemorative edition with a postscript by Kurt Diemberger. Nymphenburger Verlagshandlung, München 1958.

———: *Grosse Bergfahrten.* With an introduction by Luis Trenker and a concluding piece by Kurt Diemberger. Nymphenburger Verlagshandlung, München 1974.

———: *Allein am Nanga Parbat und Grosse Fahrten.* Steiger Verlag, Innsbruck 1984.

Diemberger, K.: *Gipfel und Gefährten.* Bruckmann Verlag, München 1990 (*Summits and Secrets.* Hodder & Stoughton, London/The Mountaineers Books, Seattle 1991).

———: *K2—Traum und Schicksal.* Bruckmann Verlag, München 1989 (*The Endless Knot—K2, Mountain of Dreams and Destiny.* The Mountaineers Books, Seattle 1991). Both Diemberger books are now included in *The Kurt Diemberger Omnibus,* Bâton Wicks, London/The Mountaineers Books, Seattle 1998.

Dumler, H.: *Grenzen des Menschenmöglichen. Alleingänger am Berg.* Verlag Das Berglandbuch, Salzburg 1970.

Dyhrenfurth, G. O.: *Der dritte Pol. Die Achttausender und ihre Trabanten.* Nymphenburger Verlagshandlung, München 1961 (*To The Third Pole: The History of the High Himalaya.* Laurie, London 1955).

Harrer, H.: *Die Weisse Spinne. Die Geschichte der Eiger-Nordwand.* Verlag Ullstein, Berlin 1959 (*The White Spider: The History of the Eiger's North Face.* Hart-Davis, London 1959; Dutton, New York 1960; Granada, London 1983).

Herrligkoffer, K. M.: *Nanga Parbat 1953.* Lehmanns Verlag, München 1954 (*Nanga Parbat: Incorporating the Official Report of the Ex-*

pedition of 1953. Elek, London 1954; Knopf, New York 1954; Panther, London 1956).

——: *Nanga Parbat. Die Geschichte eines Achttausenders*. Bayerische Verlagsanstalt, Bamberg 1979.

Hiebeler, T.: *Zwischen Himmel und Hölle. Aus dem Leben eines Bergsteigers*. Limpert Verlag, Frankfurt/M. 1965.

Höfler, H.: *Sehnsucht Berg—Grosse Alpinisten von den Anfängen bis zur Gegenwart*. BLV Verlagsgesellschaft, München 1989.

Isselin, H.: *Die Aiguilles von Chamonix*. Verlag Hallwag, Bern 1964.

Karl, R.: *Erlebnis Berg: Zeit zum Atmen*. Limpert Verlag, Bad Homburg 1980.

Lukan, K.: *Alpenspaziergang. Durch die Alpen von Wien bis Nizza*. Bruckmann Verlag, München 1988.

Messner, R.: *Alleingang Nanga Parbat*. BLV Verlagsgesellschaft, München 1979 (*Solo Nanga Parbat*. Kaye & Ward, London/Oxford, New York 1980).

Messner, R., Varale, V., Rudatis, D.: *Die Extremen. Fünf Jahrzehnte sechster Grad*. BLV Verlagsgesellschaft, München 1974.

——: *Die Grossen Wände. Geschichte, Routen, Erlebnisse*. BLV Verlagsgesellschaft, München 1977 (*The Big Walls*. Kaye & Ward, London/Oxford, New York 1978).

——: *Die rote Rakete am Nanga Parbat*. Drehbuch zu einem Film, der nie gezeigt werden kann. Nymphenburger Verlagshandlung, München 1971.

——: *Grenzbereich Todeszone*. Verlag Kiepenheuer & Witsch, Köln 1978.

——: *Überlebt. Alle 14 Achttausender*. BLV Verlagsgesellschaft, München 1987 (*All 14 Eight-Thousanders*. The Mountaineers Books, Seattle 1998).

Rébuffat, G.: *Sterne und Stürme*. Nymphenburger Verlagshandlung, München 1955 (*Starlight and Storm: The Ascent of the Six Great North Faces of the Alps*. Kaye & Ward, London/Oxford, New York 1968).

Schliessler, M.: *Beruf: Abenteurer*. BLV Verlagsgesellschaft, München 1972.

Schmitt, F.: *Das Buch vom Wilden Kaiser*. Bergverlag Rudolf Rother, München 1982.

Schmuck, M.: *Broad Peak—Meine Bergfahrten mit Hermann Buhl*. Verlag "Das Bergland-Buch," Salzburg/Stuttgart 1958.

Material was also drawn from the following sources: issues 9/1964, 7, 8 and 12/1967 of the magazine *Alpinismus*, Heering-Verlag, München; the 1954–1959 journal and the 50th Jubilee literature of

"Karwendler" Mountaineering Club, Innsbruck; the 75th Jubilee literature of the German Alpine Club, Munich Bergland Section (11/1983).

Buhl's essays were taken from the Yearbook of the German Alpine Club (1952 und 1953), the magazine *Der Bergsteiger* (issues: 4/1951, 7/1951, 7/1952, 5/1953, 7/1953 and 1/1957), Bruckmann Verlag, München and the *Österreichische Alpenzeitung* 75th yearbook, 1957.

The quotations attributed to the brothers Hugo and Luis Vigl were taken from the *Österreichische Bergsteigerzeitung* no. 10, 35, 1957.

Kurt Diemberger's texts in the chapter "The Death" were taken from the essay "Chogolisa," published in the *Österreichische Alpenzeitung* in 1958.

About the Authors

For over thirty years, **Reinhold Messner** has been one of the most successful climbers in the world. He has about 3,500 routes and expeditions to his credit, including more than 100 first ascents. He has climbed all fourteen Himalayan eight-thousanders, crossed the Antarctic on foot, made a north-south traverse of Greenland, walked through Tibet, and trekked across the Takla Makan Desert.

Horst Höfler, mountaineering journalist, archivist, and climber, has long been fascinated with the enigma that is Hermann Buhl. For this book he put together the original writings of Buhl and researched the background bibliographical matter.